Discourse, Grammar and Ideology

Also available from Bloomsbury

An Introduction to Multimodal Analysis, David Machin

Construing Experience through Meaning, M. A. K. Halliday &
Christian Matthiessen

Contemporary Critical Discourse Studies, edited by
Christopher Hart and Piotr Cap

Discourse in Context, edited by John Flowerdew

Evaluation in Media Discourse, Monika Bednarek

Language and Society, M. A. K. Halliday (edited by Jonathan J. Webster)

Multilingual Encounters in Europe's Institutional Spaces, edited by
Johann Unger, Michał Krzyżanowski and Ruth Wodak

Multimodal Discourse Analysis, edited by Kay O'Halloran

The Bloomsbury Companion to Discourse Analysis, edited by
Ken Hyland and Brian Paltridge

Discourse, Grammar and Ideology

Functional and Cognitive Perspectives

Christopher Hart

Bloomsbury Academic
An imprint of Bloomsbury Publishing Plc

B L O O M S B U R Y
LONDON · OXFORD · NEW YORK · NEW DELHI · SYDNEY

Bloomsbury Academic
An imprint of Bloomsbury Publishing Plc

50 Bedford Square	1385 Broadway
London	New York
WC1B 3DP	NY 10018
UK	USA

www.bloomsbury.com

BLOOMSBURY and the Diana logo are trademarks of Bloomsbury Publishing Plc

First published in paperback 2016

First published 2014

British Library Cataloguing-in-Publication Data
A catalogue record for this book is available from the British Library.

ISBN: HB: 978-1-4411-3357-1
PB: 978-1-4411-1741-0
ePDF: 978-1-4411-0135-8
ePub: 978-1-4411-0485-4

Library of Congress Cataloging-in-Publication Data
Hart, Christopher (Linguist)
Discourse, grammar and ideology : functional and cognitive perspectives /
Christopher Hart.
pages cm
ISBN 978-1-4411-3357-1 (hardback) – ISBN 978-1-4411-1741-0 (paperback) –
ISBN 978-1-4411-0485-4 (epub) 1. Critical discourse analysis–Social aspects.
2. Cognitive grammar. 3. Ideology–Social aspects. 4. Language and
languages–Philosophy. 5. Functionalism (Linguistics) I. Title.
P302.H348 2014
401'.41–dc23
2014014858

Typeset by Newgen Knowledge Works (P) Ltd., Chennai, India

*This book is dedicated to the memory of my grandfather.
Thanks for everything.*

Contents

Acknowledgements

This book owes a great deal to a great many people. It is not possible to name everyone who has made a contribution to it in some way or another but I hope, at least, you will know my thanks.

This book was begun while working at Northumbria University and completed while working at Lancaster University. I am exceedingly grateful to the linguistics departments in both institutions for the time and space afforded to me which has enabled this project to be pursued to fruition.

The intellectual space at the intersection between critical and cognitive linguistics has only relatively recently been opened. I am grateful to all those researchers who have had a hand in creating this highly productive space and whose work is reflected in this book. I am especially grateful to those people working in this area with whom I have been able to exchange ideas by distance or at international conferences, meetings and symposia. Particular thanks are due to Piotr Cap, Bertie Kaal, Laura Filardo Llamas, Lesley Jeffries, Monika Kopytowska and Juana Marín Arrese.

At Lancaster University, I have found an environment which is extremely warm and supportive, both personally and professionally. I am grateful to colleagues there for making me feel so at home so quickly. Lancaster is also an epicentre for critical discourse studies. This book has benefitted enormously from the many stimulating conversations I have had with Paul Chilton, Veronika Koller, Ruth Wodak and Johnny Unger in the offices and corridors of the university (as well as in train carriages and in various station cafes across the country while stranded after cancelled or delayed services). While at Northumbria University I enjoyed numerous discussions on matters of linguistics and critical discourse studies with colleagues in the department as well as with John Richardson, Majid KhosraviNik and Darren Kelsey as part of the Newcastle and Northumbria Critical Discourse Group. I am also grateful to John, Majid and two anonymous reviewers for reading draft chapters and offering useful suggestions for improvement. All remaining oversights are, of course, my own responsibility.

At the publishers, I would like to thank Gurdeep Mattu for commissioning the work (albeit in a different guise to the way it turned out) and Andrew Wardell for so efficiently handling the production process, especially in the face of repeated requests for extensions on my part.

Always last but never least, I would like to thank Heather, my shining light, for the love and support that she has shown me over the last year and for her patience during the final stages of preparing the manuscript for this book. I hope somehow I will be able to repay you.

Introduction

This is a book about grammar, broadly conceived, and ideology. I do not mean here attitudes towards grammar, such as the prescriptivism of people concerned with a perceived decay in language standards. Rather, we will be interested in the relationship between grammar and ideology in the practice of discourse. Grammar is thus understood much more widely than in traditional definitions. We are not talking about the grammars one learns at school in relation, for example, to written forms of English or a second language learned by rote. This is a sense of grammar which for many readers would conjure bad memories and prevent them from reading much further. Grammar is taken here, instead, as it is in linguistics, where scholars are concerned with describing language rather than prescribing how it ought to be used. And, as Langacker (2008: 3) puts it, 'grammar is actually quite engaging when properly understood'. Grammar in this sense refers to the system or systems that make up part of the human language capacity, as well to the theoretical models that aim to capture this system. From one theoretical perspective, grammar may be said to facilitate or realize different 'functions' of language (Halliday 1994). By function, linguists working in this tradition mean the different things that speakers can and do do with language; namely, communicate about the world, comment on the world, and try to convince one another. Thus, we can talk about grammars for representation, evaluation or legitimation. Such grammars can be described at various further levels of specificity or 'delicacy', for example, in specific domains of experience such as space or at finer levels within the system. Grammar as system is understood in linguistics as a finite set of rules, networks or structures which gives rise to linguistic output. Grammars as models all aim to explain linguistic output in terms of more restricted principles. Grammars as models are derived from language, then, but they serve subsequently as tools for doing discourse analysis, including Critical Discourse Analysis. The relationship between grammars and data is thus bidirectional and dynamic where grammars can be continually modified to accommodate new (types of) data.

Ideology is understood throughout the book in a similarly broad fashion as something akin to 'perspective'. That is, as a particular interpretation of the way things are or ought to be. Language is ideological when it is used to promote one perspective over another. Grammars as system engender ideology through the, often inhibited, choices they allow 'for representing "the same" material situation in different ways' (Haynes 1989: 119). Grammars as models, in turn, allow a handle on the ideological 'choices' presented in discourse. A grammar serves as a guide to the particular sites of ideological reproduction in text and talk. A grammar provides a plan of potential practices against which ideological differences can be clearly seen and delineated. And a grammar can act as a reference point for comparing (i) what is expressed in discourse with what is suppressed and (ii) the way something is expressed in text with other available options in the grammar. In other words, a grammar allows for a text to be compared with other potential rather than necessarily attested texts – an affordance which is crucial in the absence of competing Discourses. One area where the relation between grammar and ideology has been investigated is Critical Discourse Analysis.

Critical Discourse Analysis

Critical Discourse Analysis (CDA) is a particular form of discourse analysis which, in one guise at least, seeks to disclose the ideological and persuasive properties of text and talk which might not be immediately apparent without the assistance of a systemized descriptive framework such as a grammar or typology. CDA is not a particular method of discourse analysis but, rather, a discipline or practice which consists of several identifiable 'schools' or 'approaches', each of which has its own distinct methodology. In many cases, these methodologies are sourced from the field of linguistics and in this sense CDA can be characterized as a branch of applied linguistics. However, some approaches borrow less from linguistics (though linguistics usually remains somewhere within their purview) and operationalize instead frameworks sourced from fields as diverse as ethnography and social psychology. In its broader conceptual framework, CDA is informed by critical social theory and thinkers such as Bakhtin, Bourdieu, Habermas and Foucault.[1] Following such social scientists, CDA is not critical in the ordinary sense of the word. Rather, it is critical in so far as it is 'rooted in a radical critique of social relations' (Billig 2003: 38) and aims at illuminating the role that language plays in creating and sustaining those social relations. Ultimately, CDA aims at achieving social change.[2]

This position, of course, is predicated on the assumption that discourse is instrumental in the construction of society and that discourse analysis, and CDA in particular, may, in turn, be instrumental in its deconstruction. These assumptions are found in both Critical Theory and Post-structuralism. Habermas, for example, claims that language is 'a medium of domination and social force' (1977: 259). In CDA, discourse and social action are held to exist in a dialectical relation. Language use reflects social structures but at the same time it (re)enforces social structures (Fairclough 1989, 1995a/b). As Fairclough puts it, discourse 'is socially shaped, but it is also socially shaping, or constitutive' (1995a: 131). This arises from a view of language use as social action (Austin 1962; Wittgenstein 1953). For Fairclough, discourse refers not only to the production and consumption of text and talk but 'to the whole process of social interaction' of which text and talk are but a particular element (1989: 24). Discourse is not just a linguistic practice, then, but is in and of itself a social practice which contributes to the formation of the social systems, situations, institutions and ideologies in which it is embedded. The upshot of this conceptualization is that 'every single instance of language use reproduces or transforms society and culture, including power relations' (Titscher et al. 2000: 146). The extent to which CDA is necessary to make visible, in the sense that readers cannot see for themselves, the social values and attempts at persuasion instilled in discourse has been the subject of recent debate (see Chilton 2005a, 2011 and Hart 2011c for further discussion).

One crucial way in which language effects social actions and relations is through the 'normalization' of ideology (another is through 'legitimation'). Ideology is a difficult term to define. Eagleton (1991) identifies at least six different concepts of ideology. The definition usually adopted in CDA and the one that we will use in this book corresponds roughly with 'world view', where ideologies are seen as normalized patterns of belief and value (Hodge and Kress 1993). From a critical standpoint, however, ideology is not just any world view. Rather, it carries a pejorative meaning and is applied to perspectives promoted in the interests of specific social groups (Eagleton 1991: 29). For van Dijk (1998), ideologies involve an Us/Them polarization and, typically, positive beliefs about and attitudes towards Us and negative beliefs about and attitudes towards Them. Ideologies, as ways of viewing the world, provide guides for social action and may thus in turn give rise to inequalities and injustices. The question that arises, of course, is whose discourse is most effective in disseminating ideology?

CDA largely addresses the discourse of powerful social actors/agencies where power is defined, from a neo-Marxist perspective, in terms of privileged 'access' to socially valued resources, including wealth and status but also, crucially, channels for the dissemination of information (van Dijk 1993). Media discourse, for example, is widely consumed and recognized to be influential in the manufacture of consent (Herman and Chomsky 1988). Other individuals/ institutions, including politicians and corporations, are in turn powerful by virtue of their preferential access to (and control over the contents of) the media.[3] Other 'ordinary' actors lack power because they are not afforded access to communication channels with equal 'symbolic capital' or distributional mass.

Of course, discourse is not just consumed. It is reproduced and entered into intertextual chains where it may be commented on, countered, recontextualized, and/or further normalized inside a dominant Discourse. It therefore makes sense to study discourse at all levels of the social strata and in all settings. The discourse of 'ordinary' speakers is far from uninstrumental in the normalization of ideology and the legitimation of social action. The issue, however, relates to the degree of agency involved. Non-powerful members often have only limited access to alternative Discourses and therefore do not necessarily recognize discourse as ideological.

Following Gee (1990), we can distinguish between 'little d-' discourse and 'big d-' Discourses. Discourse in the first sense refers to particular stretches of text and talk or the unfolding activity of producing and consuming text and talk. Discourses are the conventionalized practices, including linguistic practices, which members of a discourse community both engage with and are governed by. Discourses can refer at the same time to conventional ways of thinking about the world which account for social, including linguistic, and material practices within it. Discourses in this double-sided sense are countable and exist in different domains of experience. Fairclough uses the term 'order of discourse' to refer to the totality of attested statements in some social domain (1995a: 132). CDA has studied the relationship between discourse and social action in domains as diverse as race and immigration, gender, war, crime, education and the environment.

Discourses are inherently ideological in so far as Discourses in the same domain can exist in competition with one another (Lee 1992). The relationship between discourse and Discourses is mutually constitutive. What may be expressed and how in discourse is controlled by Discourses but at the same time Discourses are formed and reinforced by the patterns of discourse which reflect them. Which competing Discourses establish themselves as dominant depends on various factors including the discourse of powerful actors (see Fairclough 2005: 55–6). On this account, discourse, and the discourse of powerful speakers/ institutions in particular, represents a site for the (re)articulation of ideology and the legitimation of (sometimes harmful) social action. This explains the micro-level focus in CDA on the strategies and structures of text and talk and why CDA critically analyses the language use of those in power (Wodak 2001: 10). The relation between discourse and dominant Discourses is one of normalization so that the ideological nature of Discourses, through repeated instantiations in discourse, is not noticed and Discourses are instead taken for granted as commonsensical (Fairclough 1995a). Or as Kress (1989: 10) states, Discourses conceal ideology by 'making what is social seem natural'. In seeking to raise to critical consciousness the otherwise opaque ideological or persuasive properties of discourse and Discourses, as well as the relation between them, CDA is sometimes characterized as 'denaturalising' or 'demystifying' (Reisigl and Wodak 2001: 32).

CDA is not directly aimed at specific ideologies and may therefore, in principle, be applied to social and political discourse of any ideological bent. However, critique is intended to lead to improvements in the social order and this necessarily implies starting from some particular normative-ethical perspective. Most CDA practitioners can be seen to adopt a broadly liberal or humanitarian philosophy and thus tend to target more conservative Discourses which run counter to this point of view and which are perceived to be more dominant.[4] As a consequence of this open political commitment, CDA faces charges of being biased leading to claims that its analyses are invalid (Widdowson 1995). To this one may respond that no research is *a priori* free from the values of scholars and that recognizing one's own position in conducting research is in fact a form of objectivity (Fairclough 1996). We may also stress that systematic, unbiased and scientifically grounded critical discourse research is perfectly possible when equipped with the right tools, including theories of language.

CDA and grammar

Models of grammar are useful for CDA because they enable systematic, theoretically driven, comparative approaches to analysis only on the back of which may well-founded observations and generalizations be made. As Martin (2000) points out, grammars, 'provide critical discourse analysts with a technical language for talking about language – to make it possible to look very closely at meaning, to be explicit and precise in terms that can be shared by others, and to engage in quantitative analysis where this is appropriate' (275–6). If we were being particularly polemical, we might argue, with Halliday, that 'a discourse analysis not based on [a] grammar is not an analysis at all, but simply a running commentary on a text' (1985: xvi). But CDA is inherently interdisciplinary, drawing on various combinations of linguistics and critical social theory in which linguistics holds a more or less central place.[5] For Fairclough (1992: 74), 'discourse analysis is in fact a multidisciplinary activity, and one can no more assume a detailed linguistic background from its practitioners than one can assume detailed backgrounds in sociology, psychology or politics'. For my money, however, linguistics must remain at the core of CDA in order that it retain not only its rigour but its originality. What sets CDA apart from other critical approaches to discourse analysis is its stringent application of linguistics. While I make every effort throughout the book to guide the reader gently through the minefields of alternative theoretical frameworks, then, I make no apology for the complex nature and necessarily technical, and often idiosyncratic, conventions and metalanguages of the linguistic models presented. This book is intended for audiences with some insight into, or at least some interest in, linguistics. This is not to say that it will be irrelevant to students and scholars of sociology, social psychology, media studies, political science and so on; only that it may require some investment from readers unfamiliar with basic principles in linguistics.

The most well-known model of grammar appropriated in CDA is Halliday's (1985, 1994) Systemic Functional Grammar (SFG). SFG is a natural framework for CDA since, as Young and Harrison (2004: 1) outline, both fields share fundamental commonalities which are not found between CDA and Generative Grammar (GG). Both SFG and CDA, for example, see language as a primary social resource. Both fields view the forms of language (at all levels) as well as the contents as meaningful. And both see the relation between language and social contexts as dialectical where linguistic 'choices' (register) are governed by the communicative situation (setting) but those choices at the same time define the nature of the communicative event (genre), including the interpersonal relationship between participants. This dialectical view is extended in CDA where language is seen as constitutive not only of the immediate situational context but also of wider social structures and relations (Discourses) which, in their turn, determine ways of using language. Most fundamentally, both SFG and CDA examine language in relation to its performative purposes. SFG, in contrast to GG, presents a model in which the systems, including the grammatical systems, of the language are 'designed' to meet the communicative needs of its users. Here, Halliday identifies three 'functions' of language. By functions, Halliday (1994) means both the different uses that language has evolved to serve and the uses it is put to by speakers in discourse. The functions are thus part of the language capacity and of the language practices which are constitutive of culture and society. They are realized, through various sub-systems, in the particular semantic, lexicogrammatical and phonological *forms* of utterances. The ideational function constitutes a grammar for **representation**. It is the 'content function of language' (Halliday 2007: 183) which allow speakers to communicate about and thereby construct reality. The interpersonal function constitutes a grammar for **evaluation**. It is 'the participatory function' (Halliday 2007: 184) in which speakers comment on reality by expressing attitudes and opinions. In doing so, speakers construct their own social identities. For Fairclough (1995b: 58), it is also the function through which the social identities of others and relationships between participants are managed and maintained. The textual function is an enabling one. It is through the textual function that ideational and interpersonal meaning is actualized and, in conjunction with context, organized into coherent strands of discourse (Halliday 2007: 184). The three functions are built into the grammar of the language such that any utterance necessarily expresses all three functions simultaneously (though one may be more prominent than the others on particular occasions). Given the constitutive role of language in society, it therefore follows, according to Fairclough (1995a: 134), that 'language use is always simultaneously constitutive of (i) social identities, (ii) social relations and (iii) systems of knowledge and belief'. On this account, discourse is always 'textured' or 'multi-layered' consisting of several different dimensions or aspects which may be separated only for analytical purposes.

Halliday's tripartite distinction captures three important facets of language. However, it fails to recognize that a fundamental function of communication is not just to exchange information or express opinions but in so doing to convince others or to coerce them into acting in particular ways. Indeed, from an evolutionary perspective, this Machiavellian function may have been the major driving force in the development of language (Dessalles 1999; Origgi and Sperber 2000). In CDA, this macro-function is described in terms of '(de) legitimation' (Cap 2006; Chilton 2004; Martin Rojo and van Dijk 1997; Reyes 2011; van Leeuwen 2007; van Leeuwen and Wodak 1999). **Legitimation** is a macro-function through which speakers seek social approval of the Self, where the Self is either the individual speaker or an institution or social group the speaker identifies with, or accreditation for social actions and relations. In neo-institutionalism, Suchman (1995: 574) defines legitimation as: 'a generalized perception or assumption that the actions of an entity are desirable, proper, or appropriate within some socially constructed system of norms, values, beliefs, and definitions'. For Chilton, legitimation establishes positive face and the right to be obeyed (2004: 46–7). It is defined by Martin Rojo and van Dijk as the act of 'attributing acceptability to social actors, actions and social relations within the normative order' in contexts of 'controversial actions, accusations, doubts, critique or conflict' (1997: 560–1). Legitimation, then, is inherently dialogic. According to van Dijk (1998: 256) it is related to the speech act of defending, the preparatory conditions for which require that the speaker be responding to or pre-empting potential criticisms. Delegitimation is the effective counterpart. It challenges the negative face of others and involves speech acts of blaming, accusing, insulting and so on (Chilton 2004: 46). Legitimation and delegitimation go hand in hand such that, as part of what van Dijk calls the 'ideological square', legitimating the self often involves the delegitimation of others. Three 'fields of action' (Reisigl and Wodak 2001) in which legitimation is particularly important are politics, law and socio-economics. According to Cap (2006: 7), for example, attaining legitimacy is the 'principal goal of the political speaker'. Speakers in political, media and corporate contexts often have to do linguistic work to (re)establish legitimacy in the face of actions – past, present or future – which are potentially inconsistent with normative backgrounds, as when, for example, politicians seek sanction for wars, when the press report police violence, when people call for policies restricting the rights and freedoms of immigrants or when large corporations must defend harmful business practices. Pragmatic means of (de)legitimation include argumentation, appeals to logic and reason, appeals to emotion, claims to authority, attacks on claims to authority, acts of Self-praise and acts of Other-deprecation. However, legitimation and delegitimation are also achieved through strategies (whose instantiations may operationalize particular, meso-level pragmatic strategies such as argumentation) in the ideational and interpersonal functions of language.[6] SFG has therefore remained a theoretical mainstay of much of CDA such that, as Wodak (2001: 8) states, 'an understanding of the basic claims of Halliday's grammar and his approach to linguistic understanding is essential for a proper understanding of CDA'.

SFG, however, is not the only grammar available to CDA. In linguistics, various models of grammar have been advanced. These are oriented to three major genera: Generative Grammar, Functional Grammar and, more recently, Cognitive Grammar. There is no reason, in principle, why CDA should restrict itself to the application of SFG. As Fairclough (1995: 10) points out:

> Textual analysis presupposes a theory of language and a grammatical theory, and one problem for critical discourse analysis is to select from amongst those available. While systemic linguistics is a congenial theory to work with, in the

longer term critical discourse analysis . . . should be informing the development of a new social theory of language which may include a new grammatical theory.

Indeed, some authors have explicitly called for CDA to turn its attention to new theories of language as found, for example, in Cognitive Linguistics (e.g. Chilton 2005; Hart 2010; O'Halloran 2003). One reason for this is that while SFG may be ideal for description-stage analysis of representation and evaluation in discourse and their (ideological) communicative functions, it is less well furnished for interpretation-stage analysis, which, according to Fairclough, involves 'more psychological and cognitive concerns' (1995a: 59) with how hearers construct meaning in discourse. Interpretation-stage analysis, in other words, addresses *the effects* of ideological or perspectivized language use on hearers' mental representations and evaluations of reality. Appropriating models better equipped for interpretation-stage analysis is an especially important move if CDA is to address some of its criticisms and substantiate some of its claims. More recently, therefore, CDA researchers have begun to dabble with the virtues of Cognitive Grammar (Hart 2013a/b; Marín Arrese 2011), a model intended to provide a 'psychologically plausible' account of grammar and meaning construction (Langacker 2008). We discuss later in the book the particular advantages of incorporating Cognitive Grammar in CDA as well as the consonance of such an appropriation. Suffice it for now to say that Cognitive Grammar and SFG share broadly similar orientations in so far as both belong to the greater functional tradition and can be seen in opposition to GG (Nuyts 2007). Both offer very semantic characterizations of grammar. Differences between them are that SFG is largely founded on textual properties while Cognitive Grammar is founded on mental phenomena studied in cognitive psychology. Accordingly, they may complement one another in CDA deployed at the description versus interpretation stage, respectively.

Critical discourse analysts, then, have at their disposal a range of grammatical as well other linguistic models. To pursue the toolkit analogy a little further, which one the analyst selects will depend on which is most appropriate for the task at hand, where different models provide different perspectives on language and communication and afford a handle on the alternative functions, features and modalities of discourse which, depending on the particular research context, analysts may be interested in. In this sense, CDA cannot be identified by a specific methodology (Weiss and Wodak 2003: 12). CDA is, rather, multifarious and can only be presented 'with reference to particular approaches and . . .

their specific theoretical backgrounds' (Titscher et al. 2000: 144). Such different approaches can, however, be identified as being more or less concerned with linguistic structure (syntagmatic, paradigmatic, cohesive, conceptual) versus propositional content (recurring topics, themes, presuppositions, arguments and so on) and, correspondingly, relying to greater or lesser extents on specific theories of language to present detailed linguistic analyses (see Hart and Cap 2014; see also Wodak and Meyer 2009: 21–2). In this book, we are concerned with functional and cognitive perspectives on linguistic structure. Three more structurally oriented approaches to CDA are Critical Linguistics, Kress and van Leeuwen's Grammar of Visual Design and the Cognitive Linguistic Approach to CDA.[7] I briefly introduce each of these below.

'Grammatical' approaches to CDA

Critical Linguistics is centrally preoccupied with the theory and practice of representation and draws heavily on SFG (Fowler 1996). It insists that all representation is mediated, moulded by the values ingrained in the speaker and the medium of expression itself (ibid.). The aim of this approach is then to use grammatical analysis 'to expose misrepresentation and discrimination in a variety of modes of public discourse' (Fowler 1996: 5). For example, analysts have shown that grammatical devices in the ideational function, including nominalization and passivization, as well as transitivity choices, reflect and reinforce particular ideological points of view (Fowler 1991; Fowler et al. 1979). Much of this research has addressed how issues of public order are reported in news discourse where the press have been found to favour representations which refrain from challenging dominant power relations and instead preserve the social *status quo* (e.g. Fowler 1991; Montgomery 1986; Trew 1979). Within the tradition of Critical Linguistics, van Leeuwen (1996) proposes a model for social actor analysis in which he outlines a grammar specifically for the representation of social actors. He illustrates this model with data taken mainly from a single newspaper text on immigration. More recently, the principles of Critical Linguistics have been extended to analyse the practice of evaluation in public discourse. For example, Fuoli (2012) has shown how multinational corporations use the interpersonal function of language to manage public perceptions in the face of growing concern over their social and environmental policies.

For many researchers in CDA, the concept of discourse as a semiotic social practice extends to the production and consumption of visual material. Kress and van Leeuwen (2006) develop a **grammar of visual design** largely inspired by Halliday's functional grammar. For Kress and van Leeuwen, meanings belong to culture rather than specific semiotic modes and, although realized quite differently, many of the same meaning potentials may find expression in both linguistic and visual discourse. The mapping between semiotic channels is not absolute, however, where some meanings may only be expressed verbally and others only visually. The point is that visual structures and linguistic structures are functionally comparable in that they both 'point to particular interpretations of experience and forms of social interaction' (Kress and van Leeuwen 2006: 2). And, as instantiations of the same semiotic capacity, linguistic and visual products may be analysed in terms of the same underlying (systemic functional) principles. Multimodal CDA and the grammar of visual design on which it draws thus incorporates many of the same analytical categories as Critical Linguistics, including those outlined in the Social Actor Model (Kress and Van Leeuwen 2006; Machin 2007).[8] For example, in a comparative study of images of soldiers in the Iraq war, Machin (2007) shows how social actors can be activated or passivated in the image and, if activated, how alternative 'transitivity' choices are realized as the soldiers are presented as engaged in different kinds of processes. Machin (2007) also shows how more connotative, evaluative meaning may be communicated by the particular participants, objects, settings and styles in an image.

The **Cognitive Linguistic Approach** represents a relatively recent development in CDA. It is concerned with the cognitive reflexes of representation and evaluation in discourse.[9] The Cognitive Linguistic Approach, then, explicitly theorizes the relationship between linguistic structures in texts and conceptual structures in the minds of discourse participants. It thus addresses the problem of cognitive equivalence, which we discuss later in this book. However, this approach provides more than a theoretical account of the conceptual import of linguistic choices already identified as potentially ideological. It also affords a lens on ideological properties of texts and conceptualization which have hitherto been beyond the radar of CDA. Much of this research has been concentrated on metaphor, particularly in immigration discourse (e.g. Charteris-Black 2006a; Hart 2010; Santa Ana 2002). Here, metaphorical themes such as WAR and WATER have been shown to play an important structuring role in media Discourses of immigration. More recently, however, researchers in this tradition have turned to forms of representation and evaluation in discourse and conceptualization beyond metaphor (Chilton 2004; Hart 2011a/b, 2013a/b; Marín Arrese 2011). For example, from the methodological perspective of Force Dynamics (Talmy

2000), Hart (2011a) investigates indicators of force-interactive conceptualizations in immigration discourse. He shows that grammatical elements including certain conjunctions and adverbial particles such as *still* serve to invoke conceptualizations of immigrants as instigators of forceful actions. Drawing on Langacker's Cognitive Grammar, Hart (2013b) investigates the image schemas recruited to conceptualize interactions between police and protestors during the 2010 student fees protests. In accordance with earlier findings from Critical Linguistics, he finds that the majority of the British press rely on transitivity choices which invoke conceptualizations of the violence that occurred as either one-sided or where police involvement is otherwise cognitively backgrounded or mitigated.

This book

This book is intended to show how different grammatical models can contribute to CDA. As we have already suggested, some grammars have by now been extensively applied in CDA. SFG, for example, is recognized as 'centrally important to the critical study of situated language events' (Young and Harrison 2004: 1). Other 'younger' grammars, such as Martin and White's (2007) model of Appraisal, are yet to have been as widely applied. And others still, like Langacker's (2008) Cognitive Grammar, have hardly been taken up at all in CDA. As we progress through the chapters, therefore, the ground will, for most readers, become gradually less familiar.

This book is organized into two parts. The division reflects, in part, more established tools versus new methodological territories. The case being made in Part 1 is that the models presented remain relevant for CDA in contemporary discursive contexts. The case being made in Part 2 is for a more cognitively grounded CDA. The two parts also reflect alternative perspectives from which one may address the communication of ideology: as it is encoded in texts (description stage) and as it is cognitively constructed in discourse (interpretation stage). As we progress through the book, then, we slowly shift from a more text-level perspective to a more discourse-level perspective. This shift begins in Chapter 2 when we encounter a distinction between 'inscribed' and 'invoked' evaluation. Chapter 3, on multimodality, and Section 4 on vectors and viewpoints in particular, represents a pivotal moment when the audience themselves is brought in as an essential component of the meaning of texts. It is no coincidence that the transition should come at this point for, as we shall see, various aspects of visual experience show up in the cognitive basis of linguistic meaning. This book can therefore be read as evolving both a narrative, as we move from one model to the next, highlighting the kinds of analyses they are good for, and the field of CDA, which is advanced both theoretically and methodologically.

It is not my intention in this book to report specific, large-scale, empirical studies. Rather, for the most part I aim to show, qualitatively, how particular linguistic theories can contribute to CDA. In order to demonstrate this, throughout the book I draw on data instantiating several salient Discourses relating to globalization, including Discourses of immigration, war, corporate practice, political protest and economics. It should not be taken, however, that the range of any particular model is restricted to analysing data of any particular type or that particular types of data are only approachable from particular methodological perspectives. Indeed, any 'complete' empirical analysis of a particular Discourse will require multiple methodologies to account for the different linguistic and visual dimensions involved in its articulation. And if I am guilty of not being representative with any of my data, then it is because the selected data are being used to illustrate the pragmatic significance of (potential) semiotic differences rather than with any claims to statistical significance. It should be clear, however, that the analytical techniques presented could, in principle at least, be deployed across large corpora of texts to allow more quantitative, comparative analyses.

Chapter 1, on representation, signals a departure point relying on concepts familiar from SFG and Critical Linguistics: transitivity and grammatical metaphor. We see how these concepts can be applied, in the vein of Critical Linguistics, to reveal ideology and the concealment of responsibility in the reporting of 'hard news' events. We then home in specifically on the representation of social actors, illustrated with reference to media discourse on immigration. In this chapter, we also highlight a number of theoretical and methodological issues relating to Critical Linguistics which the developments discussed in Part 2 can be seen as partially responding to.

In Chapter 2, we explore how speakers express evaluations. The most natural framework for this is Appraisal Theory (Martin and White 2007), which has been developed as an extended account of the interpersonal function in the tradition of Halliday. Through the various sub-systems of ATTITUDE, speakers communicate moral, emotional and aesthetic values in relation to the entities, events and processes represented in discourse. Through the sub-system of ENGAGEMENT, speakers acknowledge, to lesser or greater extents, intertextual voices and engage with them in alternative ways. We see how this grammar for evaluation is exploited in different ways by speakers in two different genres. We examine corporate social reports from three multinational companies, Coca Cola, Nike and Nestlé, and a political speech by George W. Bush. We also see how evaluation may be expressed more covertly in anti-immigration discourse.

In Chapter 3, we see how the principles of SFG may be extended to multimodal CDA. We see that many of the ideational and interpersonal categories of functional grammar, as well as those which traditionally lie outside linguistic grammars but which can be approached within a systemic functional framework, find expression through different visual parameters, which constitute a 'grammar of visual design'. We explore these multimodal dimensions of discourse by examining images of immigration and political protests. Images, we will see, do not simply capture reality but, like language, contribute to constructing it as images come with different ideological connotations which have the power to persuade.

In Part 2, we switch firmly to a more discourse-level perspective and introduce more cognitively motivated theories of language and meaning construction. There has been a recent 'cognitive turn' in CDA (e.g. Hart 2011d; Hart and Lukeš 2007). This turn has been largely driven by the advent of Cognitive Linguistics and the consequent availability of new analytical frameworks. One of the major claims of Cognitive Linguistics is that language is not an autonomous cognitive faculty but, rather, linguistic processes are seen as being based on the same underlying principles as processes in other, non-linguistic domains of cognition, such as visual perception. A closely related claim is that aspects of the language system do not exist in the mind as discrete 'modules' or 'components' that require distinct models of description. Rather, lexicon and grammar are considered as two backs of the same beast. Words and constructions 'form a gradation consisting solely in assemblies of symbolic structure' (Langacker 2008: 5). One important finding has been that the meaningful basis of linguistic – lexical and grammatical – forms lays in image-schematic conceptual representations of prior (embodied) experience. In the case of grammar, these form-meaning pairings constitute what Langacker calls a Cognitive Grammar. One further, major finding of Cognitive Linguistics is that these image schematic representations also enter into metaphorical mappings with more abstract, social domains of experience to provide them with content and structure. These conceptual metaphors are indexed in and invoked by metaphorical expressions in discourse.

Metaphor, of course, has always been linked with imagery and so the leap from visual discourse to metaphor in linguistic discourse is not too great. It is much more unorthodox, however, to think of grammar in symbolic or imaginative terms. Although, as Langacker points out, this does not necessitate that such a view is wrong. One upshot of thinking this way is that grammar is seen not just as form but, rather, grammatical constructions have conceptual content and are therefore in and of themselves meaningful. Alternative constructions expressing the same proposition are not formal equivalences but are functionally and *experientially* different. A second upshot is that we may need to reconsider the direction of influence between grammars proposed in linguistics and those proposed in multimodal discourse analysis. For example, as we have suggested, Kress and van Leeuwen's grammar of visual design is based, in part at least, on Halliday's functional linguistic grammar. However, on the assumptions of Cognitive Linguistics, it may be more prudent to derive our linguistic grammars from the kind of 'grammars' developed in disciplines like Graphic Design and Game Studies where researchers are concerned with the way that physical domains like vision, action, force and motion get manipulated. Although we will not make contact with these disciplines in the present work, we will at least start to think about the meaningful basis of grammatical constructions as being grounded in the parameters of these experiential domains. As Langacker states, 'grammar reflects our basic experience of moving, perceiving, and acting on the world' (2008: 4).

In Chapter 4, then, we explore cognitive grammars of action, force, space and motion as they are exploited in online press reports of contemporary political protests. We also investigate point of view shifts in linguistic discourse and see that certain grammatical constructions may realize some of the same spatial positioning strategies as images encountered in Chapter 3 as they invite conceptualizations from different 'vantage points'. We argue that the conceptual operations which those grammatical constructions invoke in the hearer to constitute their experience of the situations and events described in discourse are the proper site of ideological reproduction.

We turn to metaphor in Chapter 5. Metaphor is not traditionally associated with grammar. However, Cognitive Linguistics sees no principled distinction between grammar and semantics with both being grounded in the same conceptual system and more general cognitive capacities. And conceptual metaphors, like grammar, are at the same time productive and restrictive. Moreover, conceptual metaphors are expressed in discourse through what, in Halliday's terms, we would call transitivity choices. In Chapter 5, then, we explore the ideological and legitimating potentials of metaphor in political and media discourse in times of austerity. Specifically, we consider the metaphorical construction of the London Riots and David Cameron's discourse on the economic crisis in the Eurozone.

Finally, in Chapter 6, we further investigate the grammar of space in conceptualizations of discourse 'beyond the sentence'. Here, building on the work of Chilton (2004), we focus on the positioning of textual elements inside a deictically specified conceptual space. Crucially, in such deictic spatial positioning the audience themselves is placed 'onstage' as part of the conceptualization. Again, following findings in Chapter 3, we see that certain visuo-spatial variables may be indexed in linguistic expressions to different ideological effects. The grammar of space may also be mapped metaphorically to constitute a grammar of time and evaluation. In this chapter, then, we examine representations of space and spatialized representations of time and evaluation in Tony Blair's discourse on Iraq as well as in the English Defence League's discourse on 'Islamisation'.

The use of grammatical models is not new in CDA. Grammar has been at the heart of CDA methodologies since the genesis of Critical Linguistics. It is SFG, however, which has almost exclusively 'provided the toolkit for deconstructing the socially constructed (and thus linguistically constructed) machinery of power' (Chilton 2005: 21). In this book, we also explore the efficacy of alternative grammars. The methodological import of these models will be demonstrated in the analytical handle they allow on the different dimensions of discourse from the alternative perspectives of description versus interpretation. The theoretical import of some of the claims made remains just that: theoretical. The 'psychological reality' of Cognitive Grammar is, at this point in time, plausible but not yet proven. On top of a cognitive turn in CDA, then, we may need to go one step further and take an experimental turn. For the moment, however, we restrict ourselves to theorizing and satisfy ourselves that if linguistics, and so by extension CDA, does not entertain speculation then it becomes a rather tedious enterprise.

Part 1

Functional Perspectives

Representation

1. Introduction

In the introduction, we identified a number of different dimensions of discourse where ideology may lurk. In this chapter, we address the ideological potential of linguistic representation. Representation concerns the depiction of social actors, situations and events. However, linguistic expressions do not correspond directly with the realities they describe. Rather, the grammar of representation, located in the ideational function of language, yields a linguistic product which reflects but a particular take on reality which may thus be ideologically infused. In this chapter, we apply tools sourced from SFG and developed for ideological discourse research primarily in the framework of Critical Linguistics to shed light on the ideological functions of linguistic representation. We do so in the context of media Discourses concerning State and Citizen. In Section 2, we introduce the basic principles of SFG. In Section 3, we show how the system of TRANSITIVITY affords ideological differences in Discourses of civil (dis)order. In Section 4, we discuss VOICE and GRAMMATICAL METAPHOR as means of mystifying responsibility for criminal acts of State power. In Section 5, we outline a grammar for the representation of social actors and illustrate the ideological potential of different options within this system with examples from discourse on immigration. Finally, in Section 6, we highlight a number of potential problems with Critical Linguistics which motivate the adoption of new complementary tools in contemporary approaches.

2. Systemic Functional Grammar

Systemic Functional Grammar (SFG) presents a theory of language based on purpose and choice (e.g. Halliday 1973, 1978, 1994). In other words, it is concerned with what speakers are doing when they use language and why on particular occasions of use they formulate their utterances in the way they do. This is in contrast with other models of grammar such as Chomsky's GG, which, as Fowler (1991: 5) states, 'is not interested in the role of language in real use'. Here, for example, the active and passive constructions are seen as formal equivalences derived from some underlying deep structure. Similarly, GG would analyse two sentences 'the police forced the rioters back' and 'the police moved the protestors back' as realizations of the same syntactic structure [S[NP[VP[NP[PP]]]]] without any reference to differences in meaning, which, for Chomsky, is not the proper business of linguistics. SFG, by contrast, is 'specifically geared to relating structure to communicative function' (Fowler 1991: 5). Its focus point, in analysing language, is therefore meaning rather than form. Here, such alternative formulations are recognized as being used for different purposes on different occasions, as is partly evidenced by their context-dependent distributions. It is this functionalist orientation that makes SFG an ideal tool for CDA (Fairclough 1989: 11; Fowler 1991: 5).

In SFG, Halliday seeks to describe the systems of choices open to a speaker in the three (ideational, interpersonal and textual) functions of language he identifies. In CDA, researchers seek to interpret the ideological functions of these choices. On this account, language is said to provide a system of semiotic resources which exists as a **meaning potential**. The system is organized into strata at different levels of abstraction which are connected by means of **realization**. Meaning potentials are actualized through choices at each level in the system. The three strata are semantics (meaning), lexicogrammar (coding – both wording and ordering) and, relevant to spoken language only, phonology (sounding).[1] These three strata overlap with the three functions as shown in Figure 1.1.

The semantic stratum constitutes the speaker's basic experience of what is described. This basic experience is then subject to further construal as is it is coded at the level of **lexicogrammar**.[2] Realization takes place through choices in various sub-systems of the lexicogrammar, each of which serves particular functions. Language conceived this way exists as a semiotic pool of both syntagmatic and paradigmatic choices realized through various sub-systems. These sub-systems consist of networks which have entry conditions and output features and are presented left-right according to a scale of delicacy. Crucially, the output of one sub-system may provide the entry conditions for the operation of another. Similarly, more than one sub-system may share the same entry conditions. Hence, sub-systems enter into systemic networks. For example, a fundamental choice the speaker makes in English is in the MOOD system

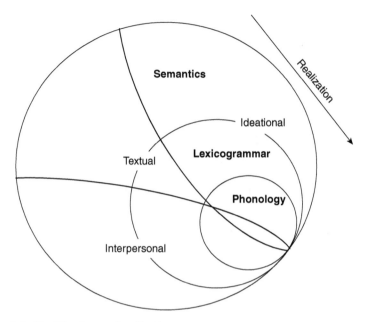

Figure 1.1. Stratification and realization

between imperative and indicative forms. If the speaker selects indicative, then he/she faces a choice between declarative and interrogative forms. At the same time, the speaker must make choices in TRANSITIVITY (process, participant and circumstance types) and THEME (marked or unmarked ordering of the clause). These three systems reflect the interpersonal, ideational and textual functions of language, respectively.

The system of a language (i.e. the totality of all the specific systems that would figure in a complete and comprehensive network) is instantiated in the form of text – the material (no matter how ephemeral) manifestation of the system as a meaning-making potential. System and text, then, define two poles of a cline from potential to particular instance. Between these two poles are intermediate stations which, adapted from Halliday, we can think of as context-dependent constraints on the system which are responsible for statistical probabilities in instantiation and are associated with particular Discourses and genres (see Figure 1.2.). In examining the representational dimension of discourse, we are concerned with choices made in the ideational function, which is served primarily through the system of TRANSITIVITY. In Critical Linguistics, practitioners have been primarily occupied with ideological patterns of representation which result from transitivity choices in Discourses of law and order. In the following section, we consider TRANSITIVITY as ideological means in Discourses of civil disorder.

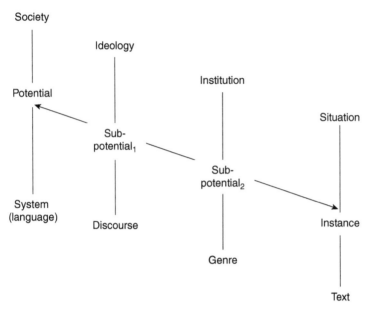

Figure 1.2. Instantiation

3. Transitivity analysis

Transitivity in CDA is a broader concept than the number of complements required by the semantics of a verb. It refers instead to the type of process designated in the clause and the consequences of this for the types of participants that can occur in the clause. TRANSITIVITY, then, provides a system of resources for referring to entities in the world and, crucially, the way that they interact with or relate to one another. It involves speakers analysing situations and events as being of certain types. Here, three elements of a canonical semantic configuration are distinguished: PARTICIPANTS, PROCESS and CIRCUMSTANCE. These elements are typically realized, at the level of lexicogrammar, in nominal, verbal and adverbial groups, respectively, and reflect functional categories in the clause structure Subject/Complement, Finite-Predicator and Adjunct as in Figure 1.3.

Lexicogrammatic	Nominal group	Verbal group	Nominal group	Adverbial group
Semantic	PARTICIPANT$_1$	PROCESS	PARTICIPANT$_2$	CIRCUMSTANCE
Functional	Subject	Finite-Predicator	Complement	Adjunct

Figure 1.3. Canonical clause structure at three levels of realization

For Fowler, transitivity is the 'foundation of representation' (1991: 71). It is a particularly powerful notion and much used concept in CDA for, following Fowler, the system

> has the facility to analyse the same event in different ways, a facility which is of course of great interest in newspaper analysis . . . Since transitivity makes options available, we are always suppressing some possibilities, so the choice we make – better, the choice made by the [D]iscourse – indicates our point of view, is ideologically significant. (ibid.)

The process is the 'core' component of the clause and the starting point in any ideational analysis. A relatively small number of general process types can be identified. Major process types are material, mental, relational and verbal while more minor types include existential and behavioural processes.[3] These process types are associated with particular participant roles. For example, **material processes**, perhaps the largest category of processes, necessarily involve an ACTOR or AGENT (the 'doer') and may also involve a GOAL or PATIENT (the 'done to').[4] By contrast, verbal processes necessarily involve a SAYER and may also involve a RECEIVER. Note that these requirements pertain to the semantic level and are not necessarily rendered explicit in the clause, sometimes to ideological effect, as we will see below.

A significant part of a Critical Linguistic analysis of transitivity involves identifying the process types and thus the participant roles that different social actors are represented as engaged in. This includes distinguishing, for example, whether certain social actors are more frequently represented as AGENTS or PATIENTS in material processes, or whether some social actors are more frequently represented as AGENTS in material processes while others are more frequently represented as SENSERS or SAYERS in mental and verbal processes, respectively. At a greater level of delicacy, it may involve distinguishing particular types of material, mental or verbal processes. Here, for example, we can distinguish between processes in terms of their modality, their intensity or the effect they have, if any, on a second participant. Let us now demonstrate how close comparative analysis of transitivity can reveal patterns in discourse which, it is argued, are indicative of ideology. Take, by way of illustration, the following analysis of reporting during the 1984–1985 British Miners' Strike.

3.1 An example from the 1984–1985 Miners' Strike

The Miners' Strike is one of most pivotal moments in British industrial relations history. It greatly divided public opinion but many claim that significant factions of the national press were institutionally biased against the strike (Williams 2009). Throughout the period, there were several flashes of violence between police and striking miners on the picket line. Among the most controversial of these occurred at Orgreave on 29 May 1984 when police used riot gear for the first time in the strike.[5] The events left 48 police officers and 28 miners injured.

Press coverage of industrial disputes and civil actions tends to focus on the disruptive effects of protests rather than the causes behind them (Glasgow Media Group 1976). This is problematic for it reduces the protest to a spectacle rather than a legitimate form of political action and prevents serious discussion of the issues at stake (Murdock 1973). Both papers in the data below conform to this conventional practice. However, there are some subtle differences. Trew (1979: 118) suggests that 'when social norms are infringed, there is a response in the media which tends to show most visibly the existence of specific and differing ways of perceiving things'. Such alternative perceptions reveal themselves in alternative transitivity patterns. The data below are taken from *The Sun*, a staunch critic of the strike, and *The Morning Star*, a paper hostile to the policies of the then British Prime Minister Margaret Thatcher and sympathetic towards the plight of the miners.[6] Given the opposing political stances of the two papers, then, we should expect to find subtle differences in transitivity structures which reflect these conflicting ideological positions. And indeed, this turns out to be the case. Consider the contrast between the examples presented in Table 1.1.

Table 1.1. Material processes in the Miners' Strike

The Sun	The Morning Star
Picketing miners <u>caused</u> a bloody riot with a mass attack on police yesterday.	Police <u>provoke</u> violent clashes as 7,000 miners <u>tried to stop</u> lorries ferrying coke from the Orgreave plant to the steel works.
One mounted policeman had his leg <u>broken</u> when he was <u>dragged</u> from his horse and another suffered a broken jaw when he was <u>hit</u> in the face with a brick.	Mounted police and police in riot gear <u>moved into</u> the picket lines after <u>splitting</u> the pickets into two groups.
Squads of riot police were <u>forced to put on</u> full riot gear for the first time since the twelve-week strike began.	

In the first instance we can see a difference in the ascription of agency in the 'creative' process designated by 'cause' and 'provoke'.[7] The AGENT in *The Sun* is 'picketing miners' while the AGENT in *The Morning Star* is 'police'. Further asymmetries can be seen where in *The Sun* the police are cast as PATIENTS in material processes of violence acted out by the miners. The only process of which police are AGENTS is the 'putting on' of riot gear which they are presented as doing only reluctantly and in response to the actions of the miners. By contrast, in *The Morning Star*, the police are presented as AGENTS acting on the miners and when the miners are cast as AGENTS they are not acting on the police but on 'lorries'. These differences represent the events in ideologically different ways and serve to apportion blame and agency along alternative lines commensurate with institutional stances. In a more contemporary context, let us consider two newspaper reports covering the G20 protests in 2009.

3.2 A contemporary example: the G20 protests in 2009

Around 35,000 people attended the initial G20 protests in London on 28 March 2009 with 5,000 people involved in the 'G20 Meltdown' protest outside the Bank of England on 1 April. A Royal Bank of Scotland (RBS) branch was also broken into and a 'climate camp' set up outside the European Climate Exchange on Bishopsgate. The protests, which were targeting a range of policy issues pertaining to capitalism and climate change, witnessed outbreaks of violence and police use of a controversial crowd control technique known as 'kettling'. One bystander, Ian Tomlinson, died after being beaten by a Metropolitan Police Officer Simon Harwood. The data presented below are taken from online reports published in *The Guardian* and *The Telegraph*.[8] These papers take alternative political stances and appeal to different audiences with the papers and their readers likely to hold more liberal versus more conservative values, respectively.

Both texts focus on the violence that occurred. However, some subtle differences can be seen which constitute alternative Discourses of political protests.

Let us take the headlines first, reproduced in (1) and (2):

(1) G20 protests: Rioters loot RBS as demonstrations turn violent.
    (*The Telegraph*)
(2) G20 protests: Riot police clash with demonstrators. (*The Guardian*)

We can break down the semantic and associated functional constituents of (1) as follows:

Rioters	*Loot*	*RBS*	*as demonstrations turn violent*
ACTOR	PROCESS: MATERIAL	GOAL	CIRCUMSTANCE
Subject	Finite/Predicator	Complement	Adjunct

Here we can see that the process in *The Telegraph* is focussed on 'looting' with protestors (referred to as 'rioters') as agents of the action, thus serving to 'criminalise' the protestors. Mention of the violence that occurred between police and protestors comes only in the CIRCUMSTANCE of the clause, which bears some semantic load but is not integral to the process and provides only 'additional' information. Moreover, the ACTOR in the clausal CIRCUMSTANCE is not agentive but occurs in the form of an abstract nominal 'demonstrations'. This serves to gloss over details of the interaction including issues of causality and agency thus avoiding reference to any role the police played in the violence (see next section). This is in direct contrast to the headline in *The Guardian* where the police are represented as agents in the violent process 'clash'.

This ideological dissociation is continued throughout the texts. If we examine the two texts for processes in which protestors are AGENTS we can extract the instances given in Table 1.2 (not including nominalized processes or those in reported clauses).[9]

From this we can glean a certain degree of similarity. In both papers, the protestors are agents of aggressive or destructive actions such as 'throwing', 'pelting' and 'smashing'. However, there are some differences. For example, transactive processes in which protesters are AGENTS are more often directed at

Table 1.2. Material and verbal processes (protestors) in the G20 protests

	The Telegraph	*The Guardian*
Material Processes	Loot (2), force (2), smash, throw (2), carry (2), clash, surround, shake, strike, gather, climb, unfurl, pelt, scramble, grab, surge, set off	Storm (2), seek, surge (2), throw (2), target (2), ransack, tear out, smash, climb, sit down, gather, pelt, rip, let off, push, hand out
Verbal Processes	Cheer, goad	Chant, write, demand, say, complain

police or police equipment as GOAL, rather than other inanimate objects, in *The Telegraph* compared to *The Guardian*. Consider (3) and (4):

(3) At one point, a black-clad man in the crowd <u>struck</u> an officer with a long pole. (*The Telegraph*)

(4) ... a van that had been surrounded by protestors who <u>shook</u> it from side to side. (*The Telegraph*)

At the same time, *The Guardian* presents protestors in peaceful processes such as 'sitting down' and distributing milk, which *The Telegraph* does not:

(5) At least 10 protestors <u>sitting down</u> in the street close to the bank of England ... (*The Guardian*)

(6) Others <u>handed out</u> milk so that people could wash the pepper spray from their eyes and mouth. (*The Guardian*)

The main difference in material processes, however, is that certain transitivity choices in *The Guardian* seem to suggest a Discourse which attributes some degree of legitimacy to the protests. For example, 'storm' and 'target' in (7) and (8) suggest organization and principle. Indeed, a quick search of the British National Corpus reveals such a 'prosody' (see Chapter 2) where the most frequent Left-collocates of *storm* are *troops*, *police* and *the army* as AGENTS and the most frequent Right-collocate is 'victory'.[10]

(7) [A] band of demonstrators close to the Bank of England <u>storming</u> a Royal Bank of Scotland branch. (*The Guardian*)

(8) [P]rotestors <u>targeting</u> the Bank of England were met by police ... (*The Guardian*)

This is in contrast to *The Telegraph* where 'forced their way into' as in (9) and the focus on 'looting' as in (10) suggest anarchy and opportunistic crime thereby indicating a Discourse of deviancy.

(9) A small number of demonstrators <u>forced their way into</u> the building on Threadneedle Street near the Bank of England. (*The Telegraph*)

(10) G20 summit protestors <u>looted</u> a City office of Royal Bank of Scotland this afternoon. (*The Telegraph*)

Perhaps the most striking difference between these two newspapers, however, is in the designation of verbal processes, not only in the numbers that occur but in their type and co-text. In *The Telegraph*, we find the following examples:

(11) Hundreds of protestors <u>cheered</u> as office equipment including a printer
      was carried out of the building. (*The Telegraph*)
(12) One man . . . was seen to apparently <u>goad</u> officers. (*The Telegraph*)

In (11), the CIRCUMSTANCE ('as office equipment including a printer . . .')
delegitimates the SAYERS in the verbal process by presenting them as supportive
of, even jeering on, the criminal actions being carried out by fellow protestors.
The process in (12) is itself inherently negative and delegitimating presenting the
protestors as antagonistic. In *The Guardian*, by contrast, we find examples such
as the following:

(13) 'It's our street, it's our street', the protestors <u>chanted</u> as they were forced
      forward on to the line. (*The Guardian*)
(14) [D]emonstrators <u>complained</u> they were being blocked in by police and
      not being allowed to leave. (*The Guardian*)

In (13), protestors are cast as SAYERS in a verbal process that is typically associated
with legitimate political protest while the CIRCUMSTANCE presents the protestors
as PATIENTS undergoing rather than AGENTS acting out a material process. The
verbal process in (14) is an expressive speech act (Searle 1975). The presence
of such a speech act and the particular VERBIAGE functioning as Complement
serve to acknowledge the voice of the protestors and to call into question police
handling of events.

There is a starker contrast in the way the police are constructed in the
two texts. This is most apparent in the number of actions in which police are
presented as agentive and the types of processes involved. Consider the data in
Table 1.3, which shows all instances of police agency in material processes across
the two texts (again excluding nominalizations and those in reported clauses).

Perhaps the most striking difference between these two papers is that there
is only one reference to police kettling in *The Telegraph* ('pen in') compared to
three in *The Guardian* ('hold', 'keep' and 'pen'). More subtly, in *The Telegraph*
the police are presented as the vanguards of civil order. They are presented as
agents in peaceful, intransactive processes such as 'retreat'. Besides containment,
the transactive processes in which the police are agentive and where the GOAL
is protestors are processes such as 'force back', which similarly relates only to the
location of the protestors and does not suggest physical harm. This particular
process, moreover, is presented as a valiant effort ('managed to') made in
response to the protestors' looting. No process in *The Telegraph* is represented
as unprovoked. Indeed, even in the face of provocation, the police are explicitly

Table 1.3. Material processes (police) in the G20 protests

The Telegraph	*The Guardian*
• Hundreds of protesters cheered as office equipment including a printer was carried out of the building – which is believed to have been empty – before riot police wielding batons <u>managed to force</u> the crowds back. • Police efforts had concentrated on <u>defending</u> its [RBS's] headquarters on Bishopsgate. • A group of 4,000 were <u>penned in</u> by officers. • Clashes later erupted at Mansion House Street and Queen Victoria Street near the Bank, with police <u>forced to deploy</u> ten vans and hundreds of officers to <u>rescue</u> a van that had been surrounded by protesters who shook it from side to side. • One man, bleeding from the head, was repeatedly seen to apparently goad officers, who <u>did not respond</u>. • Dozens of protesters surged forward and forced officers to <u>retreat</u>.	• Thousands of protesters <u>held</u> in containment pens. • Police <u>tried to keep</u> thousands of people in containment pens. • The G20 protests in central London turned violent today ahead of tomorrow's summit, with a band of demonstrators close to the Bank of England storming a Royal Bank of Scotland branch, and baton-wielding police <u>charging</u> a sit-down protest by students. • Nearer the heart of the City, police <u>moved in</u> to <u>break up</u> a 'climate camp' on Bishopsgate, with baton-wielding officers said to be <u>pushing through</u> a line of tents and bicycles. • Earlier in the day, protesters targeting the Bank of England were met by lines of police whose tactics were to <u>try to pen</u> demonstrators inside multiple cordons of officers. • At one stage, after midday, riot officers and police dogs and horses <u>removed</u> some 20 protesters. • Police in riot gear inside the bank <u>tackled</u> protesters trying to climb in through the smashed windows. • At least 10 protesters sitting down in the street close to the Bank of England were left with bloody head wounds after being <u>charged</u> by officers with batons at around 4.30pm. • Police <u>responded</u> by <u>using</u> truncheons, batons and pepper spray. • Police <u>used</u> truncheons and batons to <u>beat back</u> the protesters each time they surged forward.

presented as 'not responding'. One final thing worth pointing out in *The Telegraph* is that several lexical realizations come from the domain of war: 'defend', 'deploy', 'rescue' and 'retreat'.[11] The narrative constructed, however, is not one of military aggression but peacekeeping.

By contrast, in *The Guardian* the police are presented as aggressors who do 'respond' violently in 'tackling' and 'beating back' the protestors. Furthermore, in

The Guardian the police are presented as agents of unprovoked violent actions in 'charging' a sit-down protest and 'breaking up' a climate camp. It is worth noting at this point, however, that although we find police as agents of violent actions in *The Guardian*, we also find transitivity structures which serve to euphemize violent actions. For example, in 'moved in', 'pushed through' (intransactive) and 'removed' (transactive), processes are represented in terms of motion and location. In 'moved in' and 'pushed through' (compared with, say, 'smashed their way through'), the destructive nature of the process is glossed over. In 'remove' we are not told of the resistance put up by the protestors or the police response to that resistance.[12]

Taking the processes of which both protestors and police are agents into account, then, both papers appear to steer towards a Discourse in which the protests are seen as deviations from normative behaviour focussing on the protests as a spectacle. Only transitivity patterns in *The Guardian*, however, pay heed to the protests as political rather than criminal actions and attribute any degree of responsibility for the violence that occurred to the police. The transitivity patterns upheld in each paper are reflective of what van Dijk (1998) calls an 'ideological square' – a structure of mutual opposition involving simultaneous positive Self-representation and negative Other-representation. Consistent with the contrasting political stances of the two newspapers, then, the State and its authorities are aligned with the Self in *The Telegraph* and legitimated while protestors are positioned as Other and delegitimated. The converse is seen in *The Guardian* where the protests are legitimated and the police response delegitimated. These transitivity differences, therefore, not only reflect alternative ideologies but serve to construct institutional identities.

4. Mystification analysis

Mystification analysis concerns the ability of the clause to defocus or altogether conceal aspects of the realities described in discourse to different ideological effects.[13] In Critical Linguistics, mystification analysis has been primarily concentrated on the obfuscation of responsibility in the (excessive) exercise of State power (e.g. Fowler 1991: 134–45; Trew 1979). Two grammatical devices in particular are identified as ideologically load-bearing in this way: **the passive voice** and **nominalization**. Let us illustrate the (potential) ideological functions of these discursive strategies in turn. We will take as data examples from *BBC*

Online News reports of a high-profile case of civilian death at the hands of State authorities.

In the system of VOICE, speakers select between **active** and **passive** constructions. The difference concerns the organization of the message. In the active voice, the ACTOR (in a material process) occurs in the Subject of the clause and the GOAL occurs in the Complement. The active voice is usually treated as the 'unmarked' construction. In the passive voice, the ordering is reversed and the Subject slot is taken by the GOAL and the ACTOR appears in the Complement. It is in the system of VOICE, therefore, that the ideational and textual functions of language can be most clearly seen to interact. In the textual function, SFG distinguishes two major 'constituents': the Theme and the Rheme. The Theme is defined positionally as 'the point of departure of the message' (Halliday 1967: 212). That is, the Theme is the first functional element of the clause and the Rheme is the remainder. Functionally, the Theme thus serves to locate and orient the clause within its context (Halliday and Matthiessen 2004: 64). Ideologically, it serves to 'topicalise' the entity given as Theme (van Dijk 1991). In unmarked declaratives, the Theme coincides with Subject and, in material processes, ACTOR. In marked declaratives such as the passive voice, however, it is the GOAL, in material processes, that functions as Theme.[14] Let us consider an example.

Two weeks after the London Bombings of 7 July 2005, on 22 July, Metropolitan Police shot and killed Jean Charles de Menezes outside Stockwell tube station after they had mistakenly identified him as a suicide bomber. The police were acting under a controversial 'shoot to kill' policy known as Operation Kratos. The 'suspect' was shot seven times in the head and once in the shoulder. The following examples are all taken from the opening paragraphs, which appear in bold font, of *BBC News Online* reports in the wake of the incident.

(15) Police have said they shot a man dead at Stockwell tube station in South London after he was challenged and refused to obey an order. (*BBC News Online*, 22 July 2005)

(16) A man shot dead by police hunting the bombers behind Thursday's London attacks was a Brazilian electrician unconnected to the incidents. (*BBC News Online*, 23 July 2005)

(17) The man mistaken for a suicide bomber by police was shot eight times, an inquest into his death has heard. (*BBC News Online*, 25 July 2005)

(18) No police officers are to be prosecuted over the fatal shooting of Jean Charles de Menezes at a tube station last July. (*BBC News Online*, 17 July 2006)

In the reported clause of (15), immediately following the event, we find the following basic semantic and thematic structure:

They	shot dead	a man	in South London | after he was challenged ...
ACTOR	PROCESS	GOAL	CIRCUMSTANCES
Theme	Rheme		

(15) is in the active voice. The police, realized anaphorically as 'they', appear as ACTOR in the Theme of the clause. The clause is thus 'about' the police and their actions. By contrast, the basic semantic and thematic structure of the relevant clause in (16), from the following day, is reorganized in the passive voice as follows:

A man	shot dead	by police ...
GOAL	PROCESS	ACTOR
Theme	Rheme	

Here, it is Jean Charles de Menezes, as the GOAL in the PROCESS, who functions as Theme. The clause in (16) is thus 'about' Jean Charles de Menezes rather than his killers. According to Hodge and Kress (1993: 26), the passive voice enables the speaker to place the ACTOR in the less focal Rheme so that the causal connection between AGENT and PROCESS is at least syntactically loosened (1993: 26). The separation between AGENT and PROCESS goes a step further still in (17). **Agentless passives**, such as found in (17) and analysed below, allow the ACTOR in the semantic structure to be elided entirely in the clause, thus leaving responsibility for the PROCESS unspecified (Fowler 1991: 78). Such exclusions therefore allow speakers to conjure away social actors or keep them in the semantic background (Reisigl and Wodak 2001: 58).[15]

The man	was shot		eight times
GOAL	PROCESS	ACTOR	CIRCUMSTANCE
Theme	Rheme		

In (18), from a year after the incident and following the result of a Crown Prosecution Services review, we find a **nominalization** of the process in 'the fatal shooting'. In SFG, nominalization is a form of 'grammatical metaphor', which pertains to whether or not a process is actually represented as a process in lexicogrammar.[16] One potential ideological function of nominalization, like agentless passivization, is to permit habits of concealment (Fairclough 2003: 144; Fowler 1991: 80). In contrast to agentless passives, however, nominalizations involve the reification of processes. Processes are reduced to 'things' and thereby leave no room for information relating to participants or circumstances. Recovery of the agent is therefore no longer a question of filling an 'empty slot' in the clause structure but, rather, retrieving the 'congruent' representation would seem to involve a significant amount of 'unpacking'.

Critical Linguists have suggested that when events occur which are a threat to the prevailing ideology, they cannot be ignored by the media, but subtle shifts in linguistic representation, guided by the ideology, can ultimately succeed in producing a final version of events which overcomes such local incongruities and is in best keeping with the wider normative background (Toolan 1991: 228; Trew 1979: 107). What we are witnessing in (15)–(18), it may be argued then, is a highly controversial action, inconsistent with the dominant Discourse of police as protectors but which the press must nevertheless report, being brought over time into line with that Discourse. In other words, (15)–(18) may be said to constitute a natural restoration of legitimacy managed through the mystificatory facilities of linguistic representation.

5. Social actor analysis

When social actors are included in the clause, the speaker faces a range of options in how to represent them. We have already seen, for example, that they may be **activated** as AGENTS or **passivated** as PATIENTS. The range of options open to the speaker, however, extends beyond the functional participant categories of SFG. A grammar for the classification of social actors existing at a finer level of delicacy is therefore proposed (van Leeuwen 1996). Van Leeuwen points out that there is no neat fit between sociological and linguistic categories, although there is some degree of overlap, and that limiting critical analysis to the latter may lead to other ideologically relevant forms of representation being overlooked (1996: 33). The grammar described in the Social Actor Model is therefore motivated by broader sociological rather than linguistic categories and may be said to constitute a 'socio-semantic inventory' for the representation of social actors. In this section, we partially outline this grammar and illustrate its ideological potential with examples from another discourse domain concerned with State and Citizen, and much addressed in CDA, namely, immigration. The data presented are taken from a corpus of news reports on immigration which I have analysed, from a different perspective, elsewhere (Hart 2010).[17]

A number of categories in the network relate to the 'referential scope' of the representation. With the widest scope, for example, social actors may be represented as a general class, realized in plurals without an article or, as in (19), singular forms with an article. Here the nominal refers to all entities that fall within its denotation.

(19) 'If he is to live as a British citizen, then he must have the ability to integrate into the society of his chosen home. The immigrant owes that to himself, as well as to his host society'. (Norman Tebbit in *The Independent*, 4 September 2003)

Slightly more specific in scope, speakers may refer to a particular group of social actors collected together by means of plural forms such as 'immigrants' in (21) but also by means of mass nouns denoting a group of people as in (20). Ideologically, **genericization** and **collectivization** can serve to impersonalize social actors and perpetuate social stereotypes.

(20) [W]hat we need is a comprehensive, coherent, rights-based immigration policy that . . . makes known . . . the rights and the responsibilities of the immigrant community. (*Sunday Mirror*, 14 December 2003)

(21) Immigrants coming to the UK must learn English, Gordon Brown said yesterday. (*The Mirror*, 6 June 2006)

Most narrow in referential scope, speakers may refer to social actors as specific individuals as in 'Gordon Brown' in (21). According to van Leeuwen, newspapers tend to collectivize 'ordinary' social actors and personalize powerful people.

Particularized groups of people can be quantified or 'aggregated' and treated as statistics as in (22).

(22) Almost 90,000 immigrants entered the country in the past year – the highest number since records began. (*The Mirror*, 13 September 2006)

In **indetermination**, individuals or groups can be represented as unspecified or anonymous as in (23). Such anonymous actors can also be aggregated as in (24). Indetermination strategies treat the identity of the personalized actor(s) as irrelevant and in (23) and (24) prevent the reader from forming a critical judgement on their validity or appropriateness as a source (Hart 2011c).

(23) Immigration makes <u>some people</u> feel they are being 'overwhelmed', the leader of Roman Catholics in England and Wales said yesterday. (*The Daily Mail*, 3 May 2006)

(24) [M]assive inflows from alien cultures are leaving <u>many people</u> feeling like strangers in their own land. (*The Express*, 8 August 2006)

When individuals or groups are determined, they can be nominated or categorized. **Nomination** is typically realized in proper nouns such as 'Gordon Brown' in (21). Here the speaker faces further choices in formality between formal (surname only), semi-formal (first and surname) and informal (first name only). Informal nominations are less likely to be used for powerful actors and less likely to be used at all in broadsheet newspapers compared to mid-market or tabloid papers. Nominations may also be 'titulated' either through **honorification** involving the addition of titles such as 'Dr' or through **affiliation**, often specifying a functional role in a particular institution as in (25). These kinds of titulation serve to legitimize the social actor and thus the assertion (Hart 2011c) by reference to qualifications or positions of rank in society and 'blur the dividing line between nomination and categorisation' (van Leeuwen 1996: 53).

(25) <u>Sir</u> Andrew Green, <u>chairman</u> of Migrationwatch UK, said the numbers still in Britain could be as high as 340,000 because the estimates do not include dependents. (*The Express*, 14 March 2006)

Categorization concerns identities and functions which social actors share with others. Van Leeuwen distinguishes two major types of categorization: **functionalization** and **identification**. Functionalization occurs when social actors are referred to in terms of something they do, an activity, as in (26).

(26) <u>The Heathrow worker</u>, now in jail, was one of more than a dozen suspected terrorists allowed to enter Britain, it emerged this weekend. (*The Sunday Times*, 14 September 2003)

Identification occurs when social actors are defined in terms of something they more or less permanently *are* rather than something they choose to *do*. It is further broken down into **classification**, **relational identification** and **physical**

identification. Classification involves reference in terms of 'the major categories by means of which a given society or institution differentiates between classes of people' (Van Leeuwen 1996: 54) including age, gender, race, religion, ethnicity, and social and legal status. Relational identification represents social actors in terms of personal or kinship relations and is often used to highlight human characteristics of individuals and thereby manoeuvre the reader into a position of empathy or sympathy. In immigration discourse, relational identification is therefore often reserved for perceived 'victims of immigration policy', either immigrants themselves or, as in (27), other individuals. In (27), then, we find the person responsible for the accident represented by means of classification highlighting their legal status only, without any reference to their familial identity. The victim of the accident, by contrast, is referred to by means of relational identification. The effect of this strategy is to align the victim with the Self and contribute to the construction of a delegitimated Other.

(27) An illegal immigrant was convicted yesterday of killing a father of two
      teenagers after speeding with a 'seriously under-inflated' tyre. (*The Daily
      Telegraph*, 5 June 2004)

Physical identification represents social actors in terms of physical characteristics. Such features can carry connotations which serve indirectly to classify or functionalize those actors. In (28), for example, 'bearded' might be taken to classify the actors along ethnic and religious lines.

(28) The bearded hijackers pulled down their headrobes to scrutinise the 55-
      year old aid worker. (*The Sunday Times*, 13 February 2000)

Finally, and most closely related to linguistic categories in SFG, van Leeuwen distinguishes two types of passivation: **subjection** and **beneficialization**. In subjection, social actors are commodified as 'things' which can be bought, sold, borrowed and exchanged. In beneficialization, the beneficialized social actor benefits, positively or negatively, from the process. In immigration discourse, it is usually immigrants who are commodified as in (29) and industrialized countries which are beneficialized as in (30). In positive beneficialization, this is often to the tune of economic or labour advantages.

(29) The case for bringing in immigrant workers is more complex than many
      assume. (*The Sunday Times*, 27 March 2005)
(30) This may provide evidence that immigrants bring complementary skills
      to the existing workforce. (*The Guardian*, 11 December 2002)

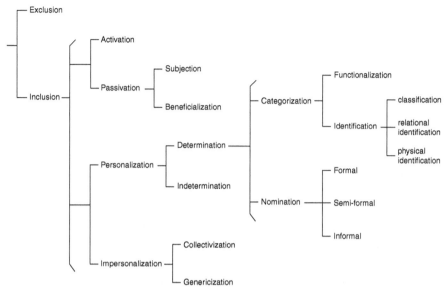

Figure 1.4. Partial system network for representation of social actors (adapted from van Leeuwen 1996: 66)

Note, then, that realization of the socio-semantic categories proposed in the Social Actor Model is not restricted to referential elements (relying on lexis for differentiation) but certain categories may be realized by other morpho-syntactic means (e.g. adjectives, quantifiers) as well as in socio-functional participant roles. Means of realizing exclusion include nominalization and agentless passivization as discussed in Section 4. A partial grammar for the representation of social actors is presented in Figure 1.4.

6. Issues in Critical Linguistics

So far in this chapter, I have presented a framework for analysing the ideological functions of linguistic representation, based on Halliday's SFG, in an unproblematized way. However, it should be noted that a number of issues have been raised against CDA and Critical Linguistics in particular (e.g. Billig 2008; Chilton 2005; Stubbs 1997; Widdowson 2004) which are worthy of attention at this point. Current issues in CDA can be oriented to three closely related and overlapping motifs as follows:

Epistemology

- Critical Instinct
- Cognitive Import

Data

- Selection
- Significance (pragmatic and statistical)

Interpretation

- Subjectivity
- Over-interpretation

There is not space in this section to deal with all the issues currently being debated in CDA, some of which I have addressed elsewhere. For example, I will not discuss the Critical Instinct issue raised by Chilton (2005). The reader is instead directed to the papers held in the debate pages of *Discourse Studies* (Hart 2011c and other papers therein).[18] Neither will I deal here with the problem of cognitive equivalence (see Hart 2013a). I will, however, briefly highlight and address some problems pertaining to data and interpretation.

Data issues in CDA concern the selection and presentation of data in analyses and the significance, both in a pragmatic and a statistical sense, of selected data. In relation to selection CDA is accused of the fragmentary and exemplificatory use of data (Fowler 1996: 8; Widdowson 2004: 102). A consequence of this is that data may have been 'cherry-picked' to fit some predefined model or political motive rather than theory and critical standpoint being derived from data (Widdowson 2004: 102). Similarly, there is the danger that the reason a particular instance has been selected is in fact because it is a rather unusual example which has attracted the analyst's attention (Koller and Mautner 2004: 218). For example, use of genericization realized by means of singular forms with an article as in (19) is actually quite infrequent in contemporary political discourse. Furthermore, as Widdowson (2004: 2013) points out, when data fragments are presented cut off from co-textual and intertextual connections, a vast amount of text necessarily goes unanalysed or unaccounted for. Consequently, information 'mystified' may in fact be given elsewhere either in the text itself or in its intertextual context.

Another data issue, related to data selection or its non-selection, concerns the pragmatic significance of linguistic structures. Critical discourse analysts may seem to attach pragmatic significance to particular types of structures when it suits them and ignore the same structures on other occasions. For example, in the context of political protests, critical analysts might highlight the use of the agentless passive voice in relation to police actions but ignore instances such as (31) where it is protestors who are excluded and where, thus, given the political stance of the newspaper, the example does not fit with expectations.

(31)   Graffiti <u>was scrawled</u> on buildings along Millbank and a war memorial <u>was defaced</u> with the words 'Fight back'. (*The Daily Mail*, 10 November 2010)

Critical discourse analysts are even themselves guilty of using agentless passives and nominalizations in their own writings (Billig 2008). However, no linguistic structure is in and of itself ideological – at least not in the pejorative sense. Rather, it becomes so in contexts where it is used as 'a form of discursive power abuse' (van Dijk 2008: 823). The same structure is not equally significant, therefore, in relation to all social actors or in every discourse genre but instead realizes an ideological potential in contexts where power is at stake and when deployed in the interests of established power. A second sense of significance, again related to the selection of data, concerns the statistical significance or representativeness of given examples. In short, it seems too often to be taken for granted that the examples presented are typical instantiations of the Discourse under investigation. In the absence of any evidence to support such an assumption, however, the analyst is in danger of making overgeneralized statements about a given Discourse and attaching too much weight to the potential ideological effects of a given linguistic structure within the order of discourse. As Stubbs (1997: 111) suggests, therefore, 'a much wider range of data must be sampled before generalizations are made about typical language use'.

Further problems pertain to the interpretation of selected data. Interpretive issues are related in part to data issues in the sense that some interpretative problems can be seen to stem from insufficiencies in data selection and sampling. A first major issue surrounds analytical subjectivity. Given the open sociopolitical position of CDA, Widdowson (1995: 516) suggests that in some analyses conviction can count for more than cogency. What we find in critical discourse analyses, Widdowson (2004: 103) argues, are precisely 'critical discourse interpretations'. In other words, we find subjective, idiosyncratic interpretations motivated by the analyst's political predispositions rather than more objective theoretically driven, predictable, measureable interpretations which satisfy usual scientific criteria. Without such constraints, and in the face of data disconnected from its co-textual and intertextual context, analysts may find themselves in danger of over-interpreting the pragmatic effects of a particular linguistic instantiation. For example, information described as 'missing' from the clause and thus 'mystified' may not be 'missing' or 'mystified' at all. It may not 'supposed' to be there given normal efficiency principles governing language use. It may instead be presupposed on the basis that it is recoverable from context or co-text. Information, then, may be presupposed when it has been previously spelled out in the co-textual or intertextual context and/or is otherwise assumed to be inferable from shared knowledge. Thus, in our earlier examples (15–18) from *BBC News*, the latter instantiations may not specify agency because this was indicated in the first instance and is therefore subsequently treated as given information. The speaker may therefore not be 'guilty' of any attempt at manipulation and the information may be perfectly accessible to the reader. As Widdowson (2000: 22) points out, people process texts 'in normal pragmatic ways, inferring meanings which have not been explicitly spelled out by reference to what they have already read and what they know of the world'. Here, the issue of over-interpretation intersects with the problem of cognitive equivalence which concerns the extent to which linguistic representations in texts impact on cognitive representations and processes in the minds of readers (Billig 2008). We discuss this more fully in Chapter 4. For now, however, it is worth pointing out that (i) the intentions of the speaker do not necessarily bear on the legitimating effects of discourse which may be a product of natural language rules, principles and processes as much as the way speakers put the system to use and that (ii) although hearers do make inferences in discourse, this requires the relevant background knowledge and/or intertextual experience in the first place as well as extra cognitive effort to recover the information. In relation to the second point, O'Halloran (2003) points out that not all readers will have the requisite knowledge or be willing to invest the additional processing costs. In some cases, as Maillat and Oswald (2011) show, readers may be cognitively blocked from accessing contextual information. Finally, it is worth noting that the presence or absence of implicit information in the 'mental picture' is not absolute. In relation to this last point, van Leeuwen (1996: 39) distinguishes two types of exclusion: **suppression** and **backgrounding**. Suppression involves a radical exclusion leaving no 'trace' of the excluded information. In the case of backgrounding, the exclusion is less radical: the information is given elsewhere and is thus 'not so much excluded as de-emphasized, pushed into the background'. Crucially, however, this 'background' may be psychologically real experienced in terms of salience and subject to scalar effects (see Chapter 4). Another issue relating to over-interpretation comes with transitivity choices involving the metaphorical realization of processes and the claim that such choices attribute particular qualities to referents. For example, an instance such as (32) may be said to compare protestors with insects and thus evoke negative associations. The extent to which such a claim can be warranted, however, is called into question by Widdowson (2004: 108–9).

(32) The glass frontage was smashed and protesters <u>swarmed</u> seven floors up to the roof. (*The Daily Mail*, 10 November 2010)

CDA, then, faces some fairly well-founded criticisms. However, much of the work highlighting perceived shortcomings in CDA is directed at early analyses in Critical Linguistics such as found in Fowler et al. (1979) and Kress and Hodge (1979) which are taken as emblematic of CDA as a whole (e.g. Sharrock and Anderson 1981). More recent research in CDA makes use of a range of analytical techniques available to help address these potential problems. One way of reducing subjectivity, for example, is through comparative analyses of the kind presented earlier in Section 3. Another is with reference to a fully fledged grammatical model whose alternative potential instantiations can also act as a point of comparison. Moreover, contemporary approaches to CDA, facilitated by new developments in linguistics, can be seen at least in part as motivated by some of these issues. For example, in so far as it allows for much larger bodies of data to be collected and analysed for typical linguistic occurrences, the Corpus Linguistic Approach responds to issues of data selection and statistical significance (Baker et al. 2008; Gabrielatos and Baker 2008). Corpus Linguistic techniques can also be used to guard against the over-interpretation of metaphor and/or provide evidence in support of one's intuitive interpretations (O'Halloran 2007). Similarly, the Cognitive Linguistic Approach can reduce subjectivity and demonstrate cognitive import by grounding analyses in psychologically plausible, potentially testable models as advanced in Cognitive Linguistics. The chapters in Part 2 of this book are dedicated to developing a Cognitive Linguistic Approach to CDA.

7. Conclusion

In this chapter, we have pursued an analytical framework, based in Halliday's SFG, for the treatment of ideology in linguistic representation. We have seen that choices across a number of systems in the ideational function of language, including TRANSITIVITY and VOICE, can serve in certain discursive contexts to present social actions in particular, ideologically vested ways and thus contribute to their (de)legitimation. We have also illustrated a grammar for the representation of social actors and shown the ideological functions of different options within this system. In the final section, we have highlighted a number of potential problems for CDA, including, under the heading of pragmatic significance, attaching universal effects to particular linguistic forms. In keeping with the 'restricted relativism' of Critical Linguistics, however, we have argued that representational choices in specific Discourses are not ideologically innocent but, on inspection, can be shown to betray the speaker's particular ideological position. In this sense, representation cannot be truly separated from evaluation. Since all linguistic products are based on choices, both representations and evaluations involve **perspectivization** – 'an omnipresent feature of linguistic realisation' (KhosraviNik 2010: 58). The distinction, however, is that in (inscribed) evaluations the speaker's ideological perspective is explicitly signalled by lexico-grammatical resources designed specifically for this purpose. In the following chapter we explore the grammar of evaluation located in the interpersonal function of language.

Evaluation

1. Introduction

In the last chapter, we discussed representation in discourse. In this chapter, we discuss evaluation. If the grammar of representation, as we saw, provides a resource for reflecting on the world, then the grammar of evaluation provides a resource for reacting to it and thus serves the interpersonal function of language. In grammatical approaches to CDA, the study of evaluation has been predominantly confined to the region of modality (Fairclough 1989; Fowler 1991). More recently, however, researchers have begun to point to other aspects of evaluation as relevant for CDA (e.g. Koller 2011b; van Dijk 2011). Evaluation, more broadly construed, concerns the way that speakers code or implicitly convey various kinds of subjective opinion in discourse and in so doing attempt to achieve some intersubjective consensus of values with respect to what is represented. Evaluation in all its forms, thus, plays a crucial part in legitimation. There is a considerable body of literature on evaluative phenomena in discourse going under several different headings, including most visibly 'stance' (e.g. Biber and Finegan 1989) and 'appraisal' (e.g. Martin and White 2007).[1] The more developed framework, and a direct extension of Halliday's SFG, is Appraisal Theory (Martin and White 2007). Appraisal Theory therefore provides a particularly useful and appropriate grammatical tool for analysing aspects of evaluation beyond modality in CDA (Koller 2011b: 125).[2] We discuss the ideological functions of evaluation in the context of three quite different domains: corporate discourse, political discourse and media discourse. We start, in Section 2, by introducing Appraisal Theory and situating it with respect to SFG. In Section 3, we illustrate the different aspects of the system and demonstrate their potential ideological functions through critical analyses of instantiations found in corporate social reports. In Section 4, we apply the framework in a single text analysis of a political speech seeking to justify American involvement in Iraq. In Section 5, we explore how Corpus Linguistic techniques can reveal the presence of more covert evaluations in discourse taking by way of example media discourse on immigration.

2. Appraisal Theory and SFG

Recall from the introduction that while the ideational function of language allows the speaker to communicate about the world, the interpersonal function allows the speaker to comment on the world. According to Halliday, it is through the interpersonal function that the speaker 'intrudes himself into the context of situation, both expressing his own attitudes and judgements and seeking to influence the attitudes and behaviour of others' (Halliday 2007: 184). In SFG, the interpersonal function is said to be realized through the system of MODALITY which allows for the expression of opinions relating to probability/usuality (modalization) and obligation/inclination (modulation). In a programme of research further elaborating the interpersonal function, Martin and White (2007) advance a grammar of APPRAISAL. This grammar describes a more comprehensive system for the expression of subjective opinions and the realization of intersubjective positioning strategies. Specifically, APPRAISAL is defined as a system of semantic resources for 'reacting emotionally (affect), judging morally (judgement) and evaluating aesthetically (appreciation)' as well as resources for amplifying and engaging with these evaluations (Martin 1995: 28). Appraisal Theory thus incorporates research relating to style, stance, evaluation and evidentiality within a unified systemic framework.

In contrast with ideational meanings, interpersonal meanings are not so readily identifiable with particular functional elements. Rather, interpersonal meanings find expression across the full range of grammatical categories, though adjectives, adverbials and modals are perhaps prototypical realizations. Neither are interpersonal meanings necessarily associated with a single element in a clause but may be strung throughout it.[3] Interpersonal meanings may not, in fact, be explicitly coded in any element of the clause but may instead rely for recognition on the hearer's 'reading' of the text which is, in turn, partly dependent on their predefined values and assumptions. Such meanings are said to be 'invoked' rather than 'inscribed'. To account for this, following Martin and White, we can add an extra station to the cline of instantiation presented in Chapter 1. A text then becomes characterized as an 'affording instance' and its uptake and interpretation an 'actualised instance'.

For Martin and White, APPRAISAL exists as a meaning potential in the semantic stratum which is realized in the lexicogrammar through three particular sub-systems: ATTITUDE, ENGAGEMENT and GRADUATION. These three systems may each be progressively subdivided left-right reflecting greater levels of delicacy which allow for a more fine-grained analysis. The system of ATTITUDE, for example, may be broken down into sub-systems of AFFECT, JUDGEMENT and APPRECIATION constituting resources for the expression of emotion, ethics and aesthetics, respectively. We discuss the system of ATTITUDE in the proceeding sections followed by the systems of ENGAGEMENT and GRADUATION. The basic APPRAISAL system is presented in Figure 2.1.[4] In the following section we illustrate the ideological functions of evaluation, across the whole system, with examples extracted from a small corpus of corporate social reports. We then, in the subsequent section, apply the general framework in a critical analysis of a single political speech produced by George W. Bush in the War on Terror. Both of these discourse genres have as their principal goal the legitimation of social action. In contrast to media discourse, however, this goal is overtly manifest. Both of these genres rely much more heavily on explicit evaluation and are more concerned with establishing the *ethos* of the speaker than media discourse. In

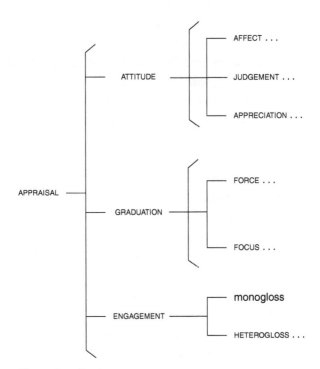

Figure 2.1. Basic APPRAISAL system

the final section, we explore more covert means of evaluation in media discourse on immigration.

3. Appraisal in corporate social reports

Corporate discourse has only recently fallen under the lens of CDA (e.g. Fuoli 2012; Koller 2010, 2011; Merkl-Davies and Koller 2012). Critical analysts of public-facing corporate discourse agree that it involves some form of 'impression management' (Merkl-Davies and Koller 2012). The precise (linguistic) form of impression management involved, however, differs according to particular activity and intended audience type. These **field** and **tenor** variables give rise to different sub-genres of corporate discourse, all of which are aimed at instilling confidence in the company and ultimately at profit-making, but which relate to different aspects of business practice and are associated with different strategies and structures of discourse. Advertising and branding, for example, are aimed at retaining and attracting customers on the basis of products and services. Financial reports are aimed at preserving and securing investors on the basis of financial performance. And social reports are aimed at maintaining positive 'face' in the public eye (and thus satisfying shareholders of the company's financial stability) in spite of business practices which negatively impact on people and the environment. The form of impression management involved in corporate social reporting, thus, corresponds most closely with the concept of legitimation as understood here.[5] Multinational corporations are now much more accountable for their actions as their practices are more publicly scrutinized and subject to official regulation. Various movements such as the Fair Trade movement reflect public expectations that corporations behave in just and responsible ways. However, large corporations routinely engage in practices which are harmful to individuals and the environment. Heavily mediatized scandals include, for example, the BP Oil Spill in the Gulf of Mexico in 2010 and the collapse of a Primark factory in Bangladesh in 2013. More ongoing are general issues concerning working conditions, exploitation and climate change. When harmful business practices are revealed, it can be damaging to reputations, sometimes resulting in mediatized boycotts and consequent falls in share prices. Corporate social reporting is a particular genre of corporate discourse which has evolved to restore or maintain public faith in light of such threats to the perceived legitimacy of the corporation. As Fuoli (2012: 57) puts it, corporate social reports are 'directed at (re-)establishing congruence between social norms and values and organizational conduct'. The CDA research on corporate discourse and social reporting specifically has been concentrated primarily on representation (with a focus on metaphor) where, as we saw in the previous chapter, speakers 'manage' ideational meanings in order to promote particular, ideologically vested, versions of reality and to 'deal with' difficult facts. Research into interpersonal resources and their legitimating role in corporate discourse has been comparatively sparse (though see Fuoli 2012; Merkl-Davies and Koller 2012). Evaluation in discourse, however, plays a crucial part in the construction of identity, including corporate identity, and thus serves equally in steering public perceptions. In the next section, then, we examine the ideological and legitimating functions of evaluation in the context of corporate social reports. Instances are taken from a small corpus of three reports published in 2009 by Coca Cola (CC), Nike (Nk) and Nestlé (Ne).

3.1 ATTITUDE

ATTITUDE is a general system responsible for expressions of appraisal including emotional reactions, social judgements and aesthetic evaluations. It may be broken down into three sub-systems accordingly: AFFECT, JUDGEMENT and APPRECIATION. The system of AFFECT focuses on the appraiser (who does not necessarily co-identify with the speaker) and may be directed or not. The system of JUDGEMENT focuses on other individuals with whom the appraiser shares his/her social environment. The system of APPRECIATION focuses on objects in the environment which the appraiser interacts with. Each of these systems can in turn be further sub-categorized as described below.

3.1.1 AFFECT

The system of AFFECT allows speakers to talk about different kinds of emotions and is realized in a range of lexicogrammatical structures including descriptions and attributes of participants and manners of process (affect as quality), processes themselves (affect as process) and modal adjuncts (affect as comment). Two important parameters operating over the whole ATTITUDE system relate to whether categories are realized as **positive** or **negative** instantiations and whether they are realized in terms of a **disposition** or a **behaviour** (as the physical manifestation of a disposition).

Categories in the system of AFFECT include: HAPPINESS, which concerns moods construed broadly as feelings of happiness or sadness; SECURITY, which concerns feelings of peace and anxiety; and SATISFACTION, which concerns feelings of achievement and frustration. Perhaps unsurprisingly, given the functions of the particular genre, we find very few negative instantiations of HAPPINESS in corporate social reports except where it is absolutely necessary. For example, in response to tragedies in the workplace as in (1) and (2):

(1) We <u>regretfully</u> had four associates and three contractors who lost their lives while performing work for our Company. (CC)

(2) Despite all continuous efforts, we deeply <u>regret</u> four fatalities in 2009 due to accidents while at work. (Ne)

Much more common are positive instantiations as in (3)–(5):

(3) Ensuring our associates are <u>happy</u>, healthy and treated fairly and with respect is at the core of our business philosophy and success. (CC)

(4) 'I am really <u>happy</u> that I had the opportunity to participate in this nutrition programme at my child's pre-school'. (Ne)

(5) As a global business, our ability to understand, <u>embrace</u> and operate in a multicultural world – both in the marketplace and in the workplace – is critical to our long-term sustainability. (CC)

In (3) and (4), the feeling does not relate to the speaker, the corporation, but is attributed to a third party. This is employees in (3) which thus presents the company as caring for the general mental well-being of its workforce. In (4), the appraisal is part of a quotation. The purpose of this quotative seems to be to provide an endorsement of the outreach activity at which the appraisal is directed and thus present the corporation as extending its care and responsibility beyond its own workforce to local communities. In (5), the appraisal is realized as a behavioural surge directed at multiculturalism and therefore shows the company as sharing presumed desirable values.

Expressions of SATISFACTION mainly occur as positive instantiations in endorsements of corporate practices as in (6) and (7) or in relation to employee satisfaction as in (8):

(6) 'We are <u>pleased</u> to have found a partner like Nestlé to share this approach with us'. (Ne)

(7) Through this 'green fleet' scheme, which was <u>awarded</u> second prize in the International Green Fleet Award 2009 in November, we have reduced CO_2 emissions by 17%. (Ne)

(8) NIKE, Inc. has an <u>energized</u>, <u>engaged</u> work force with a <u>passion</u> for the company, their consumers and their jobs. (Nk)

Negative instantiations of SECURITY are mainly attributed to the outside world as in (9) but presented as shared by the corporation as in (10):

(9) In the face of growing <u>concerns</u> regarding water scarcity and its impact ... (Ne)

(10) Water scarcity is one of the central environmental and human health <u>issues</u> facing the world. It is also a key <u>concern</u> for our company. (Nk)

Positive instantiations of SECURITY are expressed in relation to the remedy of insecurities as in (11) and (12) which thus present the company as responding to issues of public concern:

(11) I am <u>confident</u> this initiative will strengthen economic opportunities for women in the communities we serve and help us grow our business in markets around the world. (CC)

(12) 'I feel <u>reassured</u> that support programmes are in place and that I can get advice from my mentor'. (Ne)

3.1.2 JUDGEMENT

Through the system of JUDGEMENT, speakers convey moral evaluations of other people, their character and their behaviour. The system is divided into two major categories, SOCIAL ESTEEM and SOCIAL SANCTION, each of which can be further sub-categorized and polarized between positive and negative. The distinction between them, according Martin and White (2007: 53), can be captured where someone appraised negatively in terms of SOCIAL ESTEEM might be recommended a therapist while someone appraised negatively in terms of SOCIAL SANCTION might be recommended a lawyer.

Sub-categories of SOCIAL ESTEEM include: NORMALITY, which concerns how special someone is; CAPACITY, which concerns how capable someone is; and TENACITY, which concerns how dependable someone is. Positive and negative instantiations of SOCIAL ESTEEM are thus associated with acts of admiration and criticism, respectively. In our corporate social reports, SOCIAL ESTEEM is mainly directed at employees and consultants in positive instantiations of TENACITY and CAPACITY:

(13) This report is a reflection of the efforts being made today by the <u>dedicated</u> men and women of The Coca-Cola Company and our bottling partners around the world. (CC)

(14) Thanks to the <u>dedication</u> and efforts of our employees, every day we make a difference to the lives of many consumers around the world. (Ne)

(15) Nestlé follows the principle of 'healthy minds in healthy bodies', knowing
      that a loyal and productive workforce is the key driver of its success. (Ne)
(16) In 2009, we asked respected third-party experts, including The Nature
      Conservancy and Global Environment and Technology Foundation, to
      work with us. (CC)

Appraising consultants as dependable ('respected') and capable ('experts') as in
(16) serves to legitimize Coca Cola's practices by presenting them as conducted
in light of advice from an external source that the hearer is expected to consider
independent and authoritative. TENACITY is also directed at corporations
themselves to highlight their commitment to responsibility:

(17) Nestlé remains committed to delivering integrated, science-based
      nutrition solutions and feeding guidance. (Ne)
(18) Our associates play a vital role in the success of our business, and we
      strive to be a great place to work for all our associates globally. (CC)
(19) Through this partnership, we are dedicated to conserving freshwater
      basins around the world. (CC)

Sub-categories of SOCIAL SANCTION include VERACITY, which concerns how
truthful someone is, and PROPRIETY, which concerns how far beyond reproach
someone is. Positive and negative instantiations of SOCIAL SANCTION are thus
associated with acts of approval and condemnation, respectively. In corporate
social reports, we mainly find positive instantiations of PROPRIETY used to present
the corporation as upstanding and socially and environmentally responsible:

(20) Nestlé's Corporate Business Principles guide our behaviour in relation
      to all relevant stakeholders. They reflect the basic concepts of fairness,
      honesty and respect for people and the environment in all our business
      actions. (Ne)
(21) We support policies that deliver efficient, cost-effective delivery of NIKE,
      Inc. products in a responsible manner. (Nk)
(22) Care was taken to use environmentally sustainable products and to follow
      socially responsible manufacturing processes to ensure a minimized
      environmental impact. (CC)

3.1.3 APPRECIATION

The final sub-system of ATTITUDE, APPRECIATION, allows speakers to aesthetically
evaluate 'things', including objects (material and semiotic) and processes, and is

divided into REACTION (expressions of quality or effect), VALUATION (expressions of value and uniqueness) and COMPOSITION (expressions of balance, complexity and functionality). Positive instantiations of REACTION in corporate social reports occur mainly in relation to products and practices:

(23) With the Pegasus 25, fewer materials in the upper reduced the shoe's weight by 1.4 ounces, making it an <u>impressive</u> 13-percent lighter than the previous Pegasus. (Nk)

(24) These decisions drive us to innovate to meet those evolving needs, while at the same time providing consumers with <u>great</u> taste, refreshment and hydration. (CC)

(25) The protection and propagation of <u>superior</u> 'fine' cocoa' varieties for use in our premium chocolate brands is also ongoing in Ecuador and Venezuela. (Ne)

(26) Engaging in closer relationships with suppliers has proven to be an <u>excellent</u> way of contributing to Nestlé's Creating Shared Value model. (Ne)

VALUATION is also only really realized in positive instantiations and is used to highlight (technological) innovation in products as in (27) and (28) and practices as in (29) and (30):

(27) This <u>unique</u> athletic performance shoe was designed <u>specifically</u> for Native Americans to help reduce Type 2 diabetes and increase participation in sport. (Nk)

(28) Among hundreds of general e-courses offered at a global level, more than 240 have been <u>specially</u> developed for Nestlé. (Ne)

(29) We have projects under way in Australia, Belize, Brazil, El Salvador, Guatemala, Honduras and South Africa to demonstrate <u>innovative</u> growing and production methods that can help meet Bonsucro standards. (CC)

(30) We know we can't achieve this alone and are committed to partnering and collaborating to find <u>creative</u> solutions. (Nk)

COMPOSITION is similarly realized in positive instantiations used to indicate high 'standards' in practices:

(31) We support policies that deliver <u>efficient</u>, <u>cost-effective</u> delivery of NIKE, Inc. products in a responsible manner. (NK)

(32) By designing a hyper-<u>efficient</u>, 'nested' pattern for Air-Sole production, we were able to further reduce post production waste. (Nk)

(33) Our principles and policies are applied <u>consistently</u> and <u>rigorously</u> in all countries through our auditing and assurance standards. (Ne)

(34) Stevia extract's safety has been established by more than 25 years of scientific research and the publication of safety studies from a <u>rigorous</u>, <u>comprehensive</u> scientific research program commissioned by The Coca–Cola Company and Cargill. (CC)

Positive instantiations of APPRECIATION, then, particularly those directed at business practices, present the corporation as equipped to meet their social and environmental responsibilities. The system of ATTITUDE more generally seems to be exploited in corporate social reporting to construct an identity according to which the corporation exists in a position of alignment with the values and expectations of target audiences. In the next section, we see how speakers explicitly signal their position with respect to the values and voices of others.

3.2 ENGAGEMENT

So far in this chapter, we have considered texts as if they exist in a textual vacuum. However, we have seen already in Chapter 1 that texts exist in chains of intertextuality. More specifically, following the theories of Voloshinov and Bakhtin, texts can be said to exist against a backdrop of intertextual 'voices'. Texts, on this account, not only have histories, but have futures too. Texts are influenced by prior articulations but also anticipate future articulations, construing the potential positions of putative readers and 'responding' accordingly. Texts are therefore dialogic or 'heteroglossic' in nature. That is, they contain traces of multiple voices. As Voloshinov (1995: 139) puts it, 'The printed verbal performance engages, as it were, in ideological colloquy of a large scale: it responds to something, affirms something, anticipates possible responses and objections, seeks support, and so on'. In analysing ENGAGEMENT, as modelled in Appraisal Theory, we are interested in the extent to which speakers acknowledge these alternative voices and, if they do, the different ways in which they then interact with them. That is, we are interested in whether speakers present themselves as in positions of alignment, antagonism or neutrality with respect to previous speakers' value positions and whether speakers anticipate the value positions of putative readers as being in alignment, antagonism or neutrality with respect to the positions they are advancing. Crucially, of course, we are interested in the linguistic resources that allow all of this to be played out in discourse. A number of such resources have been studied under various headings including concession, hedging, polarity, mitigation, modality, attribution and evidentiality. All these linguistic phenomena serve to realize intersubjective positioning strategies in so far as they negotiate 'solidarity', either by agreeing with alternative points of view or, more rhetorically, by attempting to bring the audience into positions of alignment with the particular points of view the speaker is advancing. They are all brought together in Appraisal Theory and distributed through the system of ENGAGEMENT.

The first choice the speaker faces in the ENGAGEMENT system is whether or not to acknowledge the dialogistic nature of texts in either a **monoglossic** or a **heteroglossic** utterance. Key to the choice is whether the speaker construes the position of the text as given or at issue and up for debate. In electing a monoglossic, or 'undialogised', utterance, the speaker presents the position communicated as undisputed and/or indisputable fact.[6] Such utterances usually take the form of categorical or bare assertions as in (35).

(35) Saccharin is permitted for use in foods and beverages in more than 100 countries around the world and <u>is</u> safe for all populations. (CC)

When speakers do acknowledge the dialogistic nature of texts they may engage with other voices in **contractive** versus **expansive** ways as modelled in Figure 2.2. The distinction pertains to whether the locution makes room for dialogically alternative positions (expansion) or whether the locution instead acts to close down alternative positions (contraction).[7] The modalized proposition in (36), for example, serves to expand the dialogistic space by allowing for the possibility that the price and availability of water might not become increasingly volatile.

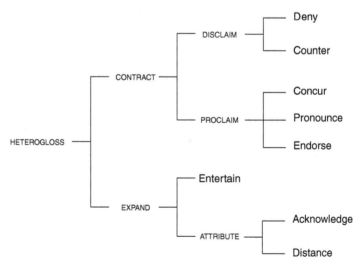

Figure 2.2. ENGAGEMENT system (HETEROGLOSS)

(36)   What will be the cost of fresh water in the future? Price and availability
        <u>may</u> become increasingly volatile. (Nk)

In cases of expansion, the speaker can choose to **entertain** the proposition or
attribute it. In examples of entertainment, such as (36), the speaker explicitly
presents a statement as grounded in their own subjectivity and thereby allows
for the possibility of dialogic alternatives. The strategy of entertaining finds
expression in epistemic modal auxiliaries (*may, might, could, will*), modal adjuncts
(*possibly, probably, definitely*) and certain first-person mental process verbs
which Halliday characterizes as modal (*I think, believe, suspect, am convinced
that*). It may also be realized in certain evidentials based on sensory observation
(*it seems, appears that*) and certain inferring evidentials (*the research suggests
that*). In attribution, the speaker similarly presents the proposition as one in a
range of possible positions but does so by grounding it in the subjectivity of an
external voice. Attribution is thus achieved through 'the grammar of directly
and indirectly reported speech and thought' (Martin and White 2007: 111) and
realized in verbal process verbs (*X said, claimed, warned that*) and third-person
mental process verbs (*X thinks, believes that*). In attributions, the speaker can
choose to simply acknowledge (and implicitly agree with) the external voice or
distance themselves from it. This latter strategy is typically realized in the verbal
process verb 'to claim' through which the speaker 'detaches him/herself from
responsibility for what is being reported' (Caldas-Coulthard 1994: 295). While
attribution belongs to expansion, it should be noted that depending on the level
of authority vested in the attributed speaker, the appraisal can be considered
functionally more or less contractive. For example, in acknowledging a third
party the hearer is expected to consider authoritative, the speaker might in
fact close down the dialogical space as a consequence of the epistemic weight
attached to the source.[8]

In cases of contraction, the speaker leaves no space in the dialogic colloquy
for the possibility of alternative, past or potential, positions. The speaker can
achieve this in two ways: **disclaim** or **proclaim**. In disclaims the speaker invokes
some alternative position by virtue of denying or countering it and thus directly
supressing it. In proclaims, the speaker indirectly supresses alternative positions
by virtue of their contrary relation with the position the speaker is emphatically
adopting. Three types of proclaim are identified. Speakers may **concur** with
other dialogic voices through evidential adjuncts which indicate a common
knowledge or value system (*obviously, naturally*). They may **endorse** dialogic
voices through evidential verbs which amount to 'proof' (*show, demonstrate*).

Or they may overtly **pronounce** the truth or warrantability of a position through phrases such as *the fact of the matter is* or *it can only be concluded that.*

Perhaps unsurprisingly, corporate social reports make use of the resources for contraction much more than expansion and when they do engage expansively it is in the form of an acknowledgement which the reader is expected to accept as authoritative as in (37) and (38). These acknowledgements are used to highlight the corporation's environmental credentials in (37) and the economic benefits that they bring to local communities in (38).

(37) This figure ranks Nike as the third-largest retail user of organic cotton in the world (<u>according to</u> the Organic Exchange, an NGO committed to increasing production and use of organically grown fibres). (Nk)

(38) <u>According to</u> an International Finance Corporation and Harvard Kennedy School report conducted in 2008, MDC owners and their employees are likely to support an estimated 48,000 dependents in East Africa. (CC)

In contractions, corporate social reports use endorsements to close down positions which might be detrimental to the reputation of the company, such as concerns over the safety of their products as in (39) and (40):

(39) Numerous studies <u>have shown</u> . . . that sucralose can be safely consumed by people with diabetes. (CC)

(40) [M]ore than 75 scientific studies <u>have proven</u> it [cyclamate] to be safe for human consumption. (CC)

They are also used to constitute 'proof' that the corporation is compliant with demands made of them and thus supress the alternative position that they are failing to satisfy expectations:

(41) Our actions also <u>demonstrate</u> Nike, Inc.'s commitment to being transparent with key stakeholders. (Nk)

(42) Nestlé Brazil <u>demonstrates</u> a high level of commitment to the three pillars of CSV (nutrition, water and rural development) through its existing Nutrir, Cuidar and Saber programmes. (Ne)

Concurrences do not occur with evidential adjuncts in our small corpus. However, certain mental process verbs such as *understand* and *recognise* in (43) and (44) seem to suggest intersubjective agreement on the position advanced at the expense of alternative positions.

(43) We <u>understand</u> that sustainability is core to our business continuity and
       how we create long-term value. (CC)
(44) We <u>recognize</u> our responsibility to advocate for greater local
       government engagement in our efforts to monitor contract factory
       conditions. (Nk)

Similarly, deontic modals such as *must* and *need to* suggest a shared value
system which confers socially sourced obligations on the corporation and
thereby disallows alternative positions. Concurrences in particular, then, are
used to directly signal alignment and close any perceived value gap between
corporations and the public.

(45) We <u>must</u> be able to address future needs for materials, to find ways to use
       materials again and again. (Nk)
(46) We recognize <u>the need</u> to create innovative new products, packaging and
       systems; strengthen the world's most advanced supply chain; enhance our
       presence in communities and manage our impact on the world's natural
       resources. (CC)

Finally, we find several disclaims in the form of denials realized through
negation. These denials are used to directly rebut, responsively or pre-emptively,
accusations of moral wrong-doing as in (47) and (48):

(47) Today, we <u>do not</u> directly target children younger than age 12 in our
       marketing messages or our advertising, and we <u>do not</u> show children
       drinking any of our products outside the presence of a parent or caregiver.
       Additionally, we <u>do not</u> directly market in primary schools. (CC)
(48) We <u>do not</u> use crude palm oil and we have no direct link to the
       plantations. (Ne)

3.3 GRADUATION

The final sub-system of APPRAISAL to discuss is GRADUATION. As we have seen,
ATTITUDE and ENGAGEMENT allow speakers to express (inter)subjective positions
of various kinds. GRADUATION is a third, *modulating*, system which acts upon
the other functional systems to 'up-scale' or 'down-scale' evaluations.[9] Critically,
choices in graduations of ATTITUDE and ENGAGEMENT betray strength of feeling
and level of commitment to value positions. GRADUATION plays a dialogistic role
in that it allows speakers to present themselves as more or less strongly aligned
with the value advanced in a way that is sensitive to the anticipated (aligned or

alternative) positions of the construed reader. The system operates across two axes of scalability: FORCE and FOCUS.

Through the sub-system of FORCE, evaluations are graded according to intensity (**intensification**) or quantity (**quantification**). The system has as its natural domain inherently scalar categories which can be graded according to, for example, strength of feeling and speaker commitment, as well as size, strength, amount, speed, extent, proximity, volume and so on. Graduations are said to be **isolated** when they are realized in a distinct lexical item whose primary function is to modify another. Reconsider the following examples in which feelings expressed through the ATTITUDE system undergo isolated intensification:

(49) Despite all continuous efforts, we <u>deeply</u> regret four fatalities in 2009 due to accidents while at work. (Ne)
(50) 'I am <u>really</u> happy that I had the opportunity to participate in this nutrition programme at my child's pre-school'. (Ne)
(51) By designing a <u>hyper</u>-efficient, 'nested' pattern for Air-Sole production, we were able to further reduce post production waste. (Nk)

Graduations are said to be **infused** when degree of force is an inherent meaningful component of a single lexical item which can be measured in comparison to degrees of force inherent in the meaning of other items belonging to the same semantic set. A clear example is in the sets of epistemic and deontic modal verbs. In SFG, modality is modelled in scalar terms with the different modals oriented to three stations on a cline of modal commitment: low, median and high (Halliday and Matthiessen 2004). In epistemic modality this scale is represented by *could < may < will*. In deontic modality it is represented by *can < should < must*. In Appraisal Theory, modality is distributed through the ENGAGEMENT system but degree of modal commitment is a product of intensification operating on the output of the ENGAGEMENT system. Consider the contrast between (52) seen earlier and (53) in which the degree of epistemic commitment is comparatively intensified:

(52) What will be the cost of fresh water in the future? Price and availability <u>may</u> become increasingly volatile. (Nk)
(53) Nike <u>will</u> begin using those shoeboxes in 2011, saving the equivalent of 200,000 trees annually. (Nk)

Degree of modal commitment, in the epistemic domain, serves several context-dependent strategies. For example, low levels of commitment might be selected to play down the possibility of undesirable outcomes. Conversely, high levels of commitment might be selected to convince audiences of the certainty of desirable outcomes. Hence, *will* frequently occurs in corporate pledges. Low levels of epistemic commitment also allow speakers to avoid accountability for the evaluation in the case that the proposition evaluated fails to transpire.

Similarly, in the deontic domain, speakers can oscillate between modal values depending on degree of commitment to the position advanced and how prepared they are to be accountable if the obligation is not fulfilled.

(54)   Nike is aware of this situation and works with contract manufacturers to stress that workers of all nationalities <u>should</u> be treated equally and with dignity, and that factories <u>must</u> adhere to either local labor law or Nike's Code Leadership Standards. (Nk)

In the sub-system of FOCUS, phenomena are graded according to prototypicality. That is, in terms of how closely something corresponds with what the speaker construes to be a good example of a particular category. FOCUS has as its most natural domain categories which are not normally scalar (at least in the way described above) but which FOCUS operates on to *reconstrue* in gradable ways. Within FOCUS, it is then possible to 'sharpen' (*real, genuine, proper*) or 'soften' (*kind of, sort of*) the specification to indicate that something either does or does not constitute a good example of the category. Explicitly, FOCUS relates to experiential notions such as category membership, resemblance, authenticity and actuality. Implicitly, however, the vocabulary of FOCUS often serves to index ATTITUDE, especially in cases where ATTITUDE is not already inscribed in the amplified item. In our corporate social reports, for example, we find instances of sharpening such as (55) and (56). 'Real' in these contexts, then, does not just specify actuality but also serves to convey ATTITUDE as appraised items are reconstrued and situated along gradable lines. In (55), for example, 'real' appraises the action designated by 'work of reducing energy consumption' as not only one with immediate material effects but as one which is therefore *more important* than setting targets. (55), thus, indexes APPRECIATION: VALUATION. Similarly, in (56), 'real' indirectly appraises future 'breakthroughs' as *more significant* than previous breakthroughs and therefore also indexes APPRECIATION: VALUATION.

(55)   We realized that the attempt to set targets was distracting us from the <u>real</u> work of reducing energy consumption. (Nk)
(56)   To build greater understanding and achieve <u>real</u> breakthroughs we need to address key issues more broadly, more collectively. (Nk)

The use of 'real' in (55) and (56), thus, serves to legitimate Nike by presenting it as a company that really cares about its impact on the environment and which is committed to taking steps to ensure that significant improvements are made in this area.

Finer levels of specification are possible in all three systems of APPRAISAL (see Martin and White 2007). However, we have explored the system in sufficient detail to allow a handle on the ideological functions of evaluation. In illustration of this, we have presented examples from a small corpus of corporate social reports. In the next section, we use this grammatical tool to analyse evaluation in a single text extract from a completely different context.

4. Appraisal in George W. Bush's justification for war

On 19 March 2003, the United States and allied forces began a military campaign in Iraq.[10] Such serious actions, which bring devastating consequences to many people, as well as jeopardize international relations, clearly require a great deal of justification to (sometimes sceptical) publics. And this, of course, involves various linguistic dimensions. Chilton (2004: 138) therefore asks 'what is the discourse make-up of the justification of war?' It is not, of course, possible to point to particular discursive strategies as forming the justificatory basis for all wars. The strategies pursued depend on the particular context and changes in the situation can lead to shifts in discursive strategy. In the case of the Iraq war, for example, Cap (2006) shows a marked rhetorical change in official justifications which corresponded with the discovery that Saddam Hussein did not, in fact, possess weapons of mass destruction. One particularly prominent feature of initial justifications, however, comprised strategies for Self-legitimation and Other-delegitimation realized through positive and negative instantiations of appraisal resources. In what follows, we conduct an appraisal analysis of part of a speech delivered by George W. Bush on 17 March 2003. This speech seemed to perform at least two functions. On the one hand, it constituted an ultimatum directed at Saddam Hussein in which he was given 48 hours to leave Iraq or else war would be declared. At the same time, and perhaps more saliently, the speech served to justify to domestic audiences the almost inevitable US intervention in Iraq. The opening five paragraphs of this speech are reproduced in Box 2.1. The text is marked for inscriptions of APPRAISAL according to the key below.[11] Further type specifications are given in brackets to the finest level of categorization defined so far in this chapter.

Single <u>underlining</u> = AFFECT
Double <u>underlining</u> = JUDGEMENT
Dashed <u>underlining</u> = APPRECIATION
+/-ve = positive/negative ATTITUDE
Italics = ENGAGEMENT
Bold = GRADUATION

Box 2.1. Bush 'ultimatum' speech: inscribed appraisal

My fellow citizens, events in Iraq have now reached the final days of decision. For more than a decade, the United States and other nations have pursued <u>patient and honorable</u> [+ve PROPRIETY] efforts to disarm the Iraqi regime without war. That regime pledged to reveal and destroy all its weapons of mass destruction as a condition for ending the Persian Gulf War in 1991.

Since then, the world has engaged in 12 years of diplomacy. We have passed more than a dozen resolutions in the United Nations Security Council. We have sent **hundreds of** [QUANTIFICATION] weapons inspectors to oversee the disarmament of Iraq. Our <u>good</u> [+ve PROPRIETY] faith has not been returned.

The Iraqi regime has used diplomacy as <u>a ploy</u> [-ve VERACITY] to gain time and advantage. It has **uniformly** [QUANTIFICATION] <u>defied</u> [-ve PROPRIETY] Security Council resolutions demanding full disarmament. Over the years, U.N. weapon inspectors have been <u>threatened</u> [-ve PROPRIETY] by Iraqi officials, electronically bugged, and **systematically** [QUANTIFICATION] <u>deceived</u> [-ve VERACITY]. <u>Peaceful</u> [+ve PROPRIETY] efforts to disarm the Iraqi regime have failed **again and again** [QUANTIFICATION] because we are not dealing with peaceful men.

Intelligence gathered by this and other governments *leaves no doubt that* [PRONOUNCE] the Iraq regime continues to possess and conceal some of the **most** [INTENSIFICATION] <u>lethal</u> [COMPOSITION] weapons ever devised. This regime has already used weapons of mass destruction against Iraq's neighbors and against Iraq's people.

The regime has a <u>history of reckless aggression</u> [-ve PROPRIETY] in the Middle East. It has a **deep** [INTENSIFICATION] <u>hatred</u> [-ve HAPPINESS] of America and our friends. And it has aided, trained and harbored <u>terrorists</u> [-ve PROPRIETY], including operatives of al Qaeda. The danger *is clear* [PRONOUNCE]: Using chemical, biological or, one day, nuclear weapons obtained with the help of Iraq, the <u>terrorists</u> [-ve PROPRIETY] *could* [ENTERTAIN] fulfill their stated ambitions and <u>kill</u> **thousands or hundreds of thousands** [QUANTIFICATION] of <u>innocent</u> [+ve PROPRIETY] people in our country or any other.

Recall that ATTITUDE is made up of three sub-systems: AFFECT, JUDGEMENT and APPRECIATION. As Martin (2000: 146) points out, however, 'some texts foreground one or another of these three systems' depending on the purpose of the discourse. Similarly, texts of different types will favour different positive/negative values of ATTITUDE and different forms of ENGAGEMENT and GRADUATION.

In the text in Box 2.1, Bush can be seen to employ JUDGEMENT resources over and above the other sub-systems of ATTITUDE. More specifically, the text relies on resources expressing SOCIAL SANCTION. Actions of the United States, for example, are appraised in terms of positive PROPRIETY as 'patient and honourable' and 'peaceful'. The people of the United States are similarly appraised in terms of positive PROPRIETY as being 'innocent' and having 'good' faith. Actions of the Iraq government, by contrast, are appraised in terms of negative PROPRIETY as well as negative VERACITY. Negative PROPRIETY is instantiated in the processes 'defy' and 'threaten' as well as in the attribute 'history of reckless aggression'. 'Terrorists', in contrast to 'innocent people', also instantiates negative PROPRIETY. Negative VERACITY is instantiated in 'ploy' and 'deceive'. Instantiations of JUDGEMENT appraising the United States, then, are all positive in orientation whereby the people and the government of the United States are presented as virtuous and above reproach. Instantiations appraising Iraq are all negative in orientation; Saddam Hussein and the Iraq government are presented as immoral – secretive, devious and aggressive – and therefore contemptible. This binary opposition in JUDGEMENT realizes a clear strategy of Self-legitimation and Other-delegitimation which plays a major part in justifying US involvement in Iraq. Crucially, however, as van Dijk (2011: 47) points out, the boundary between knowledge and opinion in the description of social actors and actions is often blurred. Bush is describing a state of affairs based in facts but these facts, through APPRAISAL, are furnished with subjective evaluations based in opinion and ideology. The critical question is then whether readers are able to separate knowledge from ideology in the course of discourse or whether they take these subjective colourations as simply objective descriptions of the way the world really is (ibid.).

The mark-up of the text in Box 2.1 highlights three instances of heteroglossia. The first instance, 'leaves no doubt that', is an example of CONTRACT. It closes down the dialogic space leaving no room for the counter possibility that the Iraq government no longer has access to weapons of mass destruction. This is especially significant in the speech because at this point in time the presence of weapons of mass destruction in Iraq was a major premise for the invasion.

Bush could therefore not afford to open the dialogical space and allow for any alternative assessment of the situation to be considered. The fact that this pronouncement is made on the back of 'intelligence', moreover, serves to 'objectify' (Hart 2010) the evaluation by presenting it as based on evidence gathered by an external source. The second instance, 'is clear', is similarly an example of PRONOUNCE. This evidential also objectifies the evaluation by grounding it in potentially intersubjective perceptual experience (Hart 2011c). Conversely, the third instance of heteroglossia in 'could' is an example of EXPAND: ENTERTAIN. It recognizes that 'terrorists' using weapons of mass destruction to kill US and other civilians does not follow automatically from Iraq possessing weapons of mass destruction but that this is only one in a range of possibilities. The evaluation is therefore down-scaled through GRADUATION. Implicitly, however, as Richardson (2007: 60) points out, *could* suggests a degree of likelihood beyond mere possibility. This is further reinforced where the 'danger' appraised as 'clear' in the second instance of heteroglossia refers to the possibility entertained in the third.

Infused intensification can also be seen to operate on instantiations of ATTITUDE. For example, 'deceived' can be considered as upscaled compared to the potential alternative *misled*. 'Threatened', likewise, can be considered upscaled compared to *warned*. And similarly, 'hatred', which instantiates negative AFFECT: HAPPINESS, is upscaled in comparison to an alternative option such as *dislike*. This latter example undergoes further graduation as infused intensification is combined with isolated intensification in the form of 'deep'. A similar thing can be seen in the appraisal of Iraq's weapons as 'the most lethal'. 'Lethal' instantiates APPRECIATION: COMPOSITION in so far it is describes the functionality or effect of the weapons. It can be considered upscaled in comparison with other options such as *harmful*. The degree of negative effect, however, is not just upscaled but 'maximised' by 'most'. According to Martin and White (2007: 142), maximizers such as *most* 'construe the up-scaling as being at the highest possible intensity'. These graduations all serve to heighten anxiety in relation to Saddam Hussein by presenting him not just as a threat to American and global security but as a *serious* threat which, if not immediately addressed, will lead to *severe* consequences.[12]

Other examples of GRADUATION occur in quantifications. Different types of QUANTIFICATION can be specified, including but by no means being limited to: amount (*some, many, all*), mass (*small, large, enormous*), and extent in both space (*partial, widespread, total*) and time (*sometimes, often, always*). Extent quantifications in the text are used to up-scale actions of Saddam Hussein and the Iraq government appraised in terms of negative JUDGEMENT in 'uniformly defied' and 'systematically deceived' as well as disarmament efforts of the United States which are said to have failed 'again and again'. Amount quantifications are used to up-scale the number ('hundreds') of weapon inspectors sent to Iraq and the number ('thousands or hundreds of thousands') of people who could be killed if the United States does not intervene in Iraq. Like intensification, then, these quantifications serve to reinforce JUDGEMENTS of Saddam Hussein as non-cooperative, highlight the futility of diplomacy, emphasize the severity of the threat posed and thereby justify immediate military action.

4.1 Inscribed versus invoked JUDGEMENT

So far in this chapter, we have only considered instances of ATTITUDE which are **inscribed** in the text. That is, those which are coded by specific lexical items and which can therefore be easily identified within the text. However, as we said at the beginning of this chapter, the meaning of a text is not in the text itself. Rather, texts provide a meaning affordance which is actualized when readers take up representations and positions based on texts. And texts may prompt value positions without containing explicit markers of evaluation. Such instances of ATTITUDE are said to be **invoked** rather than inscribed. The distinction between inscribed and invoked evaluation is not absolute but, rather, exists on a cline relating to the degree of freedom the reader has in aligning themselves with the attitudes conveyed by the text. In inscribed appraisal, the reader's linguistic knowledge constrains them into adopting the position advanced in the text, at least for purposes of local understanding (though they are, of course, free to refute the position). Invoked appraisal, by contrast, is not associated with specific functional units and uptake is reliant on the reader's prior world knowledge and predefined value orientations. Such positions, however, form part of the ideological backdrop which speakers take for granted, or **presuppose**, as common axiological ground. In the Bush extract, this is most clear for JUDGEMENT where certain actions or events may connote positive or negative PROPRIETY but where uptake of this value position is dependent on particular world views. The extract is reproduced in Box 2.2 with positive and negative invoked JUDGEMENT marked according to the key below.

<u>Single underline</u> = Positive JUDGEMENT: PROPRIETY
Bold = Negative JUDGEMENT: PROPRIETY

Box 2.2. Bush 'ultimatum' speech: invoked appraisal

My fellow citizens, **events in Iraq** have now reached the final days of decision. For more than a decade, the United States and other nations have pursued patient and honourable efforts to <u>disarm the Iraqi regime</u> without war. That regime <u>pledged to reveal and destroy all its weapons of mass destruction</u> as a condition for <u>ending the Persian Gulf War</u> in 1991.

Since then, the world <u>has engaged in 12 years of diplomacy</u>. We have passed more than a dozen resolutions in the United Nations Security Council. We have sent hundreds of weapons inspectors to oversee <u>the disarmament of Iraq</u>. Our good faith **has not been returned**.

The Iraqi regime has used diplomacy as a ploy to gain time and advantage. It has uniformly defied Security Council resolutions demanding <u>full disarmament</u>. Over the years, U.N. weapon inspectors have been threatened by Iraqi officials, electronically bugged, and systematically deceived. Peaceful efforts to disarm the Iraqi regime **have failed** again and again because we are not dealing with peaceful men.

Intelligence gathered by this and other governments leaves no doubt that the Iraq regime **continues to possess and conceal some of the most lethal weapons ever devised**. This regime has **already used weapons of mass destruction against Iraq's neighbors and against Iraq's people**.

The regime has a history of reckless aggression in the Middle East. It has a deep hatred of America and our friends. And it has **aided, trained and harbored terrorists, including operatives of al Qaeda**. The danger is clear: Using chemical, biological or, one day, nuclear weapons obtained with the help of Iraq, the terrorists could **fulfill their stated ambitions and kill thousands or hundreds of thousands of innocent people in our country or any other**.

In the text in Box 2.2, the speaker makes certain **presumptions** (Chilton 2004) in relation to the actions designated. These presumptions relate broadly to ideas of 'right' and 'wrong' and thus constitute judgements of PROPRIETY. Such presumptions make up part of the speaker's naturalized world view and are therefore ideological by definition.[13] At a higher level, the speaker further presumes that this world view is shared by his audience and that designation of the actions alone is sufficient to invoke similar judgements in readers. For example, 'events in Iraq' in the opening line of the speech not only presupposes a great deal of background knowledge about the situation in Iraq but also seems to presume a negative assessment of the situation. In the underlined stretches that follow, it is presumed that disarming Iraq is a right and desirable course of action and that references to this process will invoke positive PROPRIETY judgements in the hearer. By the same token, it is presumed that the actions marked in bold are wrong and undesirable and that references to them will invoke negative PROPRIETY judgements. These presumptions, however, rest on a number of deeply engrained 'Western' perspectives. For example, the presumption that Iraq continues 'to possess some of the most lethal weapons ever devised' will invoke a negative judgement depends on a common value system according to which Western countries are allowed to possess nuclear weapons while non-Western countries are not. Similarly, the invocation of negative judgements based on the proposition that Iraq has 'aided, trained and harbored terrorists, including operatives of al Qaeda' relies on the audience sharing a world view in which Western causes in the War on Terror are seen as just and warranted while non-Western causes are seen as wicked and without foundation. These implicit judgements, thus, simply presume the legitimacy of the United States and the delegitimacy of Iraq and Saddam Hussein. The critical question is then, again, whether these judgements are recognized as subjective orientations or are further naturalized as they go unquestioned in the course of the discourse.

5. Covert evaluation in media discourse on immigration

In the previous section, we have made a distinction between inscribed and invoked evaluation. Inscribed evaluation is explicitly coded and dependent on semantic knowledge. Invoked evaluation, by contrast, is not coded and depends instead on predefined knowledge existing outside of the linguistic system. Located somewhere on the cline between these two types of evaluation lies a further type of evaluation which is dependent on linguistic knowledge but which is only implicitly coded. Following Coffin and O'Halloran (2006), we may refer to this type of evaluation as 'covert evaluation'.

In Corpus Linguistics, it is recognized that the meaning of any lexical item is, in part, a function of its distribution and, specifically, the collocational relations it enters into with other words and phrases (Louw 1993; Sinclair 1991, 1996; Stubbs 1995). When a given word (the 'node') *regularly* co-occurs in discourse with other words (its 'collocates'), the meaning of the node word may 'take on' elements of meaning associated with its collocates, including their evaluative orientation.[14] In other words, a denotationally neutral lexical item may, as function of the broad evaluative bent of its principal contexts of use, come to have a consistent, more or less positive or negative 'aura' about it (Louw 1993: 157), which language users are somehow aware of.[15]

This connotative layer of meaning, referred to technically as the **semantic prosody** of a word, serves, in other contexts of use, to signal ATTITUDE indirectly, thereby allowing speakers to convey evaluations covertly and avoid accountability for the appraisal. This is particularly important in the context of hard news discourse where reporters are supposed to remain relatively impartial. As Coffin and O'Halloran (2006: 78) state, through semantic prosody 'people and events can be represented in such a way that the journalist cannot so easily be accused of bias, racism etc. while nevertheless communicating a negative message to the target readership'. Let us consider, by way of illustration, a few examples from media discourse on immigration which covertly instantiate negative ATTITUDE. Since such semantic prosodies are dependent on repeated patterns in general discourse, this type of evaluation can only be detected or confirmed with reference to a large corpus of attested linguistic data.[16] In our discussion, we consult the BNC*web* (CQP Edition).[17]

Consider example (57) from the *Daily Mail*. There are no explicit markers of negative evaluation in the extract. The extract nevertheless seems to suggest a negative attitude towards immigration. This may be attributable to more than one lexical item in the text. However, let us take the use of *cause* in particular.

(57)   The Home Office said a major <u>cause</u> of the increases were huge numbers
        of people coming through the Channel Tunnel. (*The Daily Mail*, 1
        December 2001)

From a restricted semantic point of view, *cause* means something like 'to bring about'. However, when Stubbs (2001) examined the lemma CAUSE in the Bank of English he found that among its 50 most frequent collocates, within a span of 3;3, there were only words (most frequently abstract nouns) with negative value orientations. We find similar results if we search BNC*web* for CAUSE with the same criteria. Figure 2.3 shows the 15 most frequent collocates of CAUSE. Overwhelmingly, one can see that it is bad things that get caused. CAUSE is thus likely to connote negative evaluation and in (57), therefore, implicitly appraise increases in numbers of immigrants in a negative way. More specifically, given the particular distributions of CAUSE seen in Figure 2.3, where a number of collocates are semantically related ([damage, problems, trouble], [concern, alarm, distress]), its use in (57) implicitly defines or **frames** increases in immigration numbers as a problem or area of concern. The seemingly neutral statement in

No.	Word	Total No. in written texts	Expected collocate frequency	Observed collocate frequency	In No. of texts	Log-likelihood value
1	damage	6,727	1.923	123	94	783.4711
2	problems	24,900	7.119	173	138	774.2477
3	concern	8,972	2.565	114	103	644.0417
4	death	19,268	5.509	131	93	580.6401
5	action	20,891	5.973	97	32	359.4157
6	trouble	7,064	2.020	60	54	291.612
7	effect	21,640	6.187	78	63	252.1457
8	root	1,763	0.504	33	33	211.6362
9	Injury	4,460	1.275	37	28	178.1078
10	confusion	2,693	0.770	32	32	176.4804
11	harm	2,080	0.595	29	20	169.0579
12	alarm	1,788	0.511	25	24	145.8768
13	distress	1,401	0.401	22	22	133.4165
14	cancer	4,007	1.146	29	25	131.9338
15	anaemia	358	0.102	15	4	120.4641

Figure 2.3 Collocates of CAUSE

(57) may in fact, then, as a function of the semantic prosody of CAUSE, covertly instantiate an AFFECT: INSECURITY appraisal.

In a similar vein, consider the GRADUATION: QUANTIFICATION in (58).

(58) The appointment of a lawyer who has opposed immigration and asylum decisions comes as <u>mounting</u> numbers of visitors to Britain . . . (*The Daily Mail*, 2 December 2003)

Semantically, *mount* may be taken to mean something evaluatively neutral like 'to increase or accumulate'. However, a search in BNC*web* reveals the most frequent collocates of MOUNT to be negative in value orientation where it is mainly unwanted things that are seen to mount (see Figure 2.4). Consequently, the use of the term in (58) may indicate an implicitly negative appraisal of rises in number of visitors to Britain as something undesirable (AFFECT: UNHAPPINESS).

Consider one final example in (59). At the strictly semantic level, the meaning of *spread* has something to do with expansion, distribution, dissemination and so on. However, when we feed the term into BNC*web* the results reveal that the most frequent collocates of SPREAD are predominantly of negative value. At the more pragmatic level, its prosody thus gives an implicitly negative evaluation, in (59), of the dispersion of immigrants. More specifically, as Figure 2.5 shows,

No.	Word	Total No. in written texts	Expected collocate frequency	Observed collocate frequency	In No. of texts	Log-likelihood value
1	pressure	11,026	0.641	51	43	346.3135
2	tension	3,131	0.182	24	20	186.9433
3	criticism	4,523	0.263	21	21	142.6508
4	excitement	2,431	0.141	18	18	138.9473
5	concern	8,972	0.522	22	21	121.7995
6	exhibition	5,234	0.304	19	15	119.8205
7	debts	1,805	0.105	15	14	119.2324
8	costs	11,291	0.657	18	16	84.5846
9	exhibitions	1,249	0.073	10	10	78.7371
10	challenge	5,009	0.291	12	12	65.8708
11	holes	2,422	0.141	10	4	65.5894
12	unrest	898	0.052	8	8	64.691
13	campaign	8,680	0.505	13	13	59.5148
14	evidence	20,291	1.180	17	16	59.1134
15	screws	372	0.022	6	5	55.648

Figure 2.4 Collocates of MOUNT

No.	Word	Total No. in written texts	Expected collocate frequency	Observed collocate frequency	In No. of texts	Log-likelihood value
1	hands	16,689	4.727	97	69	402.4203
2	infection	2,636	0.747	47	29	297.7651
3	disease	8,638	2.447	57	47	250.2536
4	rumours	1,238	0.351	31	31	217.3802
5	intracommodity	21	0.006	14	1	202.0151
6	aids	3,036	0.860	32	28	169.5401
7	hiv	1,637	0.464	27	18	166.8637
8	arms	10,217	2.894	45	38	162.9897
9	bread	3,003	0.851	31	23	162.9783
10	wings	2,265	0.642	28	26	157.102
11	height	3.513	0.995	31	6	153.495
12	word	16,464	4.663	51	50	151.5273
13	wildfire	35	0.010	12	12	151.0752
14	Legs	5,584	1.582	34	22	144.0067
15	Fire	11,259	3.189	42	30	139.1133

Figure 2.5 Collocates of SPREAD

SPREAD frequently collocates with lexical items from the semantic field of illness. SPREAD may therefore have a particularly strong association with a medical frame and serve in examples such as (59) to metaphorically attribute to immigrants meanings connected with disease (see also Musolff 2003; see Santa Ana 2002).

(59) The newcomers, mostly young and without dependants, have <u>spread</u> across the country, transforming communities which have rarely experienced migration on this scale. (*The Observer*, 27 August 2006)

6. Conclusion

In this chapter, we have introduced a framework, in the form of Appraisal Theory, which models the resources available in the interpersonal function of language and have highlighted the equal role that evaluation plays in (de)legitimation. We have shown the ideological and (de)legitimating potential of appraisal resources through critical analyses of instantiations taken from three corporate social reports. We have also applied this framework in a single text analysis of a George W. Bush's speech given on the eve of the 2003 Iraq invasion and in a corpus-assisted analysis of covert evaluation in media discourse on immigration. Across these analyses, we have seen that Appraisal Theory, and the grammar of ATTITUDE in particular, allows a systematized analysis of some of the lexicogrammatical means available for positive self-representation and negative other-representation. We have also seen, in its grammar of ENGAGEMENT, that Appraisal Theory provides a structured handle on several phenomena which should be of more interest in CDA, including reported speech, modality and evidentiality, but also more general discursive strategies aimed at achieving an intersubjective consensus of knowledge and opinion. Finally, in examining the distinction between inscribed, invoked and covert ATTITUDE, we found that representation is rarely free from evaluation, even in the absence of explicit evaluative markers. We explore this further in the next chapter in relation to the connotative values of images.

Visuation

1. Introduction

So far, we have considered two dimensions of discourse, representation and evaluation, as they are instantiated in linguistic modes of communication. As we pointed out in the introduction, however, semiosis is not restricted to linguistic modalities but also occurs through non-linguistic, including visual, channels. Many researchers in CDA contend that linguistic and visual communication operate on the same underlying capacities and principles and that they display, albeit in different forms of realization, some of the same meaning-making potentials. Consequently, visual texts, such as photographs, and visual aspects of multimodal texts, that is, those involving both written and visual material, can be studied through the same systemic functional lens. Proponents of multimodal CDA have therefore applied tools developed in Critical Linguistics, including mystification analysis and the Social Actor Model, to instances of multimodal discourse. In an elaborated and integrated Multimodal Approach, these researchers have also developed functionally motivated systemic grammars to account for semiotic features which are fundamental to the visual modality, although which serve the same general functions of communication (Kress and van Leeuwen 2006; Machin 2007). In this chapter, we consider how visuo-grammatical choices presented in texts may serve ideological strategies in representation and evaluation. In Section 2, we introduce multimodal discourse analysis and its relation to SFG. In Section 3, we explore TRANSITIVITY and SOCIAL ACTOR REPRESENTATION in images of immigrants. In Section 4, we explore the role of vectors and viewpoints in pictures of political protests. And in Section 5, we discuss the presence of metaphor and intertextuality in multimodal Discourses in the British Miners' Strike.

2. Multimodality and SFG

There are, of course, a number of similarities and differences between language and image. For instance, language is purely **symbolic** with words existing in only arbitrary relations with their designations. Images, by contrast, are **iconic** and display various degrees of similarity to their subject. Although they are iconic, however, images also perform a symbolic function as they can 'stand for' particular people, places and time periods which may, in turn, invoke attitudes and emotions. Images are also subject to **construal**. This is especially the case in the digital age where computer software programmes allow images to be easily manipulated along various lines. As with lexicogrammar, therefore, choices in visual representation may reflect particular ideological Discourses. And as we can study lexicogrammatical choices in text with a view to revealing underlying Discourses, so we can study the choices presented by the system of visual semiotic resources and show how different strategies in this system can serve to legitimate social action (Abousnnouga and Machin 2011: 327).

Another similarity relates to compositionality. As Lim (2004a: 56) points out, 'just as the grammar of language concerns itself with the chains of words to form coherent sentences, the grammar of visual images is about the piecing of one item with another to bring across a coherent message' (Lim 2004a: 56). A major difference, however, is that while the assembly of visual texts might be compositional and their different aspects can be analysed separately, images, in contrast to language, are experienced along gestalt lines rather than decompositionally (O'Halloran 2011). The appropriateness of adapting linguistic models of grammar for multimodal analysis may therefore be called into question (Machin 2009). Nevertheless, a number of CDA researchers interested in multimodal features of discourse develop and apply analytical frameworks inspired by SFG (e.g. Kress and van Leeuwen 1996; Machin 2007).

In multimodal CDA, then, visual text, like linguistic text, is said to be an instantiation of a stratified system which operates across three meta-functions of communication, namely, ideational, interpersonal and textual functions.[1] The three strata are represented in Figure 3.1. They are semantics (meaning), visuogrammar (design) and graphics (drawing, sculpting, photographing). The semantic stratum constitutes the text-producer's basic experience of what is depicted. It is realized through sub-systems of a 'visuo-' rather than a lexico-grammar, which is, in turn, realized in graphic rather than phonological properties of text.

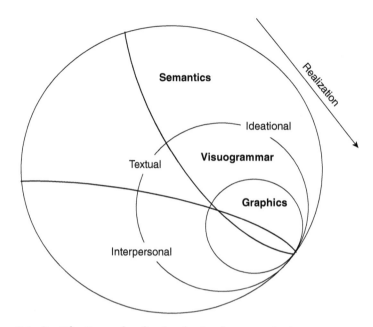

Figure 3.1. Stratification and realization in visual communication

The system of **visuogrammar** consists of some of the same sub-systems that make up lexicogrammar, including TRANSITIVITY and MODALITY.[2] However, it also comprises additional systems which are assumed to operate only in the visual realm, including those relating, for example, to space, viewpoint, colour and shape. Lim (2004b) advances a model of visuogrammar which organizes these aspects of visual design into two major categories: PERSPECTIVE and FORM. FORM contains four further sub-systems: COLOUR, SHAPE, LINE and STROKES. PERSPECTIVE concerns the way the text-producer controls space in the picture and can be broken down into two further sub-systems: DEEP SPACE and POINT OF VIEW. DEEP SPACE is responsible for the illusion of a three-dimensional world represented in a two-dimensional image. It is realized in contrasting size, convergent lines and chiaroscuro (light and shadows). POINT OF VIEW relates to the vantage point that the audience is manoeuvred into with respect to the image and is realized in different values for ANCHOR, ANGLE and DISTANCE. The sub-system of PERSPECTIVE is represented in Figure 3.2.

In an elaborated Multimodal Approach to CDA, we can further identify and analyse the 'cultural' artefacts present in a multimodal text which, too, contribute to its overall meaning. Such artefacts include, for example, clothing and other material objects, as well as semiotic products referenced intertextually. These artefacts come with specific associations or **connotations** which may

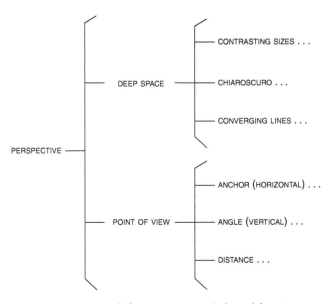

Figure 3.2. System network for PERSPECTIVE (adapted from Lim 2004b)

be shared by all or particular subsections of a given society. Consider, by way of example, the image in Figure 3.3, which was widely published across the UK press in the immediate aftermath of the London Riots. There is, of course, much that can be said concerning the saturation of the colour in the background. For present purposes, however, we just highlight the cultural artefacts contained in the image in the form of full sportswear including a hooded sweatshirt. For many readers, this form of clothing is likely to be associated with a certain class of urban youth stereotypically imagined as belonging to gangs and being involved in petty crimes. Thus, clothing in this image works to indirectly classify the social actor and for some readers may invoke negative JUDGEMENT: PROPRIETY evaluations.[3] Not only does the image serve to sustain a social stereotype, then, but it also serves to delegitimate the London Riots. The image proposes to the reader a metonymic elaboration in which the specific actor depicted stands for the type of actor involved in the riots. This metonymy, thus, operates to construe those involved as a homogenous group rather than reflect the diverse range of backgrounds represented by participants and, further, to depoliticize the riots by suggesting that the actions amounted to instances of gang crime rather than displays of political disaffection. While an image might purport to 'document' reality, then, this documentation is never neutral (Machin 2007: 24). Images are inherently ideological. They necessarily capture only part of the picture or

Figure 3.3. London Rioter. (©European Pressphoto Agency ID 50463189)

paint a particular picture, the visuo-grammatical properties of which carry connotations that invite evaluations.

Of course, given their number and variation, cultural artefacts such as clothing and their potential connotations are not easily approached within a grammatical framework. However, connotations are not restricted to the cultural artefacts present in an image but occur also on the back of representational parameters which can be studied within a grammatical framework and therefore form an important part of a systemic multimodal analysis. These connotations may be grounded in prior cultural or embodied experience. For example, options in BRIGHTNESS within the COLOUR system may, in specific contexts, connote 'warmth' or 'coldness' and thus invoke feelings of SECURITY or INSECURITY, respectively. There is a considerable amount of work in multimodal CDA on FORM (e.g. Abousnnouga and Machin 2011; Koller 2008). In this chapter, however, we shall be primarily concerned with PERSPECTIVE, and POINT OF VIEW in particular, as well as the cross-modal systems of TRANSITIVITY and

SOCIAL ACTOR REPRESENTATION. In the next section, we turn to TRANSITIVITY and SOCIAL ACTOR REPRESENTATION in immigration Discourses.

3. Actors, actions and visual implicatures:
images of immigrants

We saw in Chapter 1 that social actors can, through the system of TRANSITIVITY, be represented as engaged in different types of process. TRANSITIVITY similarly operates in visual representation and is similarly subject to GRADUATION. For example, actors can be depicted as 'deep in thought' or not really thinking about anything in particular (PROCESS: MENTAL). They can be pictured talking or shouting (PROCESS: VERBAL). Or they can be depicted in different types of material process such as walking, running (intransactive), blocking or hitting (transactive) (Machin 2007). We also saw in Chapter 1 that speakers can cast actors in different grammatical and socio-functional roles. Grammatically, for example, participants can be activated as AGENTS in the process or passivated as PATIENTS. Socio-functionally, for example, they can be referred to as individuals or groups or in terms of their different roles or places within society. Images too can 'label' social actors in this way (ibid.). Through the presence and direction of vectors in the image, actors can be presented as more or less agentive in different types of action. Actors can be pictured on their own or in groups. And they can be categorized in different ways by artefacts in the image. For example, an actor might be functionalized by a uniform or the presence of a particular object or they might be identified in terms of relation by the presence of another actor such as a child. Images, then, reflect and construct ideological Discourses when actors are routinely depicted in particular types of process and role. By way of example in this section, let us consider a small sample of images instantiating Discourses of immigration. The following images are representative of those returned earliest, and found in online editions of UK newspapers, in a Google search for 'immigrants UK'.[4] Although a crude search, the results are nevertheless indicative and seem to reveal several recurring strategies. Besides graphs presenting facts and figures, the most prominent images involve either immigrants standing in a line as represented by Figures 3.4 and 3.5 or pictures of busy pedestrian streets as represented by Figure 3.6.

In Figure 3.4, immigrants are presented lined up at the border port of Calais awaiting transport to Britain. This context is provided by the caption accompanying the image: 'Migrants in Calais queue up to board a van bound

Figure 3.4 Immigrants queuing in Calais (published in Express.co.uk, 12 December 2012)

Figure 3.5. Immigrants in dole queue (published in Express.co.uk, 9 December 2008)

Figure 3.6. Busy streets (published in Express.co.uk, 12 December 2012)

for Britain'. From a critical perspective, the most striking thing about this image is visuo-grammatical choices which serve to de-individuate and impersonalize the immigrants. De-individuation is achieved as the actors are pictured in a group. Such a strategy overlooks the various complex motives and specific circumstances that might cause different individuals to migrate to Britain (Machin and Mayr 2012: 101). It is, moreover, made easy for the reader to ignore such human dimensions of migration by the presentation of the actors with their back to the viewer. This physical orientation serves to anonymize the actors and prevent any personal affiliation with them. The headline of the article which the image accompanies reads '7.5 million migrants live in Britain'. The implication here is that this is already too many and yet, as the image suggests, many more immigrants continue to come. Indeed, the image carries a **visual implicature** along the lines 'there is no end in sight'.[5] This implicature arises where, although only a small number of immigrants appear in the image, the viewer does not get to see the end of the queue, which is depicted as 'unbounded'. Consequently, the viewer is presented with the possibility that the queue extends continually and is cut off in the image only by the restrictions of the VIEWING FRAME.

In Figure 3.5, immigrants are similarly presented collectivized in a line. The context here, however, provided by the caption 'WARNING: Policy is bound to enrage critics as dole queues grow', is a queue for social benefits inside the United Kingdom. The image, in conjunction with its co-text, thus not only confines the debate to economic issues at the expense of cultural and humanitarian issues but also ignores the economic contributions that immigrants do make. In terms of TRANSITIVITY, it is relevant that immigrants are depicted as actors in a PROCESS: EXISTENTIAL (being located in a queue) as opposed to a PROCESS: MATERIAL (such as working). The representation of immigrants drawing on state resources instead of contributing economically may for many readers invoke a negative JUDGEMENT: PROPRIETY appraisal. As with the previous image, no definitive end to the line is presented, suggesting that substantial numbers of immigrants are claiming benefits. It is similarly worth mentioning, here, the visual realization of CIRCUMSTANCE, a semantic category which, recall, provides 'additional', contextual information. Such information pertains, for example, to the LOCATION in space and time of a particular PROCESS. In visual texts, CIRCUMSTANCE is realized in the 'backdrop' held within the image in contrast to foregrounded elements.[6] In Figure 3.5, no specific circumstantial information is presented. There is no clue in the background as to where or when the image was taken. Such information might be provided, for example, by signs on buildings or the presence of identifiable landmarks. This lack of any information in the background decontextualizes the image, creating a visual implicature that the events depicted are not restricted to a particular place or time but are reoccurring around the country. These visual discursive strategies construct a stereotype of immigrants and asylum seekers as 'dole-seekers' and, by suggesting that this phenomenon is significant and widespread, support a visual argument (Richardson and Wodak 2009) legitimating a more restrictive immigration policy. In contrast to the previous image, it is worth noting that the actors in Figure 3.5 are more personalized with their faces presented to the viewer. The identification of actors found here, however, could be interpreted as a 'naming and shaming' strategy which, in this context, the image-producer considers pragmatically more pertinent than an impersonalization strategy.

The image in Figure 3.6 occurs with the caption 'The opening of British borders has led immigration to nearly double in a decade' and the headline 'Soaring immigration is unsustainable, slams MigrationWatch UK'. A major argument theme in anti-immigration discourse is that continued immigration is unsustainable because the country is full and there is no room left for further immigrants (Reisigl and Wodak 2001). The image in Figure 3.6 seems to be a visual instantiation of this argument where the minimal distance between actors creates a density in the image which gives the impression of overcrowding. It is also worth noting the blurring of the bodies which not only creates a sense of 'pace' through fictive motion but also connotes a loss of identity (another major argument theme in anti-immigration discourse.[7] The representation in this image may thus also invoke an AFFECT: INSECURITY appraisal of immigration.

In contrast to the images analysed so far, where social actors in each are collectivized, Figure 3.7 presents an individualized social actor in a counter-Discourse. This image is not representative of those returned in our Google search but is included here for purposes of comparison. It occurs with the caption: 'Polish delicatessen worker Dominik Wasilewski outside the Dwa Koty Polish in Crewe'. Linguistically, in the caption, the PROCESS is an (ellipted) existential process. The PARTICIPANT, however, is represented in terms of functionalization ('delicatessen worker') as well as classification ('Polish') and nomination ('Dominik Wasilewski'). The reader is also given a CIRCUMSTANCE realized in the locative 'outside Dwa Koty Polish in Crewe'. Correspondingly, in the visualization, we find the actor in an existential process (standing outside the delicatessen) but functionalized, indirectly, by the articulation of detail in the backdrop which specifies a particular location, in the form of a workplace, with which the actor is implicitly linked (graphically, by a non-vectorial, 'relational line' (Kress and van Leeuwen 2006: 59)). The visual information contained within this image, then, instantiates a more celebratory Discourse which highlights the contributions that individual immigrants make to local communities. Finally, it is worth noting the orientation of the actor who, interpretable as the visual equivalent of nomination, is presented 'face-on' with the viewer. In the context

Figure 3.7. Immigrant worker (published in Guardian.co.uk, 22 February 2011. ©Getty Images ID 80457351)

of a more favourable Discourse, this personalization strategy is effected as the vector, which emerges from the image through the direction of gaze, engages the viewer and invites them to enter into a more familiar relationship with the subject. We discuss the role of vectors in visuation in the next section.

4. Vectors, viewpoints and viewing frames in pictures of protests

We have seen in the previous section that ideational categories ACTOR and CIRCUMSTANCE may be visually realized by the presence in images of people and the articulation of background details, respectively. Kress and van Leeuwen (2006) suggest that what is realized in language by 'action verbs', that is, PROCESS: MATERIAL, is realized in visuation by elements that can be formally defined as **vectors** (p. 46). In fact, they claim 'the hallmark of a narrative visual "proposition" is the presence of a vector' (p. 59). Vectors are mathematical entities possessing two properties: direction and magnitude (length). They are often represented graphically by arrows. Most images, of course, do not actually contain arrows. Rather, the claim is that our *experience* of images involves recognizing the oblique lines that connect depicted elements to provide narrative coherence – a 'story'. Such implicitly present vectors emerge from various elements of the image, including PARTICIPANTS and INSTRUMENTS. They represent, for example, paths of motion, the transfer of energy between participants, or the trajectory of limbs or other objects conceived as 'pointing'. Perhaps more abstractly, vectors also represent the gaze (or eye-line) and 'body-lines' of actors in the image. The magnitude of a vector is determined by its contact inside the image with visual instantiations of GOAL.[8] However, viewers may imagine *extensions* of the vector which 'point to' a third, imagined participant. In some cases, this third participant may be the viewer themselves. In other cases, there is no GOAL within the image and instead, the viewer may be invited into the role by a vector pointing directly 'out of' the image.[9] In both cases, the viewer is no longer just a witness to the scene but is asked to become a participant in the world depicted (Kress and van Leeuwen 2006: 117–18). In other words, the viewer themselves becomes part of the meaning of the image. The extent to which the viewer becomes entangled in the world of the image, and the freedom they have to remain a mere spectator to it, I wish to suggest, is a function of the relationship between their body and vectors or extensions of vectors imagined as emerging from the image. This, in turn, is determined by the vantage point that the image presents to the viewer.

This claim that we understand images partly in relation to our own orientations is consistent with the 'embodied mind' thesis in cognitive science (Johnson 1987; Lakoff and Johnson 1999; Mandler 2004). This thesis suggests that various cognitive tasks, including memory, judgement, reasoning and language, are tied to physical experiences we have with our bodies and their situatedness in the world. With regard to language and experience, we can point to linguistic reflections of conceptual metaphors, such as GOALS ARE DESTINATIONS, which arise as different areas of experience, in this case motion and intention, are experienced as co-relating (Grady 1997; Lakoff and Johnson 1980).[10] With regard to language and situatedness, we can point, for example, to the use of egocentric relative frames of reference in linguistically locating objects in space (Levinson 2003).[11] Here, speakers describe the location of one entity (the *locandum*) in relation to another (the reference object) in a way that is relative to the speaker's own 'co-ordinates' in space.[12] We may also point to the egocentric models of geometric conceptualization proposed by Chilton to underpin both discourse and grammatical constructions (Chilton 2004, 2007, 2010). It seems perfectly reasonable to speculate that we make sense of images in much the same way: with reference to our bodies.[13]

The embodied mind maps the space around the body in three dimensions relative to the body's coronal (head/feet), sagittal (front/back) and transversal (left/right) axes (Tversky 1998; Tversky et al. 1999). Just as we imagine eye-lines following direction of gaze, so it seems that we imagine 'body-lines' extending from the body in three directions relative to gravity and the body's orientation in space (Tversky et al. 1999). We are also capable of projecting body-lines onto others and performing mental transformations of our own orientations to simulate alternative perspectives (Zacks et al. 1999).[14] Our imagined body-lines are represented schematically in Figure 3.8.

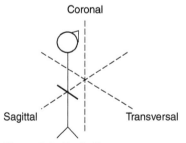

Figure 3.8. Body-lines

When we encounter images, the image presents to us a particular perspective, or vantage point, from which we are asked to view the scene depicted. In the visuo-grammatical system for PERSPECTIVE outlined earlier (Figure 3.2), we identified three main variables (or sub-systems) for POINT OF VIEW: ANCHOR, ANGLE and DISTANCE. Parameters in this region of the grammar reflect the basic visuo-spatial experiences we share as human beings and enable us to externally represent those experiences. Such externalizations, in the form of images, of course, may be ideologically vested with alternative options in the system performing alternative ideological functions (see van Leeuwen 2008: 136–41). Crucially, I wish to suggest, the ideological functions of options in PERSPECTIVE are a consequence of bringing the viewer's body into particular alignments with elements in the scene depicted and prior universal embodied experiences. We discuss these three variables in turn below in the context of pictures of political protests.

In the last few years there have been a significant number of high-profile political protests around the world. In North Africa and the Middle East, of course, the Arab Spring began on 18 December 2010. In Europe, protests have been largely in response to capitalism and corporate greed, austerity measures, environmental issues and military interventions. In the United Kingdom, the most recent, particularly high-profile protests have been: the G20 protests, the Student Fees protests and the Trades Union Congress (TUC) protest.[15] The images below are all taken from image banks such as Getty Images and the European Pressphoto Agency. Image banks hold digital stocks of images ranging from abstract designs and posed photographs which can be used in marketing to photographs of real events which can be used in news reporting. Large agencies like advertising companies, publishing houses and newspapers regularly buy the images they use from image banks like Getty.[16] Machin (2004) points to the importance of image banks in defining the visual language of various media. Image banks like Getty provide a pre-structured world of categories from which users can choose. They can be searched for multiple keywords attached to images as well as the presence of particular design elements including number, age, gender and ethnicity of participants, angle of shot, and whether the image presents a head shot, a full body shot or a shot from the waist up. The search will return images which combine these features. In this sense, image banks represent a visual grammar. The examples below are intended to illustrate, in relation to representations of political protests and interactions between police and protesters in particular, some of the options in this grammar and their potential ideological functions. What I do not do here but which would make for an interesting study is to investigate whether news agencies with alternative ideological positions exploit this grammar in systematically different ways and whether the selections they make in visual representations correspond, systematically, with selections in linguistic representation (see next chapter).

Options in visual representations of protests include, of course, those within TRANSITIVITY and SOCIAL ACTOR REPRESENTATION. For example, there is ideological significance in whether participants are routinely presented as activated or passivated and in what kind of process. If protesters, say, are typically shown as AGENTS in transactive material processes in which police are the PATIENT while police are presented as AGENTS primarily in existential processes, this asymmetry might indicate a Discourse in which police are legitimated as peaceful and protestors are delegitimated as violent aggressors, and vice versa of course. Similarly, if one newspaper tends to use images in which protestors are collectivized but the police are individualized while another favours images in which the police are collectivized and protestors are individualized, this may suggest alternative Discourses. In the first case, we may say that the image instantiates a Discourse of 'mob rule'. In the second, we may say that the image instantiates a Discourse of State 'heavy-handedness'. Our focus here, however, is on parameters in the system of PERSPECTIVE.

The examples below share a common event structure as schematically represented in Figure 3.9. The dotted arrows in the schema are potential vectors representing the possible transfer of energy between participants. The realization of these vectors in the image depends on whether the participant at the tail of the vector is activated or passivated in a transactive process. Note that laterality is irrelevant for present purposes but let us assign, arbitrarily, the police to participant A and protestors to participant B.

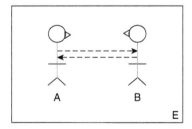

Figure 3.9. Basic event-structure in pictures of protests

4.1 ANCHOR

The ANCHORAGE point is a POINT OF VIEW variable on the horizontal plane. Potentials in ANCHORAGE are analogous to film frames involved in **panning**. Although there is an indefinite number of such possible positions depending on how discriminate we are being, we can identify four cardinal ANCHORAGE points as depicted in Figure 3.10. These alternative positions should not be taken as absolute locations in space but as imagined viewpoints relative to the internal structure of the event depicted, which is fixed in space (and time).

Alternative ANCHORAGE points mean that the viewer's sagittal axis, possibly the primary axis due to the importance of forward motion in our experience (Franklin and Tversky 1990), is aligned with participants and vectors in the image in different ways. Consider the image in Figure 3.11 depicting scenes in the TUC protest. Vectors present in this image represent the body-lines and, since both are activated, the transfer of energy between both participants. Given the ANCHORAGE point we are presented with, close to cardinal point 0 assuming the event structure in Figure 3.9, these vectors exist in a perpendicular relationship with the viewer's sagittal axis.

The viewer is thus not part of the event depicted in the image but rather a 'bystander' in the wider situation. Moreover, where the viewer's sagittal axis can be seen to intersect with the vectors emerging from both sets of participants at equal magnitudes, the viewer is encouraged to adopt a relatively neutral stance. The connection between position in space and stance is encoded in a **conceptual metaphor** STANCE IS POSITION IN SPACE which gives rise to metaphorical expressions such as 'taking sides' or 'sitting on the fence'. In this conceptual metaphor, which is probably grounded in our embodied experience of being physically located close to those we identify with, stance is conceptualized in terms of position in space. The argument being made here is that visuo-grammatical selections in PERSPECTIVE connote evaluations and encourage the viewer to adopt a similar stance based on associations built in this conceptual metaphor. The argument is based on a reversed logic of the metaphor. If

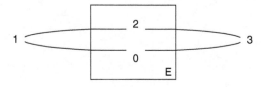

Figure 3.10. Cardinal points of view: ANCHOR

stance is conceptualized in terms of location in space, then, through positive feedback within the metaphor, location in space suggests a particular stance. In Figure 3.11, the viewer is literally occupying the middle ground, a position which in the conceptual metaphor is associated with neutrality.

The point of view is not entirely neutral however. Consider the contrast with Figure 3.12 where the vantage point presented (assuming the configuration

Figure 3.11. TUC (published in *The Telegraph*, 27 March 2011. © EPA)

Figure 3.12. G20 (published in *The Guardian*, 8 April 2009. © PA)

in Figure 3.9) is from cardinal point 2. The two perspectives see the left/right alignment of participants as a mirror image of one another. In other words, from one perspective, cardinal point 0, participant A (the police) appears to the left of the viewer and participant B (the protestors) appears to the right. From the other perspective, cardinal point 2, this is reversed and participant B (protesters) appears to the left and participant A (police) appears to the right. The alternative perspectives are schematized in Figure 3.13.

Now, if we interpret the symbolism of left/right as Kress and van Leeuwen (2006: 179–85) do, then left is associated with knowledge that is 'commonsensical' while right is associated with knowledge that is 'contestable'.[17] This association is probably grounded in the embodied construal we have of time moving linearly from left to right (Evans 2004). In this cognitive model, what is left of the speaker has already happened and can therefore be known while what is right of the speaker is in the future and therefore necessarily undetermined.[18] In any case, the views from cardinal points 0 and 2 do, therefore, involve some degree of stance-taking. Actors positioned in the left region of an image are presented as more familiar to the viewer than those positioned in the right region. We may thus say that the perspective encoded in Figure 3.11 legitimates the police by presenting them as 'safe' and their right to intervene as established but delegitimates the protesters by presenting them as unknown and disputing their right to take action. Conversely, the perspective in Figure 3.12 legitimates the protesters by presenting them as more familiar and their right to action as recognized but delegitimates the police, conferring on them a less familiar status

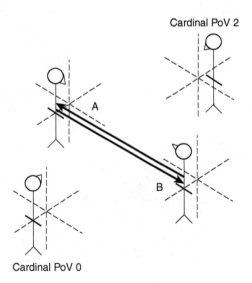

Figure 3.13. View from cardinal points 0 and 2

and calling into question their right to arbitrate. This axiological asymmetry can be seen more starkly in the opposition between cardinal points of view 1 and 3 where the viewer is forced to literally take sides.

From cardinal points of view 1 and 3, the viewer's sagittal axis is brought into line with vectors in the image. The viewer thus becomes embroiled in the event depicted such that their position forms part of the overall meaning of the image. The points of view identified in Figure 3.10 are, of course, cardinal locations and any number of perspectives may be taken in between. The extent to which the viewer is invited into the scene of the image is thus a matter of degree. In general, the more acute the angle between the sagittal axis of the viewer and vectors in the image, the more involved the viewer is asked to become and the less freedom they have to remain outside the scene. This is likely a product of our embodied experience of things directly in front of us being immediately relevant and personally consequential. Ideologically, in visual texts, the distinction between cardinal points of view 1 and 3 has to do with the ordering of participants, including (and relative to) the viewer, and the direction and extension of vectors in the image.

Consider the alternative points of view presented in Figures 3.14 and 3.15 showing scenes from the Student Fees protests. In both images, the police are activated and the protestors passivated in a transactive material process. However, the images differ in PERSPECTIVE. Assuming again the event structure in Figure 3.9, the image in Figure 3.14 encodes a view from near cardinal point

Figure 3.14. Student Fees (© Getty ID 107459525)

Figure 3.15. Student Fees (© Getty ID 107477384)

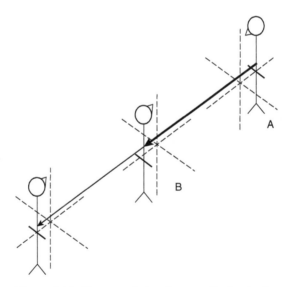

Figure 3.16. Vector and view from cardinal point 3

3 whereas the image in Figure 3.15 presents a view directly from cardinal point 1.

These alternative points of view may have a number of ideological and affective consequences as they invite the viewer to share the perspective of a particular participant. The perspective presented by Figure 3.14 may be schematized as in Figure 3.16. The viewer sees the scene from the perspective of the protestors, the GOAL in the transactive process. Ideologically, the viewer is positioned literally on the side of the protestors. In the STANCE IS POSITION IN SPACE metaphor, being on the same side as someone is associated with metaphorical 'positions' of support and affiliation. Conversely, being on the opposite side to someone is associated with antagonism. The perspective presented thus promotes sympathy and empathy with the protesters and antipathy towards the police. The alternative perspectives from cardinal points 1 and 3 also have consequences for the ordering of participants relative to the viewer. From cardinal point 3, as in Figure 3.14, the protesters are closest to the viewer with the police further away. Chilton (2004) has argued, based on a closely related conceptual metaphor MORALITY IS DISTANCE, that concepts of NEAR and FAR are associated with right and wrong, respectively. In this system, actors and actions the speaker considers moral are imagined as 'close' while actors and actions considered immoral are imagined as 'remote'. Based on a reversed logic of this metaphor, near/far values carry moral connotations. The perspective in Figure 3.16 may thus invoke legitimating and delegitimating evaluations of protesters and police in terms of positive and negative JUDGEMENT: SOCIAL SANCTION: PROPRIETY, respectively.

These **involved** versus **observer** perspectives may have one further, crucial, consequence. In Figure 3.14, for example, not only is the viewer positioned on the same side as the protesters but as a consequence the direction of the vector representing the violent action is now also pointing towards the viewer. The viewer may thus imagine themselves as a second GOAL in the process located at the head of an extended vector (represented by the non-weighted arrow in Figure 3.16). The perspective presented in Figure 3.14 may therefore have a rhetorical effect of inviting feelings of AFFECT: INSECURITY.

In contrast to Figure 3.16, the perspective presented by Figure 3.15 may be schematized as in Figure 3.17. Here, the viewer is positioned on the side of the police, literally and metaphorically 'behind' them. In terms of order of participants, the perspective thus also positions the police rather than the protesters as closer to the viewer, a location which is associated with positive PROPRIETY evaluation. This perspective may further invite a legitimating evaluation of police action where the viewer is invited to imagine themselves as an AGENT in the process (located at the tail of an extended vector as in Figure 3.17) and where we tend to think of our own actions as beyond reproach.

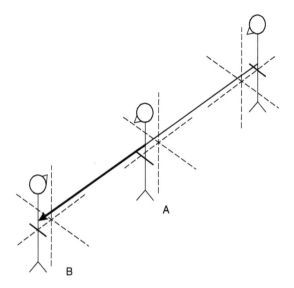

Figure 3.17. Vector and view from cardinal point 1

4.2 ANGLE

Another variable in POINT OF VIEW is ANGLE, which operates on the vertical plane. Potentials in ANGLE are analogous to **tilting** in filming. Again, although there is an indefinite number of possible angles, we may identify particular cardinal points. Figure 3.18 shows the cardinal points in ANGLE. Cardinal point

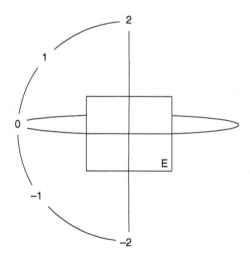

Figure 3.18. Cardinal points of view: ANGLE

0 encodes an 'eye-level' view. Cardinal points 1 and -1 encode diagonal views looking downwards and upwards, respectively. Cardinal point 2 encodes a 'bird's-eye' view. And cardinal point -2 encodes a 'worm's eye' view.

The two variables ANCHOR and ANGLE interact. The ANGLE plane as represented in Figure 3.18 can thus be thought of as rotating around a central vertical axis to provide options in ANGLE from different ANCHORAGE points. Note that cardinal points 2 and -2 coincide for each different ANCHORAGE point.

Cardinal points in the grammar reflect the basic visuo-spatial experiences we have of being located on the ground looking across, up or down at an object and being located beneath or above an object looking directly up or down at it. These visuo-spatial experiences correlate with other types of experience to give rise to conceptual metaphors. For example, being located above an object or entity may correlate with being more easily able to control it or having power over it. Conversely, being located beneath an object or entity may correlate with a lack of power and control. These correlations in embodied experience give rise to a conceptual metaphor POWER AND CONTROL IS UP/POWERLESS AND LACK OF CONTROL IS DOWN. This conceptual metaphor is reflected in language in expressions such as 'control *over* the situation', '*under* control', '*authority over her*' and '*under* her authority'. In the metaphor, then, social dynamics are conceptualized in terms of physical orientations. By the same logic as before, physical orientations therefore carry connotations in terms of social dynamics. In Figures 3.11 and 3.12 which are both *relatively* neutral, the view we are presented with on the vertical plane is more or less from cardinal point 0. In Figure 3.14, however, the view is from cardinal point -1. The vertical perspective in this image, from the point of view of protesters on the horizontal plane, may thus connote powerlessness and subjugation in the face of an authoritarian State. By contrast, the vertical perspective in Figure 3.15, from the point of view of the police on the horizontal plane, may connote legitimate (since the Self is imagined in that role) control of an unruly crowd.[19] These points of view may also be associated with fear and valour, respectively. In our physical experience, our body cowers in fright and stands tall in courage giving rise to a conceptual metaphor BRAVERY IS SIZE.

ANGLE can also serve to engage the viewer in different ways. Cardinal points −1–1 present views from 'on the ground'. The viewer is 'in the thick of things'. By contrast, the view from around cardinal point 2 represents an aerial shot which removes the viewer from the ground and thus detaches them from the situation. Consider, by way of example, the image in Figure 3.19. This point of view further results in a loss of detail – it is no longer possible to pick out individuals or

Figure 3.19. Riot police clash with students in Parliament Square (Student Fees) (©
EPA ID 02487512)

processes. The viewer is unable to see who is doing what to whom. The image
instead presents a mass of people and glosses over any interactions among them.

4.3 DISTANCE

The final variable in POINT OF VIEW is DISTANCE. DISTANCE operates across the
other two planes allowing different values for distance at each combination of
ANCHOR and ANGLE and is analogous to **zoom**. This is illustrated in Figure 3.20.

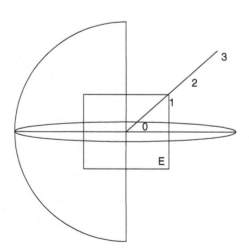

Figure 3.20. Cardinal points of view: DISTANCE

Again, we can identify particular cardinal points. Here, these correspond with long shot, medium shot, close-up and extreme close-up. In general, we can say that the closer the DISTANCE, the stronger the effect of ANCHOR and ANGLE. For example, the more removed the viewer is from the ground on the vertical plane, the less engaged he or she is with the event and the less detail is discernible. Similarly, on the horizontal plane, the further the viewer is from the foregrounded participant, the less likely they are to take their selves into account in making sense of the image. In some images, however, the viewer's perspective is not from behind another participant, as in Figures 3.14 and 3.15, but instead a 'point of view' shot is presented. Here, as in first-person video games, the viewer may be explicitly cast in the role of AGENT or PATIENT in a material process. DISTANCE is particularly important in such images when the viewer is passivated. Consider, for example, the picture in Figure 3.21. The image, which was published by news. bbc.co.uk, depicts scenes during a protest held in Kashmir on 16 September 2006 in response to comments made by Pope Benedict XVI criticizing the Prophet Mohammed.[20]

The view presented by the image is directly from cardinal point 0 on the horizontal plane. Since no other GOAL is present in the image, the zero angle between the vector pointing directly out of the image and viewer's sagittal axis

Figure 3.21. Muslim anger at Pope (©AP ID 6091504433)

means the viewer themselves is invited into this role. On the vertical plane the view is from cardinal point −1 which, alongside other visual features present in facial expression and gesture, attributes power and aggression to the protesters. On the proximal/distal plane, the perspective presented is that of an extreme close-up at cardinal point 0. Although, as we have argued above, NEAR is associated with rightness (and may also be associated with intimacy in the conceptual metaphor SOCIAL RELATIONS ARE DISTANCE),[21] it is also associated with fear. The embodied correlation here comes from our experience of peripersonal space – the zone around the body, defined by the reach of our limbs, which when entered by an unwanted entity makes us feel uncomfortable or anxious (Rizzolatti et al. 1997). The perspective in Figure 3.21, at cardinal point 0 in DISTANCE, means that the ACTOR in the image appears as located inside the viewer's peripersonal space. Given other visual features suggesting intimidation rather than intimacy, the image may thus serve to delegitimate the protesters by invoking an AFFECT: INSECURITY appraisal.[22] This is a similar strategy to that in Figure 3.14 but the effects are likely to be felt more strongly given the lack of intermediate GOAL and degree of proximity involved.

4.4 VIEWING FRAME

Values in DISTANCE have consequences for the contents contained in the VIEWING FRAME. The VIEWING FRAME defines the 'coverage' of the image. That is, it defines how much of the scene is captured in the image and how much is not. Depending on DISTANCE, a greater or lesser coverage is possible. Critically, what gets captured in the VIEWING FRAME and what does not can have different ideological effects. In our earlier examples of queues of immigrants, for example, the VIEWING FRAME did not extend to the end of the queue, suggesting an indefinite line. In pictures of protests, the VIEWING FRAME can be used to mystify aspects of reality by excluding social actors from the image. Consider the image in Figure 3.22 for example. The image is from a student protest held in Turin on 17 November 2011 against budget cuts and the appointment of bankers and business figures in the new Government just formed by Mario Monti.

We can assume a basic event structure like that schematized in Figure 3.9. However, the extreme close-up in DISTANCE results in the exclusion of any other participant presenting to the viewer only a portion of the whole event. The image may therefore be said to mystify causation and agency in the scene depicted. This may be schematized as in Figure 3.23 where the box VF represents the VIEWING FRAME presented to the viewer.

Figure 3.22. Injured protester (© AP ID 111117033428)

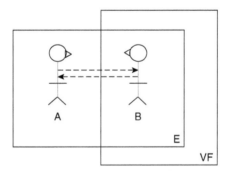

Figure 3.23. Viewing frame in visual mystification

We have seen in this section the role that metaphor plays in providing meaning to the different vantage points available in visual 'documentation'. In these examples, the source concepts in the metaphor have come from embodied experiences. In the next section, we explore the way images may instantiate metaphorical Discourses in which the source domain comes from an area of cultural experience. Here we will also see that metaphor, especially in visual texts, is closely related to intertextuality. Our data come from one of the most intense periods of civil disorder in modern British history: the 1984–1985 British Miners' Strike.

5. Visual metaphor and intertextuality in the British Miners' Strike

Conceptual metaphors are not part of language but of our conceptual system, which underlies all modes of communication including language, gesture and visual semiotics (Lakoff and Johnson 1980). We should therefore expect to find realizations of the same conceptual metaphor across communicative modalities. A number of recent multimodal studies have sought to show the role of conceptual metaphor in visual communication. These studies, however, have been focused largely on advertising or editorial cartoons (Bounegru and Forceville 2011; El Refaie 2003; Forceville 1996) – genres which do not purport to *document* reality. In this section, we address conceptual metaphor in newspaper pictures of the British Miners' Strike.

During the British Miners' Strike, the national press (on both sides) construed the strike metaphorically in terms of a war between the State and the Unions and specifically between the police and picketers. This conceptual metaphor, STRIKE IS WAR, is reflected in linguistic examples such as (1) and (2):

(1) Pit wives smash picket <u>invasion</u>. The angry housewives squared up to the <u>ranks</u> of spitting, snarling pickets. (*The Sun*, 13 March 1984)
(2) An <u>army</u> of 8,000 police were at <u>battle stations</u> last night ready for the final bust-up with Arthur Scargill's flying pickets in the bloody pit <u>war</u>. (*The Sun*, 19 March 1984)

We discuss the implications of metaphor in more detail in the following chapter. Suffice it for now, however, to point out that metaphor involves a particular **framing** of events and that the particular frame selected has specific ideological consequences. The STRIKE IS WAR metaphor, for example, asks the reader to take sides and see the other side as 'the enemy'. It thus realizes a classic ideological square. Our point in this chapter, anyway, is to show how this conceptual metaphor may be instantiated in visual texts.

Visual realizations of conceptual metaphors often involve **intertextuality**. Intertextuality refers to the presence in texts of elements of previous texts. This can involve the reuse of previous text (attributed or not) and/or broader allusions to previous texts. In relation to the latter, the text alluded to may not be a specific text but an iconic phrase or image associated with a specific event, time and/or place. Consider, for example, the newspaper cover in Figure 3.24. The phrase 'lest we forget' in the co-text of the image comes originally from a poem called *Recessional* written by Rudyard Kipling in 1897 and refers to the sacrifice

Figure 3.24. 'Lest we forget' (*The Sun*, 4 March 1985)

of Christ. However, it is often reused in the Ode to Remembrance, added as a final line to Laurence Binyon's poem *For the Fallen*, written in 1914 in honour of British soldiers who had already lost their lives in the First World War. The phrase remains irrevocably associated with the First World War. This intertextual allusion, coupled with the picture of the blooded police officer, serves to frame the Miners' Strike in terms of war and make specific comparisons between the sacrifice of soldiers in the First World War and the efforts of police officers in the strike.

Intertextual references to the First and Second World Wars were, in fact, a recurring phenomenon in newspaper pictures of the year-long strike. The image in Figure 3.25, for example, is reminiscent of the barricades in the Second World War, while the image in Figure 3.26 clearly references the celebrated Christmas Day football match between British and German soldiers during the First World War. In Figure 3.26, the viewer is invited to compare the ground in front of the colliery to the battle fields in the First World War and the police and miners to soldiers. Through intertextuality, then, an image can invoke comparisons with other particular historic moments as specific examples from the source domain. In doing so, the image conjures knowledge and emotions surrounding those historic moments.[23]

Figure 3.25. Barricades (*The Daily Mirror*, 19 June 1984)

Figure 3.26. Football match (*The Guardian*, 17 March 1984)

Figure 3.27. Arthur Scargill as Nazi (© News UK. *The Sun*, 17 March 1984)

The final two images I wish to discuss are both editorial cartoons. Editorial cartoons are interesting because, in contrast to photographs, they are largely satirical and their producers have complete control over their contents. Editorial cartoons thus more directly indicate attitude and demonstrate an intention to frame the situation in a particular way. In the conceptual metaphor STRIKE IS WAR, instantiated in specific intertextual references to the Second World War, editorial cartoons compared Arthur Scargill (the leader the National Union of Miners) to a Nazi General and Margret Thatcher (the Prime Minister) to Winston Churchill. Consider the cartoons in Figures 3.27 and 3.28.

In Figure 3.27, Scargill is depicted in the military uniform of the German army. The winding tower of the mine resembles a watch tower in a Nazi concentration camp, with Scargill presiding over the camp. The train tracks and the chimneys in the background are further reminiscent of iconic images of concentration

Figure 3.28. Margret Thatcher as Churchill (© News UK. *The Times*, 6 June 1984)

camps. In the linguistic co-text, the caption reads 'the lads think you're going over the top'. In modern usage, the phrase means something equivalent to 'going too far' suggesting that Scargill does not have the full support of the miners in taking national strike action. However, 'going over the top' is also associated with going over the parapet of the trench into the killing fields. Hence, entering in to a strike is compared with trench warfare. In Figure 3.28, by contrast, Margret Thatcher is compared to Winston Churchill. She is depicted smoking the iconic cigar associated with Churchill. She is also shown in the shape of a British bulldog – a breed of dog which Churchill was compared with. The dog is presented as guarding Great Britain. Thatcher is also depicted wearing a British military helmet with the phrase 'go to it' written on it. This phrase is associated with 'civilian soldiers' being sent to work in factories, fields, coalmines and dockyards during the Second World War.

These contextualizations serve to delegitimate the Miners' strike by comparing the strike to actions of the German army during the Second World War and depicting Scargill as the 'evil enemy'. At the same time, they serve to legitimate the Government's position by presenting their hard line as 'defending the nation' in the face of this threat and comparing Thatcher's refusal to negotiate with (the myth of) Churchill's resolve.

6. Conclusion

In this chapter we have seen that grammatical systems such as TRANSITIVITY and SOCIAL ACTOR REPRESENTATION, originally proposed in relation to language, find expression in images too. We have also seen that conceptual metaphors, as evidenced by language usages, are similarly indexed in images. Here, theories such as SFG and Conceptual Metaphor Theory, developed in linguistics and applied in CDA, can be usefully extended in analyses of multimodal discourse. In this sense, multimodal discourse analysis is informed by linguistic discourse analysis. However, we have also seen, in the grammar of PERSPECTIVE, a model grounded in visuo-spatial experience and designed in the first instance to account for features of multimodal discourse. Here, we have seen that different points of view have consequences for where participants in the image occur in relation to the viewer and that these configurations may have different ideological effects. We have also suggested that these ideological effects may be a function of a sense-making process in which viewers understand images with reference to their own bodies and embodied experiences. In an egocentric model of conceptualization, we could begin to think about alternative points of view as positioning participants in the image at different sets of coordinates relative to the viewer's sagittal (ANCHOR), coronal (ANGLE) and transversal (DISTANCE) axes. These variables are usually assumed to be specific to multimodal discourse. We have hinted, however, that such features, including vectors, may also show up in linguistic meaning. Indeed, at least in relation to DISTANCE, this is the position taken up by Chilton (2004). It is also a position strongly supported by Cognitive Linguistics where grammar is said to be grounded in visuo-spatial experience. The imaginative processes described in this chapter are ultimately, of course, conceptual in nature and, since both linguistic and visual communication are likely to be based on the same underlying conceptual system, these processes may provide meaning to linguistic discourse too. We develop this line of argument further in subsequent chapters. It should be noted presently, however, that this position has important implications for CDA as it suggests that we may need to at least balance the direction of influence in the development of linguistic and multimodal grammars. In this way, as O'Halloran notes, 'the development of theories and practices specific to MDA [can] potentially contribute to other fields of study, including, importantly, linguistics' (2011: 124).

Part 2

Cognitive Perspectives

Event-Structure and Spatial Point of View

1. Introduction[1]

In the previous chapter, we saw how visuo-spatial variables and various imaginative processes contributed ideologically to the meaning of images. The argument I wish to make in this chapter is that meanings constructed in linguistic discourse similarly involve imagination and possess certain visuo-spatial properties, including point of view. Language, of course, in the course of narrative, can lead readers to adopt alternative perspectives. This kind of spatial manoeuvring is a well-known stylistic device (Simpson 2004). The argument I am making in this chapter, however, is that certain grammatical constructions include, as part of their meaning, a simulated spatial point of view which is imposed on the conceptualization they invoke. This position is based on the claim in Cognitive Grammar, a model which seeks an 'accurate characterization of the structure and organization of linguistic knowledge as an integral part of human cognition' (Langacker 2002: 102), that language is grounded in non-linguistic experience, including visuo-spatial experience of the kind captured in a grammar of visual design. From this perspective, then, meaning draws on experiences we have with our bodies, including visuo-spatial experience, and meaning construction relies on cognitive processes whose primary domains are those involved in such experiences, including vision, spatial cognition and motor control.

The current chapter, thus, represents a cognitive turn in this book where we begin to think about the mental, or more precisely the conceptual, processes involved in meaning-making. This line of enquiry is motivated in large part by the **problem of cognitive** 'equivalence' sometimes posed in CDA (e.g. Stubbs 1997) and is facilitated by the advent of Cognitive Linguistics. In Section 2, we therefore highlight this issue and discuss how it may be resolved by pursuing a more cognitive approach. In Section 3, we introduce image schemas as a key theoretical construct in Cognitive Linguistics and show how different types of image schema may be invoked by alternative transitivity choices in press reports of violence at political protests. In Section 4, we introduce point of view and suggest that the conceptual import of certain grammatical features, including voice and nominalization, can be accounted for in terms of the alternative points of view they invoke. In this chapter, then, we are concerned with cognitive processes operating principally in service of representation.

2. The cognitive perspective

In Chapter 1, we introduced three types of analysis which are frequently presented in CDA: transitivity, mystification and social actor analysis. In all three cases, the analyst is concerned with strategies in linguistic representation. One issue often raised against CDA, however, relates to the cognitive import of representations in text (Billig 2008; Chilton 2005; O'Halloran 2003; Stubbs 1997; Widdowson 2004). The issue concerns the extent to which structures in text index and invoke equivalent structures in the minds of speakers/hearers, respectively. In relation to social actor exclusion, for example, O'Halloran (2003: 234) asks: 'does the absence at text level . . . mean there will be an absence and thus mystification at the discourse level?' Similarly, Billig (2008) questions whether nominalizations found in texts suggest any cognitive form of reification on the part of text producers and consumers. This is an important issue for CDA because the discursive legitimation of (discriminatory) social action necessarily involves cognitive dimensions (Chilton 2005a; van Dijk 2010). Discourse can only be constitutive of social identities and social relations if it is first and foremost constitutive of 'knowledge', which ultimately of course resides in human minds. The dialectic between discourse and society, then, is mediated by the ideological cognitive structures and processes of interacting members. The locus proper of ideological reproduction is therefore not language itself but rather the cognitive processes, including conceptual processes, which language invokes. Most critical discourse analysts now recognize the need for a cognitive perspective, which SFG is not equipped to provide, that shifts the focus of attention from text to discourse, taking into account the cognitive dimensions involved in meaning-making (Wodak 2006: 180).

To date, the most elaborated framework in CDA which addresses the cognitive dimensions of discourse and ideology is van Dijk's socio-cognitive approach and his theory of **event models** (van Dijk 1997, 1998, 1999, 2009, 2010, 2011).[2] For van Dijk, event models are the cognitive architectures stored in social cognition which guide discourse processes of production. They are propositional in form made up of a fixed number of semantic and affective categories (see also Koller 2011). More recently, however, a second cognitive approach to CDA has begun to emerge which, based on findings in Cognitive Linguistics, suggests that such mental models are conceptual and imagistic rather than propositional in nature (Hart 2013a/b). The Cognitive Linguistic Approach (CLA) further differs from the socio-cognitive and systemic functional approaches in so far as it focuses on discourse processes of comprehension. It is to developing this approach that we devote the remainder of this book.

The CLA to CDA (e.g. Chilton 2004; Hart 2010, 2011d; Hart and Lukeš 2007) can be characterized by an emphasis on the relationship between text and **conceptualization** in contexts of social and political discourse. Conceptualizsation is the dynamic cognitive process involved in meaning construction as language, or image, connects with background knowledge to yield local mental representations (Evans and Green 2006: 162). Such background knowledge takes the form of image schemas, frames and conceptual metaphors. To this extent, the CLA aims to theorize, within a coherent analytical framework, the conceptual effects of ideological language choices and thus directly address the problem of cognitive equivalence. It draws on a number of insights presented by Cognitive Linguistics.

Cognitive Linguistics is not a single theory but instead represents a particular school of linguistics comprising several theories, including Cognitive Grammar (Langacker 1987, 1991, 2002, 2008) and Conceptual Metaphor Theory (Lakoff and Johnson 1980, 1999; Lakoff and Turner 1989). It is defined by a specific set of epistemological commitments which can be outlined as follows (cf. Croft and Cruse 2004):

- **Meaning is grounded in experience.** Meaning is rooted in cultural and embodied experience. In the case of the latter, meaning is derived from non-linguistic physical, including visuo-spatial and sensory-motor, experience.
- **Language is not an autonomous faculty involving uniquely specific cognitive processes.** Rather, language is an integrated system dependent on cognitive processes found to function in other domains of cognition including memory, imagination, reason and perception.
- **Language is not modular, made up of distinct sub-systems for syntax, semantics and so on.** Rather, grammar and lexicon are two backs of the same beast. Language is a system of conventionalized units or 'symbolic

assemblies' in which both lexical and grammatical forms 'point to' particular conceptual structures, which are image-schematic in nature.
- **Language encodes construal**. The same situation, event, entity or relation can be conceptualized in different ways and alternative linguistic forms impose upon the scene described alternative conceptualizations.

From this perspective, then, the cognitive systems and processes that ultimately support language are the same as those involved in certain non-linguistic domains of cognition. Linguistic processes are conceptual in nature and conceptual processes are not discernibly different from, for example, perceptual processes (Langacker 2002, 2008).[3] Similarly, since all linguistic knowledge is conceptual in nature, no principled distinction can be drawn between grammar and lexicon (ibid.). Language is a system of conventionalized form-meaning pairings in which grammatical constructions are equally symbolic and therefore in and of themselves meaningful. Their meaning lies in the conceptual structures they invoke. Words and constructions, then, both similarly function as prompts for an array of conceptual operations which, in their turn, serve to constitute our understanding and experience of phenomena in the world. A number of specific conceptual operations have been identified and classified across the literature (Langacker 2002; Talmy 2000; see Croft and Cruse 2004 for a synthesis). Such conceptual operations are seen as manifestations of, and can thus be classified in relation to, abilities in four domain-general cognitive systems (Croft and Curse 2004). From a critical perspective, these conceptual operations can also, in certain discursive contexts, be seen to function ideologically by bringing into effect different types of discursive strategy. A discursive strategy is characterized, from a cognitive perspective, as a more or less intentional/institutionalized plan of discourse practices whose deployment results in a particular, systematically structured and internally coherent, representation of reality which ultimately leads to the legitimation and/or mobilization of social action. They are interpreted here as involving both a linguistic and a conceptual dimension. Discursive strategies are performed through linguistic instantiations but bring about perlocutionary effects only through the conceptualizations that those instantiations evoke. A typology may therefore be presented, as in Figure 4.1, in which conceptual operations are related to both the domain-general cognitive systems on which they rely and the discursive strategies which they potentially realize.[4]

Structural configuration is the strategy by means of which the speaker (intentionally or not) imposes upon the scene a particular image-schematic representation which constitutes our basic understanding of the internal

Strategy \ System	Gestalt	Comparison	Attention	Perspective
Structural Configuration	Schematization			
Framing		Categorization		
Framing		Metaphor		
Identification			Focus	
Identification			Granularity	
Identification			Viewing frame	
Positioning				Point of view
Positioning				Deixis

(Construal operations)

Figure 4.1. Typology of construal operations

structure of an entity, event, situation or relation. The strategy is realized through **schematization** – the imposition of an image schema – and grounded in an ability to analyse complex scenes as gestalts. **Framing** concerns how participants and processes are attributed more affective qualities as alternative categories or conceptual metaphors are apprehended in their conceptualization and, as a function of associated frame-based knowledge, project different evaluative connotations or entailments. Framing strategies are grounded in a general ability to compare experience. It should be noted at this point that the strategies presented are not mutually exclusive but are often co-extant in discourse operating at different levels. While they can be separated for purposes of analysis, then they are rarely, if ever, distinct in the practice of discourse. Categorization, for example, necessarily involves the application of a schema and in schematizing a scene in a given way one defines the scene as belonging to a particular category. In this sense, structural configuration is subordinate to framing. Structural configuration is more basic pertaining only to such structural properties of the scene as topology, sequence and causation, whereas framing operates at a higher level and involves accessing more encyclopaedic knowledge bases. **Identification** concerns which aspects of a given scene are selected for conceptual representation and to what degree of salience those aspects are represented relative to one another. Identification strategies are based in our ability to attend to different facets of a scene in alternative ways. They are realized in various construal operations which Langacker (2002) groups together under the banner of 'focal adjustments'. The argument we will make later in this chapter, however, is that distinctions in attentional distribution are ultimately a consequence of positioning strategies and shifts in **point of view** in particular. **Positioning** is based in our ability to 'see things' from a particular perspective. Specifically, positioning strategies concern where we situate ourselves in terms of space, time and evaluation and where we locate other actors and actions relative to our own 'coordinates'. Positioning can be semantic, encoded in the meaning of certain grammatical constructions. Semantic positioning is primarily spatial. Alternatively, positioning may be more pragmatic anchored in a deictically specified point of view. This form of positioning, which may be spatial, temporal, epistemic or axiological, is effected through a mental discourse space (Chilton 2004).[5]

In Chapter 1, we conducted a transitivity analysis of the material processes present in online press reports of the London G20 protests. In this chapter, we centre on the ideological significance of schematization and point of view shifts within an analytical framework inspired by Cognitive Grammar. Illustrative data are taken from online press reports of the 2010 Student Fees protests. Cognitive Grammar is a particularly useful source for CDA to draw upon because it presents a model which focuses on the mental processes that support grammar while maintaining a commitment to the communicative functions of grammar in context (Nuyts 2007). According to Cognitive Grammar, alternative grammatical devices are commonly available to code the same situation 'precisely because of their conceptual import – the contrasting images they impose' (Langacker 1991: 295). Image schema analysis in particular not only allows us to consider the conceptual reflex of transitivity structures in texts but also affords a finer-level, more semantic means of classifying and describing material process types.

3. Schematization in press reports of political protests

Images schemas are abstract, holistic knowledge structures distilled from repeated patterns of experience during pre-linguistic cognitive development (Johnson 1987; Mandler 2004). They are not images per se, but abstractions from early encounters with scenes which are perceived to have some structural commonality. Image schemas arise in basic domains of experience like ACTION, FORCE, SPACE and MOTION and enable us to make sense of the world in terms of a finite set of discrete models (see Evans and Green 2006: 190 for an inventory of those proposed across the literature). They thus function as 'folk theories' of phenomena in the world and act as heuristic guides for interpretation and action. They form the foundations of the conceptual system. The embodied language claim in Cognitive Linguistics is that these schemas are co-opted to provide the meaningful basis of both lexical and grammatical units (Hampe and Grady 2005; Lakoff and Johnson 1999; Langacker 1987, 1991). These are then later called up in conceptualization by words and constructions to constitute hearers' basic experiences of the phenomena described. To take an example, the lexical item *enter* and the grammatical structure which can be formally expressed as [NP[VP[into [NP]]]] where the verb is a motion verb are both paired in a symbolic assembly with a complex MOTION schema as shown in Figure 4.2. The schema should not be taken as a static representation (though some are). Rather, when activated it 'runs' dynamically as we imagine a smaller entity moving along a path and ending up located in a larger space.

In discourse, *enter* and all sentences of the form [NP[VP[into[NP]]]] where the verb is a verb of motion call up this schema to conceptualize the event being described. This conceptualization takes place inside a **mental space** (Fauconnier 1994, 1997). Mental spaces are conceptual pockets which continually open up and close down as discourse unfolds. They enable hearers to keep track of things like reference as

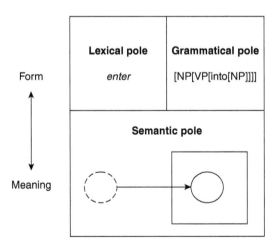

Figure 4.2. Symbolic assembly for *enter* and [NP[VP[into[NP]]]]

mappings are made between elements in different spaces representing alternative times, places and reality statuses. Meaning construction involves the **population** of mental spaces set up in discourse. They are populated, in part, by image schemas. Conceptualization, however, is not restricted to schematic representations. Rather, image schemas serve to define the structural properties of the scene and thus categorize it as being of a particular kind. This schematic representation is then 'fleshed out' through various processes of **elaboration** to provide richer information to the space making finer content specifications (Langacker 2002: 103). Elaboration of the complete schema in Figure 4.2, as prompted by the grammatical structure [NP[VP[into[NP]]]], would involve specification of at least the moving entity, the manner of motion and the location moved into.[6] These elaborations would instantiate and include within them the basic schema.

Crucially, from a critical perspective, language has the facility to recruit alternative image schemas to conceptualize the same scene and thus impose upon it alternative, ideologically vested, **construals**. The set of image schemas and alternative points of view available to construe a given scene constitute a cognitive grammar from which speakers select. This grammar can be divided into semantic regions so that we can speak, for example, about a grammar of ACTION, FORCE, SPACE or MOTION. Particular Discourses, such as Discourses of political protests, exploit this cognitive grammar in different ways. In what follows, we illustrate this with reference to interactions between police and protesters in online press reports of the 2010 Student Fees protests.

On 10 and 24 November two major student protests took place in London against rises in tuition fees for higher education in England and Wales. The first protest was attended by between 30,000 and 52,000 people. On both occasions, police used a controversial crowd control technique known as 'kettling' and both occasions witnessed violent encounters between police and protestors. The examples are taken from a small corpus of online news articles spanning the British national press published on 10 and 24 November.[7]

Based on this corpus, Hart (2013b) showed that in the immediate aftermath of the Student Fees protests, newspapers on the left and the right of the political spectrum constructed the violence that occurred in different ways.[8] One of the ways that this was achieved was through alternative strategies in schematization. At this most basic level of conceptualization, interactions of objectively the same kind can be subjectively construed in more or less violent terms as an ACTION, FORCE or MOTION event. Consider the contrasts between (1)–(3).

(1) A number of police officers were injured as they [came under attack from $_{\text{action}}$]
     the protesters. (*The Times*, 10 November)

(2) Pockets of demonstrators [pushed forward and were held back _{force}] by police. (*The Independent*, 24 November)

(3) About 50 riot police [moved in _{motion}] just after 5pm as the majority of the protesters began to leave the scene. (*The Independent*, 10 November)

In (1), the event is schematized as an ACTION event. As in SFG, the process- or event-type determines participant categories in the event. The categories here, however, are defined by purely semantic properties. In ACTION events, there is a transfer of energy between an AGENT and a PATIENT. The AGENT is defined as the participant furthest 'upstream' in the energy flow and thus the **source** of the transfer. The PATIENT is the participant furthest 'downstream' in the energy flow and the **target** of the energy transfer. Many ACTION events involve a further participant where the transfer of energy from AGENT to PATIENT is mediated by a THEME which serves as an energy **transmitter**. There is also a change in state to the PATIENT – in the case of (1) above the police officers who were injured as a result of the interaction. The image schema imposed on the scene in (1) can be modelled as in Figure 4.3. The circles in the diagram represent the participants. The straight arrow is a **vector** in this instance representing the transfer of energy between participants. The stepped arrow represents the resultant of the interaction. The diagram captures the skeletal structure which forms part of the richer conceptualization invoked by (1). Other similar constructions would instantiate the same schema.[9]

In (2), by contrast, the event is construed as a FORCE event. In a FORCE event, there is not a transfer of energy from an AGENT to a PATIENT. Rather, it is the location and freedom to move of one participant, the AGONIST, that is at issue determined by its relation, including relative strength, with a second entity, the ANTAGONIST (Talmy 2000).[10] The ANTAGONIST is thus the activated participant acting upon the passivated AGONIST. Depending on the result of the interaction,

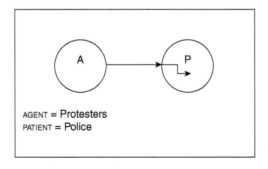

Figure 4.3. Asymmetrical ACTION schema

the AGONIST may either remain passivated or become activated. Construing the event in terms of FORCE reduces the intensity of the process so that the event becomes one of 'balance' (and its modulation) rather than violence. The schema invoked by (2) can be modelled as in Figure 4.4. The protestors are the AGONIST whose location is determined by the police. The protestors are presented with an intrinsic tendency towards action (>) but are kept in check by the stronger (+) ANTAGONIST. The resultant of the interaction is in this case is stasis (O).

Construing an event as a MOTION event, as in (3), still further reduces the intensity of the process involved. Crucially, MOTION events are not transactive. There is no interaction between animate entities. Rather, the motion path of one participant, the TRAJECTOR (in this case also an AGENT), is delineated relative to an inanimate LANDMARK (e.g. towards it, away from it or around it). The vector in the conceptualization thus represents a spatial trajectory rather than a transfer of energy with a LOCATION rather than a PARTICIPANT at its head. The particular MOTION schema invoked by (3) is modelled in Figure 4.5. The

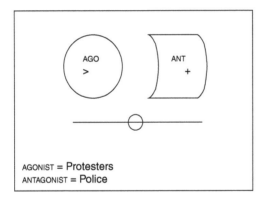

Figure 4.4. Steady-state FORCE schema (caused rest)

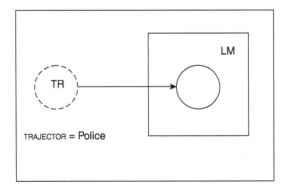

Figure 4.5. MOTION schema

dotted circle represents the starting location of the TRAJECTOR and the square the LANDMARK where it ends up. The LANDMARK is left unspecified in the clause but can be read as the event itself, conceived as a whole bounded entity which the police are there to break apart. In reality, it is difficult to conceive that this would not involve some form of physical contact between police and protesters. The conceptualization, however, overlooks this interactive dimension.

Examples (1)–(3) highlight the facility of language to invoke alternative image-schematic conceptualizations of objectively the same kind of interactive event. The examples given invoke image schemas grounded in three basic domains of experience: ACTION, FORCE and MOTION. These domains each provide for different types of experience, however. For example, in the domain of FORCE, we experience exerting force, being subject to force, and resisting or overcoming force. Similarly, in the domain of ACTION, we experience actions that are caused and actions that are not, actions which are effected directly or indirectly by means of some instrument, and actions that are performed individually or cooperatively. And in the domain of MOTION, we experience differences in rate and direction of motion and in free versus inhibited motion. These alternative embodied experiences give rise to sets of different image schemas which come to constitute regions of a cognitive grammar. There is then, of course, an ideological dimension to which schemas are recruited in discourse to construe a given scene and which roles social actors are cast in within these schemas. Across our corpus, for example, interactions in which the police are activated are more likely to be schematized as FORCE or MOTION events than events in which protesters are activated which are more likely to be schematized as ACTION events (see Hart 2013b). This pattern of distribution serves to legitimate police conduct during the protests and delegitimate the behaviour of protestors. For example, activating protesters and passivating police in ACTION events, as in further examples (4)–(6), serves to apportion responsibility for the violence solely to the protesters and present the police as innocent victims.

(4) There were scuffles at the front of the crowd, with [protesters $_{agent}$] throwing missiles and [hitting $_{action}$] [officers $_{patient}$] with [sticks $_{theme}$]. (*The Independent*, 10 November)

(5) On the ground, [sticks and other missiles $_{theme}$] [were thrown $_{action}$] at [police $_{patient}$] from [a crowd of at least 1,000 $_{agent}$]. (*The Times*, 10 November)

(6) [A number of bottles sticks and eggs $_{theme}$] [were thrown at $_{action}$] [a cordon of officers $_{patient}$]. (*The Telegraph*, 24 November)

All the examples above, then, invoke an **asymmetrical** ACTION schema as in Figure 4.6, in which there is a unidirectional transfer of energy from an AGENT to a PATIENT via a THEME. Note that (4) is in the active voice, (5) is in the passive voice and (6) is an agentless passive construction. All three instances, however, invoke the same basic structure by virtue of the valence of the verbs involved, all of which require an AGENT. The distinction between them, conceptually, lies in point of view shifts and consequent shifts in attentional distribution which we discuss in the following section.

Violent interactions can also be schematized as two-sided in a **reciprocal** ACTION schema. Compare examples (7) and (8).

(7)   A number of police officers were injured after [they ~patient~] [came under attack from ~action~^a^] [youths ~agent~], some wearing scarves to hide their faces. (*The Telegraph*, 10 November)

(8)   [Activists who had masked their faces with scarves ~agent~] [traded punches with ~action~^r^] [police ~agent~]. (*The Guardian*, 10 November)

In contrast to (7) which, similar to example (1), invokes a schema such as modelled in Figure 4.3, example (8) invokes a construal as modelled in Figure 4.7. In this schema, both participants are activated as AGENTS and there is a bidirectional flow of energy between them, represented in the conceptualization by the presence of two vectors.

Within our corpus, when the police are activated in ACTION events, this tends to be in a reciprocal (or a retaliatory; see next section) rather than an asymmetrical ACTION schema (see Hart 2013b). With the exception of *The Guardian,* in which police and protestors are activated in reciprocal ACTION events an equal proportion of the time, this is not the case for protestors (ibid.). When forced to report police violence, then, language has the facility to mitigate,

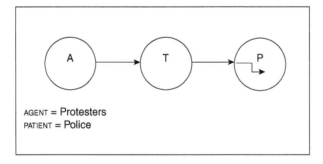

AGENT = Protesters
PATIENT = Police

Figure 4.6. Asymmetrical ACTION schema with THEME

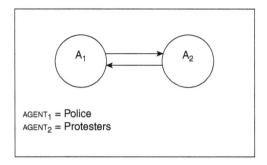

Figure 4.7. Reciprocal ACTION schema

and thus legitimate, social actions by presenting responsibility for them as shared.

Activating the police in FORCE events rather than ACTION events, casting them in the role of ANTAGONIST, further legitimates police action by presenting the police not as perpetrators of violence at all but as moral upholders of civil order in the face of protesters who, cast in the role of AGONIST, are bent on bringing disorder. The particular FORCE schema invoked by examples like (2) and (9)–(10) below, then, configures protestors as instigators of force-interactions who need to be prevented from realizing their intrinsic force tendency.

(9) [About 50 police in riot gear ₐₙₜ] [tried to drive ᶠₒᵣ𝒸ₑ] [the crowd ₐ𝗀ₒ] back away from the building at around 16.25. (*The Independent*, 10 November)

(10) [The 20 officers lining the route at Millbank ₐₙₜ] faced an impossible task of [trying to hold back ᶠₒᵣ𝒸ₑ] [thousands of demonstrators ₐ𝗀ₒ]. (*The Daily Mail*, 10 November)

FORCE schemas have inherent in them a topology which construes the event as a 'battle' between two sides locked in opposition with one another. A force-dynamic conceptualization thus lends itself to a metaphorical extension as in (11) where the event is framed in terms of WAR. This metaphorical construal further serves a legitimating / delegitimating function by comparing police, on the one hand, with the valiant soldier and protestors, on the other hand, with the deviant enemy.

(11) One constable suffered a broken arm and a second officer was knocked unconscious as he <u>battled</u> to contain protesters outside the Foreign Office . . . Huge crowds had attempted to break the security cordon outside the building but the line of police was quickly bolstered to ensure the <u>barricades</u> were not <u>breached</u>. (*The Daily Mail*, 24 November)

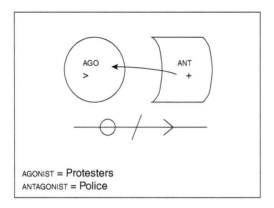

Figure 4.8. Shift-in-balance-of-strength FORCE schema

The FORCE schema invoked by examples (2) and (9)–(11) represents a **steady-state** FORCE schema. Although there is some to-ing and fro-ing, the ANTAGONIST is currently the stronger entity just about succeeding in keeping the AGONIST in check and preventing them from realizing their intrinsic tendency towards action. A further force-dynamic construal, however, is one in which there is a shift in balance of strength resulting in a change in state of affairs as the AGONIST overcomes the barrier provided by the ANTAGONIST and is able to realize their intrinsic force tendency. This schema, modelled in Figure 4.8, is the one invoked by example (12).

(12) [Protesters ₐₒ] [burst through ₍force₎] [police lines ₐₙₜ] to storm the
     Conservative party headquarters. (*The Guardian*, 24 November)

The image presented is one of a force building in mass behind the barrier until the barrier is no longer able to sustain the pressure and the balance of strength transfers to the AGONIST unleashing anarchy.

A further **shift-in-state** FORCE schema is one in which a stronger ANTAGONIST successfully able to keep the AGONIST in check disengages thereby allowing the AGONIST to realize its intrinsic tendency. This schema is instantiated in (13). It is modelled in Figure 4.9. This is the schema that structures the prototypical concept of permission (Talmy 2000). It thus reinforces the position of the police as a legitimated authority.

(13) By 7pm, [police ₐₙₜ] began to [let ₍force₎] [the several hundred protesters
     cordoned on the road in front of Millbank Tower ₐₒ] out in ones and
     twos. (*The Daily Mail*, 10 November)

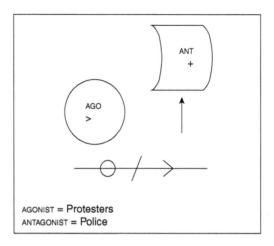

Figure 4.9. Shift-in-state-of-impingement FORCE schema

One final FORCE schema worth discussing in relation to Discourses of political protest is one in which a resistant AGONIST has an intrinsic tendency not towards motion but towards rest (as when protestors occupy a particular space), however a stronger ANTAGONIST is nonetheless able to bring about caused motion in the AGONIST. This schema is instantiated by (14) and modelled in Figure 4.10. Cast in the role of ANTAGONIST, the police are presented as restorers of public order. Note that in both (13) and (14) the processes are presented as measured, marked by 'slowly' and 'in ones and twos'. The police are thus presented as having regained legitimated control of the situation.

(14) [The police ₐₙₜ] slowly [forced 𝒻ₒᵣ𝒸ₑ] [the remaining protesters ₐgₒ] out of the courtyard of Millbank Tower. (*The Independent*, 10 November)

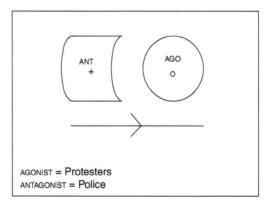

Figure 4.10. Steady-state FORCE schema (caused motion)

Activating the police in a construed MOTION event, as further exemplified in (15), reduces the process to a non-transactive one so that police actions are presented as self-contained without having any direct effect on another human participant. This strategy is thus euphemistic in serving to avoid any reference to police violence.

(15) The volatile situation started to calm down at about 4.30pm when the
      Metropolitan Police [sent in _{motion}] [hundreds of riot officers _{trajector}].
      (*The Daily Mail*, 10 November)

Note that in examples like (3) and (15), not only is the event construed in terms of MOTION rather than ACTION, but, moreover, the MOTION event is construed as one in which there is no physical impact on the unspecified LANDMARK. This is in contrast to MOTION events in which protesters are activated, such as (16), where the verb designates a violent manner of motion and expresses a change in state to the specified LANDMARK. The schema invoked by (16) is presented in Figure 4.11. The stepped arrow represents the effect of the process on the LANDMARK.

(16) A demonstration by students and lecturers descended into violence when
      [a group of protesters _{trajector}] [smashed their way into _{motion}] [the headquarters
      of the Conservative party _{landmark}]. (*The Telegraph*, 10 November)

In this section, we have shown how strategies in schematization impose upon the scene described a construal which configures the internal structure of the event in particular ideologically significant ways, defining its experiential domain and allocating the semantic roles prescribed by the conceptual complex evoked. In the next section, we see how the same basic structure is further subject to

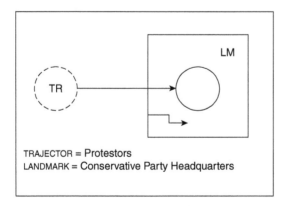

Figure 4.11. MOTION schema – impact on LANDMARK

construal as alternative grammatical constructions invite conceptualizations from different vantage points which, as we argued in the previous chapter, are ideologically and rhetorically charged.

4. Spatial point of view in press reports of political protests[11]

Positioning strategies in discourse concern the ability of the text to manoeuvre the viewer into particular positions from where the scene presented is conceptualized.[12] Positioning is at root spatial and it is spatial positioning as semantically coded in certain grammatical constructions that we deal with in this section. However, other grammatical systems, such as tense and modality, may similarly be thought of as involving metaphorical 'vantage points' in temporal, modal and axiological 'space' (cf. Cap 2013; Chilton 2004). We address temporal and evaluative positioning in Chapter 6.

The ability in narrative discourse of locative and deictic expressions to cause the reader to adopt a particular point of view in imagining the scene being described has been much studied in stylistics (e.g. Simpson 1993: 12–21). Consider, for example, the following instances:

(17) <u>Inside the severely damaged lobby of the tower,</u> a group of around 25 protesters could be seen surrounded by police. (*The Daily Mail*, 10 November)

(18) Police officers were seriously injured today as angry demonstrators protesting against the hike in tuition fees again <u>brought</u> chaos to the streets. (*The Daily Mail*, 24 November)

In (17), the locative expression 'inside the severely damaged lobby of the tower' serves to direct the viewers' attention to the scene inside the building but positions them at a safe distance from the events described at a vantage point exterior to the building.[13] In (18), by contrast, the deictic element 'brought' (as opposed, say, to 'delivered') locates the viewer in 'the streets' where the events came to take place and thus positions the viewer 'in the midst of things'.

Much less considered, at least from a stylistic or discourse-analytical perspective, is the potential of particular grammatical constructions, such as information structures, voice alternates or nominalizations, to encode a spatial point of view. These devices, as we saw in Chapter 1, may index an *ideological* point of view. That ideological point of view, I wish to suggest however, is an associated function of shifts in *spatial* point of view which these grammatical constructions invoke. This analysis is based on research in Cognitive Linguistics which postulates that certain grammatical constructions, and especially those related to event-description, have inherent in their semantic values a specific spatial perspective (Langacker 2008; Talmy 2000; Zwaan 2004).[14] That is, certain (if not all) grammatical constructions include as part of the conceptualizations they invoke a particular vantage point from which they invite the viewer to construe the scene described (Langacker 2008: 75). Event-construals are thus minimally made up of an **event-structure** plus a **point of view** coordinate. The relationship between the point of view and the event-structure constitutes a particular **viewing arrangement** (Langacker 2008).

These two dimensions of meaning – event structure and point of view – are represented during discourse inside nested mental spaces. Event-structure is conceptualized inside an **event space** (see Hart 2010). During discourse, however, there is also always a **base space** (Fauconnier 1997: 49). The base space is a grounding space which other spaces are constructed subordinate and relative to and from where those spaces are construed. This space also includes the conceptualizer (*pace* speaker and hearer) with a defined location and orientation. It is thus the space in which the viewing arrangement is configured (Radden and Dirven 2007). That is, where the viewer is positioned in a particular fashion with respect to the conceptual content in the event space. The base space and the event space may be taken together as constituting a van Dijkian event model theorized in conceptual terms. Just as in visual perception, then, where one cannot help but perceive a scene from a particular situated perspective, so in language one necessarily conceives a scene from a specific imagined perspective 'situated' in the event model. In this sense, conceptualization is egocentric.

In the framework presented here, the point of view coordinates available to language are delineated along the lines described in Chapter 3. They are thus derived from the PERSPECTIVE system in the grammar of visual design and ultimately grounded in parameters presented by visuo-spatial experience. This region of grammar, recall, is constituted by values on three intersecting planes: ANCHOR, ANGLE and DISTANCE. Reinterpreted in Cognitive Linguistic terms, the diagram in Figure 4.12, extrapolated from those in the previous chapter, represents an **idealised cognitive model** (Lakoff 1987) which codes our embodied experience of spatial perspective. It is idealized in the sense that it is abstracted (from repeated experience) and in the sense that the values marked represent cardinal points of view. Recall also that these cardinal points are not to be taken as absolute locations in space but as potential points of view relative to an internal event structure. In Figure 4.12, then, the arcs from X_1 to

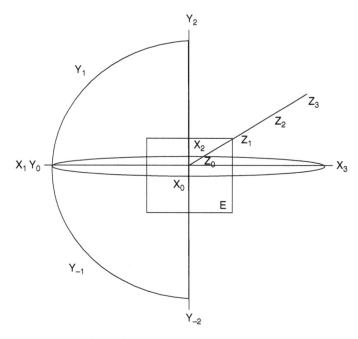

Figure 4.12. Idealized cognitive model for points of view

X_3 represent potential points of view on the ANCHOR plane. The arc from Y_2 to Y_{-2} represents potential points of view on the ANGLE plane. The two planes interact to give different potential combinations of ANCHOR and ANGLE values. The ANGLE plane can thus be thought of as rotating around the Y axis to give different options in ANGLE at different ANCHOR points. Operating across these two dimensions is the dimension of DISTANCE. The Z axis represents potential distances from which an event can be construed at any given combination of ANCHOR and ANGLE. Grammar exploits this cognitive model in different ways such that the points of view encoded by grammatical constructions can be expressed as a set of three-value coordinates within this cognitive model. In what follows, we take ANCHOR, ANGLE and DISTANCE in turn and show how alternate grammatical constructions may be theorized as invoking point of view shifts in these three dimensions.

4.1 ANCHOR

In the previous section, we saw that regular transactive versus reciprocal transactive verbs invoke asymmetrical versus reciprocal ACTION schemas, respectively. In addition to differences in internal event structure, however, these contrasting constructions may also invoke shifts in points of view on the ANCHOR plane. Further grammatical distinctions within these constructions, such as **information structure** and **voice**, may similarly involve point of view shifts in ANCHOR. Consider the contrasts between (19)–(22). The four contrasting event models invoked by (19)–(22) are represented in Figure 4.13(a)–(d), respectively.

(19) There were some minor scuffles between [protesters $_{new}$] and [police $_{given}$] in Bristol. (*The Express*, 24 November)

(20) [Police wielding batons $_{new}$] clashed with [a crowd hurling placard sticks, eggs and bottles $_{given}$]. (*The Guardian*, 10 November)

(21) [[Student protesters $_{agent}$] attacked [a police van $_{patient}$] $_{av}$]. (*The Express*, 24 November)

(22) A number of police officers were injured after [[they $_{patient}$] came under attack from [youths $_{agent}$] $_{pv}$]. (*The Express*, 10 November)

(19) and (20) are both reciprocal action constructions in which police and protestors are equally agentive. They can be analysed as linguistic manifestations of perspective parallel to the visual instantiations presented in the previous chapter by the images given as Figures 3.11 and 3.12. Accordingly, they can be characterized as encoding an **observer** perspective from PoV X_0 or X_2 performing parallel ideological functions. Which particular point of view is encoded seems to be a function of the subtle difference we find in information structure. The examples can therefore been analysed in terms of information units Given and New (Halliday 1967) rather than semantic categories. New information is information the speaker considers relevant and intends that the hearer attends to. Given information is information the speaker treats as expected. As Halliday (1994: 298) puts it, new information is news, given information is not. In line with Halliday, Given and New are not defined positionally but prosodically (new information is signalled by higher pitch and relative stress). Nevertheless, canonically, given information occurs earlier in the clause compared to new information. In news discourse, though, probably due to the urgency of delivering 'newsworthy' information, there is often a marked order of Given and New such that the latter comes earlier in the clause as in (19) and (20).[15]

From a cognitive standpoint, then, the conventional ordering of Given and New, in conjunction with the direction of writing in English, gives rise to associations between given information and spatial left and between new information and spatial right (van Leeuwen 2005: 201). The grammatical distinction between (19) and (20) can therefore be characterized as a conceptual shift in point of view which, motivated by these associations, results in an alternative left/right alignment of participants with respect to the viewer. In parallel with the images in Figures 3.11 and 3.12 in the previous chapter, and assuming an event-structure with a fixed orientation as in Figure 4.13 with police assigned as participant A1 and protesters assigned as participant A2, (19) is thus likely to invoke a construal from PoV X_0 as in 4.13(a) locating the police to the left of the viewer and protesters to the right while (20) will invoke a construal from PoV X_2 as in 4.13(b) placing protesters to the left of the viewer and the police to the right. Consequently, in (19) it is the protesters' role in the event that is contested and therefore constitutes news, while in (20) it is the behaviour of the police that is subject to question. This interpretation is consistent with our data where it can be seen that whenever newspapers do use a reciprocal action schema, those on the left of the political spectrum favour a perspective from PoV X_2 while those on the right of the political spectrum prefer a perspective from PoV X_0 (see Hart 2013b).

In contrast to (19) and (20), (21) and (22) are both asymmetrical constructions in which agency is assigned to one particular participant. Asymmetrical action constructions like this require a voice choice. The distinction between (21) and (22), then, is that (21) is in the active voice while (22) is in the passive voice. Voice alternates are similarly characterized here as point of view shifts on the ANCHOR

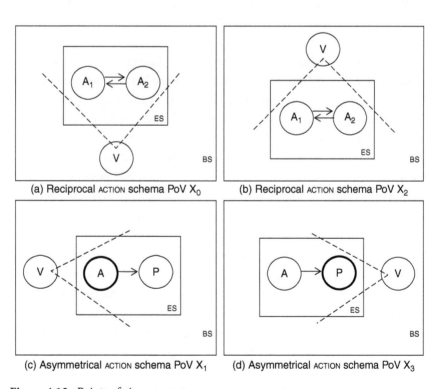

(a) Reciprocal ACTION schema PoV X_0 (b) Reciprocal ACTION schema PoV X_2

(c) Asymmetrical ACTION schema PoV X_1 (d) Asymmetrical ACTION schema PoV X_3

Figure 4.13. Points of view: ANCHOR

plane. The **active voice** is analysed as encoding a perspective from upstream of the energy flow while the **passive voice**, by contrast, encodes a perspective from downstream of the energy flow.[16] Thus, assuming again an event structure with a fixed orientation as in Figure 4.13, (21) invokes a perspective from PoV X_1 as in 4.13(c) while (22) invokes a perspective from PoV X_3 as in 4.13(d). (21) and (22) are therefore considered linguistic expressions of the same point of view operations instantiated by the images given in the previous chapter as 3.15 and 3.14, respectively, and can be described as encoding an **involved** perspective.

The viewing arrangements in 4.13(c) and (d) have a number of corollaries which can be exploited in ideological discourse. In the first instance, the different points of view entail different orientation relations with the AGENT and the PATIENT. In the active voice, the viewer's orientation is in line with the AGENT and opposed to the PATIENT. In the passive voice, the viewer's orientation is in line with the PATIENT and opposed to the AGENT. These alternative configurations, **ego-aligned** and **ego-opposed**, are associated with affiliation and confrontation, respectively. Similarly, in the second instance, voice alternates affect the order of participants relative to the viewer. In the active voice, the AGENT is closer and the PATIENT is further away. This is reversed in the passive voice. Voice alternates can thus be said to include a deictic element in their meaning. And, as we suggested in the previous chapter, proximal and distal values carry various connotations to do with affinity and morality (cf. Chilton 2004). In the third instance, voice alternates affect not only the distance of elements in the scene but also their prominence. Here, the perspectival system works in conjunction with the attentional system. In perceiving any scene, the nearest entity, the Figure, is in **focus** relative to the more distal entity, the Ground. As Croft and Cruse state, 'a particular vantage point imposes a foreground-background alignment on a scene' (2004: 59). In the active voice, it is the AGENT that achieves conceptual prominence as the foregrounded entity. In the passive voice, by contrast, the PATIENT is the focal entity while the AGENT is located in the relative background.

In our data, a number of patterns in the distribution of active versus passive voice can be found which can be taken as indicative of wider ideological Discourses. For example, when police are activated, which tends to be in FORCE or MOTION events rather than ACTION events, the active voice is preferred as in (9) and (10) and (13)–(15). In other words, when it is police behaviour under the spotlight as the focal entity, that behaviour is presented as non-violent. The active voice in these examples further serves to legitimate the police as the viewer is positioned on their side in opposition to the protesters.

When protestors are activated, which tends to be in asymmetrical ACTION events, the active voice is preferred when the PATIENT is an inanimate object as in

(21) but the passive voice is preferred when the PATIENT is the police as in (22) as well as (5) and (6). In examples like (21), then, involving a non-animate PATIENT, the point of view invoked by the active voice seems not to be about asking the viewer to see things from the protesters' side, as the closest participant, but about drawing attention to the violent actions of the protestors by placing them in the foreground of the viewer's sight-line. In other words, it is attention rather than perspective that is most important in the active construal invoked by (21).

In (22), by contrast, it is perspective that is most important. Here, the positioning of the viewer, invited by the passive construction, does seem to be predominantly a matter of asking the viewer to see things from the point of the view of the police as the nearest participant. This suggests that we may need to reinterpret the ideological and rhetorical functions of the passive voice. In orthodox interpretations, the passive voice is said to distance the AGENT and in so doing detract attention from relations of causality (Kress and Hodge 1979; Trew 1979). On our analysis, the passive voice does indeed organize things in such a way that the AGENT is distanced and thus our analysis gives some cognitively grounded weight to these claims. However, if this was the primary function of the passive voice then we might expect to find an alternative distribution of this construction across our corpus given what we can glean from other analyses about the ideological persuasions of most of the different newspapers. Here, we should not expect to see the passive voice applied to violent actions of the protesters. Overwhelmingly, however, when the protesters are activated as AGENTS of violent actions directed at the police the passive voice is preferred. The alternative interpretation that comes out of the analysis given here is that the passive voice, as a point of view operation, serves to co-locate the viewer with the PATIENT downstream in the energy flow in a position of confrontation with the AGENT so that, as a consequence, the violent action of the AGENT is symbolically directed at the viewer too. The construal may thus arouse a negative AFFECT: INSECURITY appraisal. Although the AGENT is initially distanced, then, in the dynamic schema invoked, they are construed as moving violently towards the viewer. The primary function of the passive voice, in this context at least, therefore seems to be something more akin to realizing a 'proximization' strategy as described by Cap (2013).[17]

4.2 ANGLE

Point of view shifts in ANGLE are manifested in various types of **metonymy** and certain instances of **nominalization**. Shifts in ANGLE similarly affect the way we attend to the scene under conception. The effect, however, pertains to the mode of viewing promoted by particular points of view on the ANGLE plane and the granularity rather than the relative distance of elements within the conceptualization. Let us take first nominalizations like the following:

(23) But around an hour after the protest started, [violence $_{agent}$ ^{r}] flared at Millbank Tower. (*The Independent*, 10 November)

(24) The worst [violence $_{agent}$ ^{r}] erupted after 6pm as officers let the marchers leave. (*The Guardian*, 24 November)

Linguistically, nominalizations are abstract nouns typically derived from other word classes. The abstract noun *violence* in (23) and (24), for example, is derived from the adjective *violent*. Nominalizations have their conceptual counterpart in **reification**, which involves seeing a property or relation as an OBJECT (Langacker 2002; Radden and Dirven 2007). This process of reification allows relational or attributive concepts to be treated as concrete products having, or coming into, some kind of ontological existence. In (23) and (24), the reified OBJECT is presented as spontaneously coming into being. In SFG terms, there is a creative, as opposed to a transactive, material process. A violent situation is, however, made up of a series of complex interactions with particular internal structures. Linguistically, these structures are spelled out in full clauses of the sort discussed so far in this chapter. The nominalized form *violence*, though, reduces this series of interactions to a simple OBJECT. Consequently, since OBJECTS do not unfold dynamically in space and time, properties of the interactions involved, such as those pertaining to spatial and sequential organization, get lost. In other words, the situation is glossed over by the nominalization rather than attended to in any detail. Nominalizations such as these, then, can be said to conceal, through reification, crucial features of a situation, including agency and causation (Fowler 1991; Hodge and Kress 1993).

The conceptual effects of nominalizations in reification and mystification, I suggest however, are ultimately both a function of a point of view shift in ANGLE as modelled in Figure 4.14. Nominalizations present a perspective on the event from cardinal PoV Y_1 in Figure 4.12. From this vantage point, the viewer is not looking diagonally down on the event but across the top of it in a summary fashion.[18] It is this 'skimming' of the situation from above that results in a loss in attention to detail (as when we *look over* something as opposed to when we *look into* something) and in the situation being conceived as a gestalt.

Certain types of metonymy work in a similar fashion only the perspective they invoke is from cardinal PoV Y_2 in Figure 4.12. From this vantage point, further and directly above the scene, there is a resultant loss in **granularity** or

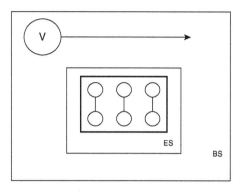

Figure 4.14. Nominalization as point of view shift (ANGLE)

'resolution'. The notion of granularity here is related to the semantic property of PLEXITY and the grammatical category of NUMBER (Talmy 2000). Consider the contrast between (25) and (26):

(25) Tuition fee protests: eight injured, five arrested as [students $_{agent}$] turn violent. (*The Telegraph*, 24 November)

(26) [Student protest over fees $_{EP\ MTNMY}$] turns violent. (*The Guardian*, 10 November)

PLEXITY refers to whether the scene under conception is conceived as being comprised of a number of individual elements, in which case the conceptualization is **multiplex** in structure, or whether it is construed as a homogenized mass, in which case the conceptualization is **uniplex** in structure. In a multiplex construal, as in (25), individual elements can be picked out and can thus be counted. This is reflected grammatically in plurality. In a uniplex construal, such as (26), those elements are collectivized and only global features of the scene are taken in. This is marked grammatically by the singular form.

In (25), then, it is individuated students who turn violent. That is, this multiplex construal attributes the property VIOLENT to participants in the event and to students in particular. In (26), by contrast, the property VIOLENT is attributed to the event itself. In reality, of course, an event is the abstracted sum of its parts – participants and processes – and cannot itself be agentive. (26) thus presents an EVENT FOR PARTICIPANT metonymy, which is a particular instantiation of a WHOLE FOR PART metonymy. This metonymy constitutes a multiplex-to-uniplex construal operation. This way of seeing the situation, though, is a product of where it is seen from. (25) presents a view from on the ground at PoV Y_0. (26) presents a bird's eye view from PoV Y_2. From a bird's eye view there is necessarily

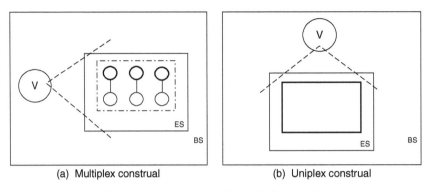

(a) Multiplex construal   (b) Uniplex construal

Figure 4.15. Multiplex to uniplex as point of view shift (ANGLE)

a loss of granularity so that the boundary of the scene can be made out but its internal components are not discernable.[19] Particular properties can then only be attributed to the scene as a whole leaving all participants potentially to blame for its outcome. The event models invoked by (25) and (26) are presented in Figure 4.15(a) and (b), respectively.

4.3 DISTANCE

The last plane on which a point of view shift can occur is the DISTANCE plane. Shifts in DISTANCE can, in principle, take place at any ANGLE and from any ANCHOR point. For present purposes, however, we consider shifts in DISTANCE from PoV Y_0 in ANGLE. We leave the ANCHOR values unspecified in the analyses but note that some perspective in ANCHOR would necessarily be taken. Shifts in DISTANCE pertain to how much of a scene is captured in the **viewing frame**.[20] The viewing frame constitutes the conceptual content which, at any moment in the proceeding discourse, is currently the subject of the viewer's attention.

In perceiving any given scene, we necessarily select only a portion of that scene to attend to, defined by the direction and limits of our visual field. Relative distance from the scene also plays a part here as the nearer we are to the scene the less of it we can take in. So in language, a text unit can encode a point of view at alternative distances from the scene under conception allowing varying ranges to be covered by the viewing frame. Information outside of the viewing frame remains within the **scope of attention** (Langacker 2002), accessible from the base space but not currently subject to conceptualization. That is, a broader schema may be evoked inside the event space but it is not currently 'in shot' within the viewing frame and thus remains unfleshed.

The most obvious means by which language directs the viewing frame on to particular facets of the reference situation is through explicit mention of that portion (Talmy 2000: 258). Linguistic devices that restrict the viewing frame therefore include the agentless passive voice, in the absence of a circumstantial clause expressing causation, and certain nominalizations which focus attention only on the resultant of interactions.[21]

In the examples given as (1), (7) and (22)[22], then, and repeated again in (28), the viewing frame extends over the whole of the evoked schema.[23] The resultant of the interaction, *injuries*, is mentioned in the main clause and the event which leads to that outcome is fully specified in the second, circumstantial clause. The circumstantial clause thus expresses the cause of the effects expressed in the main clause.[24] The vantage point permitting full coverage of the evoked schema is that from cardinal PoV Z_2 on the DISTANCE plane. In (29), by contrast, the circumstantial clause includes an EVENT FOR PARTICIPANT metonymy. The actual cause, or more pertinently the *causer*, of the injuries is not explicitly mentioned. They therefore remain beyond the purview of the viewing frame. The result is, nevertheless, expressed in a verbal form and so the process itself remains inside the viewing frame. The vantage point can be analysed as a close-up shot at PoV Z_1. In example (30), however, the resultant of the interaction is rendered as a nominalized form. No circumstantial information is therefore made available to the viewer. The vantage point is instead that of an extreme close-up at PoV Z_0 focused exclusively on the end result of the interaction. The three alternative construals invoked by (28)–(30) are modelled in Figure 4.16(a)–(c), respectively. This analysis gives some cognitively grounded weight to the claim that exclusion in discourse can push social actors into the 'semantic background' (Reisigl and Wodak 2001: 58) where the semantic background is theorized as the field of conceptualization that lies outside the current viewing frame.

(28)　[A number of police officers were injured $_{result}$] [as [they $_{patient}$] [came under attack from $_{action}$] [the protesters $_{agent}$] $_{circ}$]. (*The Times*, 10 November)

(29)　The demonstration followed a day of action two weeks ago that saw 60 arrested and [dozens injured $_{result}$] [when [a riot $_{ep\ mtnmy}$] [broke out $_{action}$] [at the Conservative Party headquarters $_{location}$] $_{circ}$]. (*The Telegraph*, 24 November)

(30)　At least 14 people were treated for [their injuries $_{result}$] in hospital and 32 arrested. (*The Times*, 10 November)

The distribution of cause-specifying ((28)) and cause-mystifying ((29–30)) constructions is ideologically revealing. Whenever it is the police whose injuries are under conception the cause tends to be specified. Conversely, however, whenever it is the protesters whose injuries are being reported the cause tends to be mystified. The only newspaper in which this pattern is not repeated is *The Guardian* in which the cause is always mystified regardless of whose injuries are at issue (see Hart 2013b). This distribution constructs and orients to a Discourse of legitimation through mystification in relation to the police as any reference (explicit or implicit) to them as causers of harmful physical effects is avoided. The distribution simultaneously constructs and orients to a Discourse of delegitimation through specification in relation to the protestors who are explicitly referenced as causers of physical harm.

In asymmetrical ACTION events of the kind discussed so far in this section, the event space is populated by a basic schema in which the AGENT is also the INITIATOR of the interaction. That is, they are the first element in a causal action chain. In a **retaliatory** schematization, however, the AGENT in the event is responding to some previous interaction. The viewing frame, in this case, is not cropped but extended to cover, ideologically, some mitigating cause or circumstance. This extension of the viewing frame involves a more distal perspective or long shot from PoV Z_3 taking in a wider array of conceptual content. Consider (31):

(31) Rocks, wooden banners, eggs, rotten fruit and shards of glass were
       thrown at police officers <u>trying to beat back</u> the crowd with metal batons
       and riot shields. (*The Telegraph*, 10 November)

To 'beat back' is a *re*action to some previous event in a sequence of causal interactions (compare (31) with (20) in which a similar police action is not construed as retaliatory). The AGENT in a retaliatory schema is presented as responding to some prior event which is encompassed within the viewing frame. They are no longer, therefore, construed as an INITIATOR but as a REACTOR. The construal invoked by (31) is modelled in Figure 4.16(d) where the circle E represents a preceding event which would of course have an internal structure of its own. Ideologically, it is only police actions which are schematized through cause-mitigating constructions. Protester actions, by contrast, are never construed as retaliatory. This distribution further contributes to a Discourse of legitimation/delegitimation as police actions are construed as provoked and justified while protester actions are construed as gratuitous.

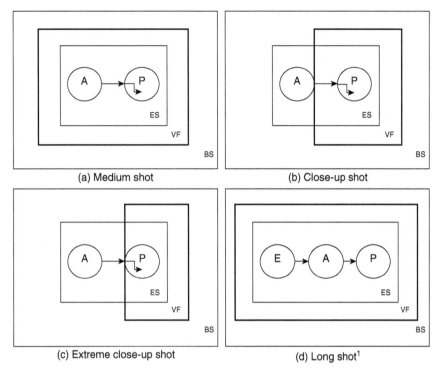

Figure 4.16. Frame shots and point of view (DISTANCE)

6. Conclusion

In this chapter, we have introduced the Cognitive Linguistic Approach to CDA and highlighted some of the conceptual lines along which, via alternative grammatical constructions in discourse, ideology is enacted in the language of press reports on political protests. From a theoretical perspective informed by Cognitive Grammar, we have suggested that grammatical constructions encountered in discourse, as a function of their conventionalized meanings, invoke in the minds of readers particular image-schematic representations experienced from a particular point of view. Here, we have argued that grammar encodes a simulated visuo-spatial experience which possesses many of the same qualities as are involved in our experience of images. We have further suggested, based on both qualitative and distributional analysis of the data, that alternative event-structures and viewing arrangements can, in specific contexts, carry particular ideological bearings. In this way, we have been able to at least speculate about the conceptual and ideological import of patterns presented by texts in transitivity and grammatical metaphor.

Overall, in the data analysed, strategies realized in schematization and point of view have been shown to steer towards a delegitimating Discourse of violence in relation to protesters, whereby civil action is seen as moral wrong doing, but towards a legitimating Discourse of peace in relation to the police, whose handling of the events is seen as normative. In terms of evaluation, these patterns of representation are thus likely to invoke positive JUDGEMENT: PROPRIETY evaluations of the authorities but negative JUDGEMENT: PROPRIETY and even AFFECT: INSECURITY assessments in relation to protesters.

The concepts that emerge from embodied visuo-spatial experience underpin much of the conceptual system. In this chapter, we have been restricted to considering the way in which they provide meaning to discourse about physical events. Visuo-spatial experience, however, is at the root of conceptualization and is extended metaphorically to structure our experience in non-physical realms. In the next chapter, we explore the ideological and (de)legitimating functions of metaphor in conceptualization. In the final chapter of this book, we see how deictically anchored points of views and shifts in relative DISTANCE of other discourse elements function ideologically in representations of SPACE and spatialized representations of TIME, EPISTEMIC MODALITY and AXIOLOGY.

Metaphor

1. Introduction

In the last chapter we were primarily concerned with the level of representation and in particular with the bare structural properties of conceptualizations invoked in discourse through schematization and point of view shifts. In focusing on metaphor in this chapter, we are still very much concerned with representation but move further towards considering the cognitive processes operating at the level of evaluation in discourse. Metaphor may impose schematic structures onto a scene when the vehicle in the metaphor instantiates a particular image schema. However, metaphor also involves the fleshing out of these basic structures with richer images recruited from encyclopaedic knowledge bases – frames. Metaphor has long been recognized as a powerful rhetorical device used to 'insinuate wrong ideas, move the Passions, and thereby mislead the Judgement' (Locke 1690: 508). It is only more recently, however, that scholars have recognized the cognitive function that metaphor performs in systematically ordering our very experience (Lakoff and Johnson 1980, 1999). On this view, metaphor is a universal means of understanding phenomena in the world. It is a cognitive adaptation which affords understanding in new and otherwise unreachable domains (Mithen 1998). Ideologically, however, metaphor may be exploited in discourse to promote one particular image of reality over another. In this chapter, we consider the ideological and legitimating role that metaphor, as a construal operation grounded in a general ability to compare experience, plays in structuring our understanding of social and political phenomena.[1] In Section 2, we discuss the cognitive and ideological workings of metaphor. In Section 3, we consider the relation of metaphor to grammar. In Sections 4 and 5, we present three case studies of metaphor in media and political discourse: metaphor in media representations of the London Riots, metaphor in David

Cameron's response to the riots and metaphor in Cameron's austerity discourse. In all three cases, we find that metaphor serves to reduce complex social situations and events to natural phenomena.

2. Conceptual metaphor, blending and ideology

Recall from the previous chapter that the various construal operations we identified are seen as manifestations of more general cognitive abilities and the locus of realization for discursive strategies. Metaphor is grounded in our ability to compare experience. Cognitively, this takes place through **mappings** or **projections** between **domains** or **spaces**. Here, we can distinguish between two levels of conceptual structure. **Conceptual metaphors** are relatively stable associations between conceptual domains in the form of a mapping from a **source domain** onto a **target domain** (Lakoff and Johnson 1980). They pertain to conceptual organization rather than conceptualization as a dynamic process of online meaning construction. **Conceptual blends**, by contrast, are *ad hoc* structures built during discourse for purposes of local understanding (Fauconnier and Turner 2002). Invoked by metaphorical expressions in discourse, they involve a projection of conceptual structure from two (or more) mental spaces into a third blended space giving rise to new *emergent* structure.[2] Conceptual blends, thus, pertain to conceptualization. The relationship between conceptual blends evoked by metaphor in discourse and conceptual metaphors is dialectic (see Hart 2010: 121–4 for further discussion). Conceptual metaphors can be treated as abstractions from repeated patterns in blending networks. At the same time, however, conceptual metaphors provide input to, and define the possibilities of, particular blends (Grady 2005; Grady et al. 1999). Conceptual metaphors thus account for the systematicity we find in metaphorical discourse.

Certain conceptual metaphors are a feature of the general conceptual system that supports 'everyday' language. These metaphors, such as STANCE IS POSITION IN SPACE, naturally show up in political discourse where they may (or may not) be exploited for ideological purposes but they are not in and of themselves ideologically constructed. Other conceptual metaphors, which we can call *Discourse conceptual metaphors*, are socially constructed and specific to social and political Discourses. They are often based on common conceptual metaphors but the target domain relates to a particular social or political context. From a critical perspective, the metaphors we should be most interested in are Discourse conceptual metaphors or those which fulfil specific ideological or persuasive functions in social and political discourse. It is Discourse conceptual metaphors which, according to Dirven et al. (2003), form the cognitive basis of ideology. These ideological cognitive systems are both reflected in and brought into being by common structures held between closely related blends which have become conventional for a given Discourse. Electing to conduct a critical metaphor analysis in terms of conceptual blending or conceptual metaphor theory is therefore just a matter of perspective (cf. Hart 2008). Which perspective one takes depends on whether one is concerned primarily with the wider patterns of belief and value (ideologies) that imbue texts or is more interested instead in the cognitive processes involved in specific instances of meaning construction during discourse. Because our primary concern in this book is with grammar in use, we will address metaphor from the perspective of conceptual blending. Perhaps the best way of introducing blending theory is through an example. We will take the visual example in Figure 5.1 commenting on British immigration policy under the Labour Party.

In the previous chapter, we came across the notion of mental spaces, defined as conceptual pockets which pop up in dynamic networks as discourse unfolds. Conceptual blending involves the construction and integration of mental spaces (Fauconnier and Turner 2002). The image in Figure 5.1 prompts for the construction of two **input spaces** which are populated by elements from **frames** for IMMIGRATION, on the one hand, and CLOTHING/TEXTILES on the other hand. Frames are areas of knowledge or memory which encode particular domains of experience (Fillmore 1982). Crucially, when one feature of a frame is activated in discourse, all other features of the frame are made available (ibid.: 111). Frames, thus, represent the richer knowledge bases which elements in discourse evoke and which, in turn, serve to flesh out meanings in discourse. Conceptual blending involves the recruitment of background knowledge from these frames. This part of the blending process is referred to as **completion**.

Elements in the input spaces are linked by different kinds of **connector**. In the case of metaphor, these are analogical connectors. In the blend evoked by Figure 5.1, which is modelled in Figure 5.2, we find the following counterpart elements linked by analogy across the TEXTILES and IMMIGRATION frames:

TEXTILES frame	IMMIGRATION frame
Bounded cloth	Britain
Filling	Population
Holes in the fabric	Border control
Packing the cloth	Current immigration policy

Figure 5.1. Bursting at the seams blend (*The Telegraph*, 16 December 2002)

In addition, we have elements 'immigrants' in the IMMIGRATION frame without a specified counterpart in the TEXTILES frame and 'bursting' in the TEXTILES frame without a clear counterpart in the IMMIGRATION frame.

Information from the two input spaces is then projected into a third **blended space**.[3] This process is referred to as **composition**. Information projected includes counterpart elements from the two input spaces which, in the case

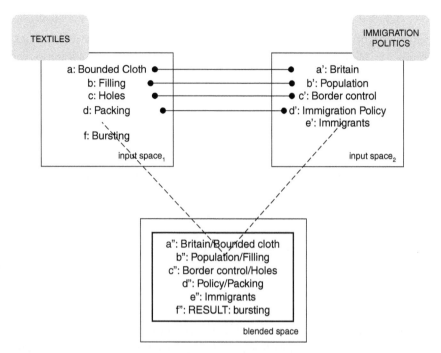

Figure 5.2. Integration network in 'bursting at the seams' blend

of metaphor, are **fused** in the blended space to forge new emergent structure unique to the blend. Thus, in this blend, 'Britain' is fused with 'bounded cloth' and the 'population' of the country becomes the 'filling' inside this bounded cloth. Crucially, it is worth noting at this point, the image invoked is not sourced solely from the TEXTILES frame mapping highly specific structure directly onto the IMMIGRATION frame, in which case the image invoked might be something like a pillow being stuffed with feathers. Rather, the emergent structure is a mix of elements from both input spaces: Britain, as a bounded material entity, is being stuffed with immigrants adding to the filling/population inside the country. Further fusions occur between counterpart elements 'holes in the fabric' and 'border control' and 'packing' and 'current policy'. Here, border control is seen as not being 'tight' enough to stop immigrants entering the country. Moreover, Labour's immigration policy, metonymically represented by David Blunkett (the then Home Secretary), is seen as actively packing the country with immigrants. Through completion and composition, frame-based knowledge accessible from elements in the input spaces also gets projected into the blended space. Only certain information, however, is selected for projection. This process is guided in part by pragmatic principles of relevance (Fauconnier and Turner 2002:

333; Tendhal and Gibbs 2008: 1844) but may also be guided by the ideological intentions or institutionalized ideology of the speaker. From the TEXTILES frame, the blend recruits inferential background knowledge which informs us that when a bounded cloth continues to be packed full of contents this will place significant pressure on the material which will eventually tear.

The most significant part in the blending process is **elaboration** – the 'running' of the blend. Elaboration is 'the simulated mental performance of the event in the blend' (Grady et al. 1999: 107). Crucially, it is this simulation that is the source of further inference and affect (Fauconnier and Turner 1996: 115). Thus, in the blended space, we find the emergent inference that continuing to pack Britain full of immigrants will result in an expanding population and the country eventually bursting at the seams. This can be expressed as a causal relation between elements in the blended space formulated as $d"(a",e") \rightarrow +b" \rightarrow f(a")$. Bursting is, of course, an undesirable outcome and therefore inscribes a negative appraisal of the situation. Moreover, it naturally follows, within the blended space, that we should mend Britain's borders and implement a more restrictive immigration policy in order to prevent the country from bursting.[4] Crucially, this inference, which is entirely logical within the blend, is projected back to the second input space where it may update the frame that structures that space and so becomes *ideological*. The construal operation of blending, then, accounts for the ideological and legitimating functions of metaphor in discourse as the dynamic conceptualization invoked by metaphor provides a local guide for thinking, feeling and acting. The particular choice of frame to populate the first input space as well as the specific knowledge selected from that frame guides these processes in different ideological directions. Moreover, through back-projection and abstraction, transitory structures built in blending networks may come to constitute more stable structures that make up world view encoded in cognitive frames and conceptual metaphors.

Metaphorical expressions can be more or less conventional where more conventional expressions are those found to occur most frequently in natural language discourse or inside a specific institutionalized Discourse. Conventional expressions are thus also those most likely to be represented in long-term memory by conceptual metaphors. Conceptual metaphors explain the conventionality of metaphorical expressions found in discourse but, at the same time, Discourse conceptual metaphors at least are derived from metaphorical forms which have become conventionalized. The BURSTING AT THE SEAMS blend discussed in this section is a relatively novel elaboration of a more general conceptual metaphor IMMIGRATION IS EXPANSION INSIDE A CONTAINER (which it also reinforces). It thus stands out as being figurative whereas more conventional metaphorical expressions, precisely because they correspond more faithfully with entrenched structures representing the way we think the world really is, are not normally recognized as being metaphorical. The example in (1) is therefore more obviously metaphorical than the example in (2) where the nature of the CONTAINER is not specified:

(1)   Britain is full to bursting point. (*The Observer*, 8 December 2002)
(2)   Ministers may not have noticed but Britain is full up. (*The Express*, 8 August 2006)

This does not make conventional metaphorical expressions any less interesting. Neither does it mean that they are in any way 'dead' in the sense that they do not still involve complex imaginative processes. Rather, exactly because the same blending operations are taking place when they are encountered in discourse yet people are largely unaware that they are dealing with an instance of metaphor, it is conventional metaphors which, from a critical perspective, are arguably the most significant. As Shimko (2004: 657) states, 'certain metaphors are so taken for granted that they usually slip into our thoughts and actions undetected'. Addressees therefore do not realize that the view of the world being presented to them in discourse is not a direct one but it is mediated and moulded by the metaphor.

In Sections 4 and 5, we consider naturalizing metaphors which have become conventional for political Discourses relating to austerity in the United Kingdom. In the following section, we turn to the relationship between metaphor and grammar.

3. Metaphor and grammar

Metaphor is related to grammar in a number of ways. From a functional perspective, metaphor, like grammar, enacts ideology in discourse through the ideational, interpersonal and textual functions of language (see Goatly 2011a for a comprehensive discussion). Although the principle function of metaphor is representation (Semino 2008: 31), where metaphors provide a means of reflecting on aspects of the world which would otherwise be beyond our cognitive reach (Mithen 1998), metaphors also offer a comment on the reality they describe; they thus inscribe or at least invoke evaluations. Indeed, metaphor is intimately bound with ATTITUDE and is a primary resource for the expression of AFFECT, JUDGEMENT and APPRECIATION. In the textual function, conceptual metaphors provide cohesion and coherence to a text. They often provide a recurring theme for a text and thus act as 'an organizing principle which gives the text a lexical cohesion' (Goatly 2011a: 172). In Koller's (2004) terms, conceptual metaphors account for 'metaphorical chains' which run through the text and bind it together. They also provide a semantic coherence to texts serving as a conceptual 'backbone' to which metaphorical expressions throughout the text are related (Semino 2008: 32).

From a cognitive perspective, the functions of metaphor, as with grammar, are to conjure imagery, albeit richer, more content-specified images than invoked by grammatical constructions. Metaphorical 'triggers' do this by virtue of the frames they evoke. Metaphors invoke a visualization in which the target situation is compared to some other (imagined) scenario. Metaphor also interacts with the attentional system. In metaphor, the target scene is not observed directly but through the refracting lens of the blend. The distorting effects of metaphor not only direct us to see the target scene in a particular way but direct us to focus on certain possible facets of the scene at the expense of others (Lakoff and Johnson 1980). Metaphors, in other words, display highlighting and hiding effects (ibid.). The BURSTING AT THE SEAMS blend, for example, focuses our attention on spatial rather than social dimensions of immigration and only on one possible negatively appraised outcome of immigration.

Metaphor also relates to grammatical realization where, as Koller and Davidson (2008: 311) put it, 'underlying conceptual metaphors may shape the surface structures of texts' (Koller and Davidson 2008: 311). This can be seen most clearly where metaphor is realized and reflected in patterns of transitivity. For example, a major finding of cognitive metaphor studies has been the systematicity with which abstract domains, including social and political domains, are structured conceptually in terms of more concrete areas of understanding salient in our embodied experience and physical environment (Beer and De Landtsheer 2004; Chilton 1996; El Refaie 2001; Santa Ana 2002). This is reflected, in TRANSITIVITY, in the use of material process verbs to designate non-material processes (Goatly 2011a: 85). As Goatly points out, the verbs most easily associated with (kinetic) imagery are those referring to physical acts and events, which Halliday would label PROCESS: MATERIAL. Conceptual metaphors thus account for the frequency with which material process verbs are used as metaphorical vehicles in referring to other types of process.

Certain argument-predicate combinations, when an argument prototypically belongs to one semantic field, or cognitive frame, and the predicate to another, necessarily encode metaphorical construals. In this way, certain structural combinations in texts trigger conceptual blending operations.[5] Similarly, certain composite noun phrases like *flood of immigrants* trigger conceptual blends where the frame accessed by the head noun (*flood*) is different to the one accessed by the object of the preposition (*immigrants*) (Lakoff 2008: 35). Certain grammatical constraints also reflect the direction of mapping in conventional conceptual metaphors (ibid.). Hence, it is possible to say metaphorically *Britain is full up* but not, in reference to a literal container, **the container is overpopulated*. Finally, conventional metaphors may be expressed with a greater degree of grammatical flexibility than more novel elaborations which are more restricted in the form of grammatical realization they permit. Hence, it is possible to use a nominalized form to express the conventional metaphor IMMIGRATION IS EXPANSION INSIDE A CONTAINER as in *Britain is expanding in population* and *Britain's expanding population* . . . but in the more novel elaboration only *Britain is bursting at the seams* and not **Britain's bursting seams* . . .[6]

4. Metaphor and the London Riots

4.1 Media reaction

The 'London Riots' took place across several London boroughs between 6 and 11 August 2011. The riots started as a relatively small protest in Tottenham in response to the police having shot dead Mark Duggan on 4 August. However, events quickly escalated after a 16-year-old girl was restrained by police for allegedly acting in an aggressive and disorderly manner. The riots that ensued witnessed mass looting, arson, and the destruction of private and retail property leading to violent confrontations between police and protesters and heavy vandalism of police vehicles. Subsequently, similar riots took place in other major cities, including Manchester and Birmingham. The riots, although relatively spontaneous, were organized and galvanized by means of social media on mobile devices like Blackberries. There has since been a great deal of debate surrounding the nature and causes of the riots with some, including David Cameron, suggesting that they were nothing more than opportunistic criminality and others attributing them to political discontent and disillusionment, felt especially by the young working class, in the face of such structural circumstances as racism, classism, lack of social mobility and general economic decline (Briggs 2012). In this section, however, we consider an initial metaphor used by the media as the riots unfolded. Consider the following examples, each of which points to conceptual blends with emergent structure in common such that the riots are construed in terms of FIRE.[7]

(3) A riot that <u>engulfed</u> north London was <u>sparked</u> when a teenage girl threw a rock at police, it was claimed last night. (*The Daily Star*, 8 August 2011)

(4) Riots have <u>raged</u> over the last few days in London. (*The Daily Mail*, 10 August 2011)

(5) Rioting has <u>spread</u> across London on a third night of violence, with unrest <u>flaring</u> in other English cities. (*BBC News*, 9 August 2011)

(6) Riots which <u>took hold</u> of London for three nights have <u>spread</u> to other parts of England. (*BBC News*, 10 August 2011)

In the particular blend invoked by (3), input space$_1$ is populated by elements from the FIRE frame, accessed by 'engulfed', while input space$_2$ is populated by elements from the RIOT frame as modelled in Figure 5.3. These counterpart elements become fused when projected into the blended space. Thus, in the blend, the riots are fused with the concept of fire, the girl throwing a rock is fused with the spark that causes a fire and, although not spelled out in the example, elements quelling the riot and extinguishing the fire are recruited through completion and fused in the blended space. Ideologically, when the

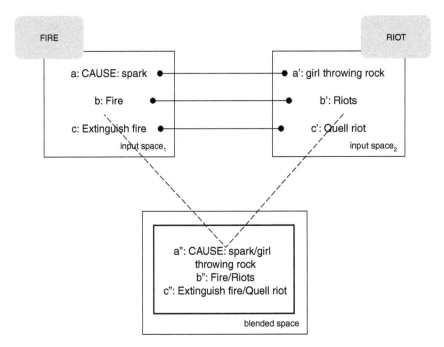

Figure 5.3. LONDON RIOTS AS FIRE blend

blend is run, or elaborated, the fusion of riot and fire is likely to invoke an AFFECT: INSECURITY evaluation of the riots since fires are generally considered dangerous. Perhaps more significantly, in the FIRE frame, there is a causal relation between the spark and the fire. By contrast, in the RIOT frame, the girl throwing the rock may be a chronologically preceding event to the riots but it cannot in reality be attributed as the cause of the riots which, of course, had multiple and complex social and political causes accumulating over time. In the blend, however, the causal relation from the FIRE frame is retained such that the riots are reduced to having been caused by a single event occurring at a specific moment in time: the spark/girl throwing the rock. Fauconnier and Turner (2002) refer to this kind of process as **compression**. Finally, recruited from encyclopaedic knowledge in the FIRE frame, the typical way to deal with a fire is to extinguish it using water. Thus, in the simulation of the event within the blend, the natural reaction to the riot/fire is to use water to quash it. This 'logic' therefore paves the way for arguments in favour of using water canon in response to future riots – a highly controversial practice in reality but one which is perfectly normal in the context of the blend. If projected back to the second input space, the use of water canon may further become a normalized feature of the general RIOT frame but one which has been legitimated on the back of a conceptual blend.

(4)–(6) similarly invoke integration networks in which riots are fused with fire in the emergent structure of the blended space. This common structure suggests a conventional conceptual metaphor RIOTS AS FIRE which served to frame the media's and potentially readers' immediate understanding of the riots taking place. This metaphor, in fact, persisted and is elaborated even in later reflections on the riots:

(7) Duggan's death . . . was <u>the spark</u> that <u>ignited</u> the worst riots in England for decades, starting in London and quickly <u>spreading</u> to other cities. (*The Telegraph*, 31 January 2013)

(8) Published today, an interim report by the Riots Communities and Victims Panel found that the 'blanket coverage' on television, online and via mobile platforms helped <u>fan the flames</u> of unrest. (*Digital Spy*, 28 March 2012)

One reason why the RIOTS AS FIRE blend might have been so resonant is that it chimes with the genuine association between riots and fires as witnessed in actual instances of arson and the media coverage of buildings on fire during the riots. Thus, references to fire in the discourse on the riots functioned both literally and figuratively.[8]

Here, the boundaries between what is literal and what is metaphorical become blurred. In (9), for example, it is not clear whether Cameron is referring to the actual fires having been extinguished or the riots having ceded.

(9) But now that <u>the fires have been put out</u> and <u>the smoke has cleared</u>, the question hangs in the air: 'Why? How could this happen on our streets and in our country?' (David Cameron, 15 August 2011)

It is worth noting that with the possible exception of (9) this metaphor does not seem to form part of official discourse on the riots. For example, the expression 'fan the flames' is a reframing not found in the interim report referred to in (8). Neither is the metaphor a feature of Government or parliamentary discourse on the riots. Vocabulary from the FIRE frame is not found in public political speeches or in the Hansard records for debates in parliament. This is in contrast to comparable riots of the past, such as the 1981 riots centred in Brixton and Toxteth but also occurring in other cities, where the RIOT AS FIRE metaphor was employed in parliamentary debates.

(10) Unemployment, housing, racial tension and policing have all played their part, but the House must also look at those who <u>fan the flames</u>. The chief constable of Manchester spoke of a conspiracy. It is certainly true that on the nights when riots <u>flared</u> in Liverpool every lunatic from the extreme wings of politics seemed to be on the streets of Liverpool.

Someone was organizing the petrol bombs. There were people in hoods overturning cars, causing disruption and deliberately helping those who wanted to <u>fan the flames</u> of the violence. People were also distributing leaflets. Other hon. Members have already referred to leaflets that were distributed in their own constituencies.

The House will recall that immediately after the riots I brought to the attention of the Home Secretary a leaflet that was deliberately designed to incite and <u>inflame</u> the situation in central Liverpool. (David Alton, MP Liverpool Edge Hill, 16 July 1981)

(11) <u>A spark</u> will not <u>ignite</u> a <u>tinder box</u> if the <u>tinder box</u> is not there for <u>the spark</u> to fall into it. We must stamp on <u>the sparks</u>. No one in the House is saying that we should allow people to be terrorized by violence or that they should not be protected, but let us not be so preoccupied with

dousing the sparks that we forget to remove the tinder box. (Sheila
Wright, MP Birmingham Handsworth, 16 July 1981)

When metaphors enter into the discourse of politicians they most directly
affect political reasoning and contribute to shaping public policy. Although
the RIOTS AS FIRE metaphor was not a general feature of official political
discourse in 2011, its employment by the media may nevertheless have had
an impact on policy making as the metaphor makes way for arguments in
favour of using water canon to quell future disturbances, a facility which
David Cameron announced in the immediate aftermath of the riots would
now be made available to police services at 24 hours notice (10 August 2011).
In the next section, we consider a metaphor which was a feature of the Prime
Minister's response to the riots.

4.2 David Cameron's response

In a televised speech delivered outside Downing Street on 10 August 2011, David
Cameron made the following statement in relation to the riots taking place in
London and other cities:[9]

(12) There are pockets of our society that are not just broken, but, frankly, sick.
(13) [T]his is a problem for our country and one which we have to cure.

Five days later at a youth centre in his Oxfordshire constituency Cameron made
a speech in which he stated:[10]

(14) Social problems that have been festering for decades have exploded in
      our face.
(15) [Gang culture] is a major criminal disease that has infected streets and
      estates across our country.
(16) I am in politics is to build a bigger, stronger society.

These examples elaborate a deeply entrenched conceptual metaphor, the BODY-
POLITIC, which has a long tradition in Western political thought (Chilton 2005b;
Musolff 2007, 2010a/b; Sontag 1978). In the BODY-POLITIC metaphor, society
or the nation state corresponds with a living biological organism. Very often,
societies and nation states are personified as human beings (Chilton and Lakoff
1995). It then becomes possible to attribute to them specifically human traits
such as personalities and emotions. A further feature of the BODY-POLITIC

metaphor, however, is that it permits societies or the nation state to be seen in various states of health and well-being. It is this potential elaboration which Cameron exploits in examples (12)–(16).

Cameron's SICK SOCIETY blend, modelled in Figure 5.4, involves knowledge from BIOLOGY and MEDICAL frames being recruited to make sense of social issues surrounding the riots. In the blend, British society is fused in the blended space with its counterpart, living organism, from the BIOLOGY frame. Through completion, just as the body can be divided into separate parts (different organs, limbs and so on), so society can be seen as divisible into distinct factions (social groups). In Cameron's blend, parts of this body/society are 'sick' putting society as a whole at risk of infection. The question that then arises is whether the body/society is sick like a patient with the flu who needs to be caringly nursed back to health or whether it is chronically ill requiring major corrective surgery. In (14) and (15), it is the latter scenario that is selected for projection from the BIOLOGY and MEDICINE frames where *fester* in particular conjures images of 'rancid' sections of society in need of radical and immediate treatment. In the blend, Cameron is the surgeon who will deliver this necessary treatment through a raft

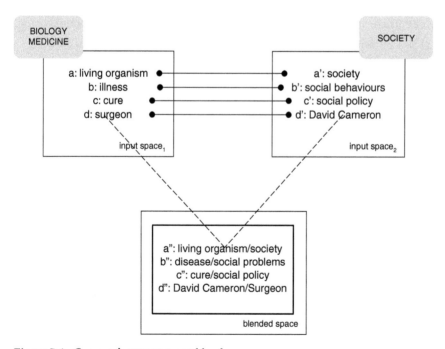

Figure 5.4. Cameron's SICK SOCIETY blend

of social policies designed to return society to a state of health.[11] The blend has a number of ideological and social consequences. For one, it reduces complex social problems which have their roots in social conditions to biological problems. There is something deterministic about this framing. It presents certain sections of society as intrinsically rather than conditionally bad. In the blend, social behaviours and the groups that enact them are the disease itself rather than the symptom of a disease.[12] The framing thus precludes the possibility of 'treating' the causes of the riots. Second, the imagery of disease invokes a mix of evaluations in terms of fear (AFFECT: INSECURITY) and disgust (APPRECIATION: REACTION) directed at the social group (mythically) held responsible for the riots. Third, the particular elaboration presented by Cameron acts as a warrant (or topos) for right-wing policies in which the 'diseased' sections of society are dealt with quickly and severely rather than more sympathetically.[13] Finally, it presents David Cameron (as surgeon) as qualified to judge the best course of action and to carry out the necessary remedies. The blend thus serves as a device to legitimate Cameron himself as well as the policies he advocates.

The idea that the nation state can fall victim to 'disease' is not a new one. It was, of course, the dominant metaphor exploited in Nazi discourse leading to the most devastating consequences when the 'logic' of the metaphor was pursued and put into practice in the real world. With such a tainted history, it is therefore somewhat surprising to find Cameron using this particular elaboration of the BODY-POLITIC metaphor. However, that he felt able to use it is perhaps emblematic of a new form of accepted classism.[14]

5. Metaphor in Cameron's austerity discourse

Metaphor is a particularly effective conceptual device in political speeches for it enables complex social, political and economic phenomena to be reduced to more tangible imagery which the audience can more easily relate to (Charteris-Black 2006). In this section, we consider the use of metaphor in a single speech delivered by David Cameron, on 17 May 2012, concerning the economic crisis in the Eurozone.[15] Two metaphors which provide a salient metaphoric chain (Koller 2004) throughout the speech are SOCIAL AND ECONOMIC POLICY IS A JOURNEY and ECONOMIC CRISIS IS BAD WEATHER. Expressions of these metaphors are highly conventional features of political and economic Discourses suggesting that they reflect conceptual metaphors in these domains

(Charteris-Black 2004).[16] These Discourse conceptual metaphors can, in turn, be seen as specific variants of more 'primary' conceptual metaphors PURPOSEFUL ACTIVITY IS MOVEMENT TOWARDS A DESTINATION and CIRCUMSTANCES ARE WEATHER (Grady 1997, 1999). Primary metaphors are those which emerge from correlations between sensorimotor and somatosensory experience and patterns of subjective judgement/feeling. For example, PURPOSEFUL ACTIVITY IS MOVEMENT TOWARDS A DESTINATION seems to be grounded in the correlation between arriving at a physical landmark and achieving goals (Grady 1999: 85). Such primary metaphors provide the foundation for more frame-based conceptual metaphors found in both the regular conceptual system as well as those located in more ideologically constructed regions of it.[17]

In David Cameron's Eurozone speech, these two conceptual metaphors are frequently combined in complex conceptual blends giving rise to a rich metaphorical **scenario** (Musolff 2006) in which the particular economic policies being advocated by Cameron are legitimated as the only sensible course of action to help steer Britain through the prevailing financial crisis.[18]

A further finding of more discourse-oriented metaphor studies is that metaphorical expressions in a text tend to occur in clusters at specific 'flashpoints' throughout the text (Koller 2004; Semino 2008). These clusters may be made up of recurring (i.e. drawing on the same source frame) or mixed metaphors. Precisely where in the text such clusters show up and the particular densities of those clusters may be functionally significant (Koller 2004). For example, when they occur towards the beginning of the text, clusters may serve to 'set the agenda' and frame the proceeding discourse; when they occur in the middle of the text they may function in laying out a particular argument; finally, when they occur towards the end of the text, they may serve to 'drive the point home' and leave the audience with a particular image in mind (ibid.: 55). The distribution of JOURNEY/WEATHER metaphors in the Carmeron text can be seen marked up in Box 5.1. Other Discourse conceptual metaphors, including ECONOMIC RECOVERY IS BUILDING and THE EUROZONE IS A CONTAINER, also occur throughout the text but they are less dominant.[19] Other 'ordinary' conceptual metaphors such as CONTROL IS GRASPING and SEEING IS UNDERSTANDING occur but are not relevant. The speech is marked up according to the following key:

Single underlining: JOURNEY
Dashed underlining: WEATHER
Double underlining: JOURNEY + WEATHER

Box 5.1. Cameron's Eurozone speech

1. We are living in **perilous economic times**. Turn on the TV news and you see the return of a crisis that never really went away. Greece on the brink; the survival of the Euro in question. Faced with this, I have a clear task: to **keep Britain safe**. Not to **take the easy course – but the right course**. Not to dodge responsibility for dealing with a debt crisis – but **to lead our country through this to better times**.

6. My message today is that it can be done. We are well **on the way** in **this journey**.

7. Since we took office two years ago, we have cut the deficit by more than a quarter. Yesterday, we had encouraging news on unemployment, too. The number of people in work – up by 100,000 in the last quarter. And the number of new business start-ups last year was one of the highest in our history. So now more than ever this is the time to stand firm.

11. Let me be clear: we are **moving in the right direction** – not rushing the task, but judging it carefully. And that is why we must resist dangerous voices calling on us to **retreat**. Yes, we are doing everything we can to **return this country** to strong, stable economic growth. But no, we will not do that by returning to the something for nothing economics that got us into this mess.

16. We cannot blow the budget on more spending and more debt.

17. It would squander all the progress we've made in these last two, tough years. It would mean tough decisions lasting even longer. It would risk our future. It's not an alternative policy, it's a cop-out.

The Challenges

20. In **keeping Britain safe** and building the recovery we face three challenges.

21. First, the struggle to recover from a long and deep recession at home.

22. Second, **the turbulence** coming from the Eurozone.

23. And third, the uncertainty over whether the world is **on the right economic path**, with debates about trade policy and how to support growth.

24. We need to find the right answer to all three. And our answers must be rooted in the reality of the global situation. This is not a conventional economic crisis, of the kind Britain has had to deal with in the recent past. This is a debt crisis.

27. Deficit reduction and growth are not alternatives. Delivering the first is vital in securing the second. If markets don't believe you are serious about dealing with your debts, your interest rates rocket and your economy shrinks.

30. Britain cannot cut itself off from what happens elsewhere. As our biggest trading partner, the problems in the Eurozone are affecting Britain too. As we prepare for the potential <u>storms</u> we should be both resolute and confident. Resolute because we will do what it takes to <u>shelter the UK from the worst of the storms</u>.

34. Outside the Euro we do have greater flexibility. We have our own currency and our own central bank with responsibility for monetary and financial stability. We have trade relationships with all parts of the world.

37. We invest more around the world per capita than America. And last month our trade in goods with countries outside the EU hit a new record at £13 billion. We will make the most of this flexibility to drive the strong deficit reduction programme, and secure the strong banks that will be necessary to keep interest rates low. And we should be confident because of our strengths.

42. Just today General Motors has given Britain and its workforce a fantastic vote of confidence by backing continued production at Ellesmere Port. The UK Government gave this its full backing. The unions supported the necessary changes. The workforce has responded magnificently. It is a British success story. And General Motors are not alone.

46. Look across the country, at Honda in Swindon, Jaguar Land Rover in the West Midlands, Toyota in Derby and Nissan in Sunderland. Britain's car industry is growing.

48. Indeed, this week our balance of trade in cars turned positive in the first quarter – for the first time since 1976 when Jim Callaghan went to the IMF. And it's not just our car industry which is strong. Life sciences, pharmaceuticals, information technology, aerospace, the creative industries, services. Britain has a stronger base from which to grow.

52. We have a global language. A time zone where you can trade with Asia in the morning and America in the afternoon. Some of the best universities in the world. And a government that's committed to making Britain the best place in the world in which to start a business.

55. With these strengths I believe we can <u>see Britain through the storm</u>. But to do so we need to act at home, and together with our European and global partners.

Recovery at Home

57. First, we must continue to get to grips with the deficit and build recovery at home. Let's be clear about what we inherited: an economy built on the worst deficit since the Second World War: the most leveraged banks; the most indebted households; one of the biggest housing booms; and unsustainable levels of public spending and immigration.

61. With a budget deficit of over 11 per cent of GDP, one pound in every four that the last government spent was borrowed. Britain still spends over £120 million every single day just to pay the interest on our past borrowing – and that amount will continue to increase every day until we start to live within our means as a country.

65. A central promise of this government – and one of the key tasks that brought the Coalition together – was to deal with this deficit. That is **the only path to prosperity**.

67. And that is exactly what we are doing. Despite **headwinds** from the Eurozone, we are **on track**. It is a long-term project. It is painstaking work. But the tough decisions we have taken on deficit reduction really are beginning to yield real results. And there can be no **deviation** from this.

...

Eurozone

71. Just as in Britain we need to deal with the deficit and restore competitiveness, so the same is true of Europe.

73. This is a debt crisis. And the deficits that caused those debts have to be dealt with. But growth in much of the Eurozone has evaporated completely. Indeed without the recent German growth figures, it would be in recession.

76. I realise that countries inside the Eurozone may not relish advice from countries outside it – especially from countries, such as Britain, with debts and difficulties of their own.

78. But this affects us too. As the Governor of the Bank of England said yesterday: 'the biggest risk to recovery [in the UK] stems from the difficulties facing the Euro area'.

80. Based on trade flows alone Britain is more than six times as exposed to the Eurozone as the United States – and that's before you factor in the impact on confidence and our closely connected financial systems.

83. This Coalition Government was formed in the midst of a debt crisis in the Eurozone. Two years later and little has changed. That's the backdrop against which we have to work. So it's only right that we set out our views. We need to be clear about the long-term consequences of any single currency. In Britain, we have had one for centuries. When one part of the country struggles, other parts step forward to help. There is a remorseless logic to it.

89. A rigid system that locks down each state's monetary flexibility yet limits fiscal transfers between them can only resolve its internal imbalances through painful and prolonged adjustment.

92. So in my view, three things need to happen if the single currency is to function properly.

93. First, the high deficit, low competitiveness countries in the periphery of the Eurozone do need to confront their problems **head on**. They need to continue **taking difficult steps** to cut their spending, increase their revenues and undergo structural reform to become competitive. The idea that high deficit countries can **borrow and spend their way to recovery** is a dangerous delusion.

98. But it is becoming increasingly clear that they are less likely to be able to sustain that necessary adjustment economically or politically unless the core of the Eurozone, including through the ECB, does more to support demand and share the burden of adjustment.

102. In Britain we are able to ease that adjustment through loose monetary policy and a flexible exchange rate. And we are supplementing that monetary stimulus with active interventions such as credit easing, mortgage indemnities for first time buyers and guarantees for new infrastructure projects.

106. So I welcome the opportunity to explore new options for such monetary activism at a European level, for example through President Hollande's ideas for project bonds. But to rebalance your economy in a currency union at a time of global economic weakness you need more fundamental support.

110. Germany's finance minister, Wolfgang Schauble, is right to recognise rising wages in his country can play a part in correcting these imbalances but monetary policy in the Eurozone must also do more.

113. Second, the Eurozone needs to put in place governance arrangements that create confidence for the future. And as the British Government has been arguing for a year now that means following the logic of monetary union towards solutions that deliver greater forms of collective support and collective responsibility of which Eurobonds are one possible example. **Steps such as these** are needed to put an end to speculation about the future of the euro.

119. And third, we all need to address Europe's overall low productivity and lack of economic dynamism, which remains its Achilles Heel. Most EU member states are becoming less competitive compared to the rest of the world, not more.

122. The Single Market is incomplete and competition throughout Europe is too constrained. Indeed, Britain has long been arguing for a pro-business, pro-growth agenda in Europe.

124. That's why ahead of the last European Council I formed an unprecedented alliance with 11 other EU leaders setting out an action plan for jobs and growth in Europe and pushing for the completion of the Single Market in Services and Digital.

127. The Eurozone is **at a cross-roads**. It either has to make-up or it is looking at a potential break-up. Either Europe has a committed, stable, successful Eurozone with an effective firewall, well capitalised and regulated banks, a system of fiscal burden sharing, and supportive monetary policy across the Eurozone.

131. Or **we are in unchartered territory** which carries huge risks for everybody. As I have consistently said it is in Britain's interest for the Eurozone to sort out its problems.

133. But be in no doubt: whichever **path** is chosen, I am prepared to do whatever is necessary to protect this country and secure our economy and financial system.

Global Economy

135. Protecting Britain's economy is not just about the measures we take at home – or even **the steps our neighbours take** in Europe.

137. In a world that is ever more connected and ever more competitive, it is also about **the steps we take** with our global partners to protect ourselves against global contagion and promote global trade.

140. So over the coming weeks I'll be flying to Camp David and to Los Cabos in Mexico to fight for what is right for Britain at the G8 and G20 summits.

142. That means committing together to make the reforms we need to our economies to get growth in the global economy working again, including involving organisations like the IMF. It means persisting with reforms to make our banks safe, by implementing high-quality, global financial regulatory standards. It means recognising the risks to the recovery from rising and volatile energy prices and working together to ensure our energy security. And most of all it means getting together to give the world economy the one big stimulus that would really make a difference an expansion of trade freedoms, breaking down the barriers to world trade.

150. We all know the Doha trade round is going nowhere. But that doesn't mean we have to give up on free trade. Far from it. There is good work from Doha that we can salvage. Like the measures to break down the bureaucracy over getting goods across borders. I want to see a commitment to open markets and to rolling back protectionist measures already in place.

155. And most importantly, I want us to **move forwards** with 'coalitions of the willing', so countries who want to can **forge ahead** with ambitious deals of their own because we all benefit from the increased trade and investment these deals foster.

158. For us that means getting EU agreements finalised with India, Canada and Singapore, launching negotiations with Japan and, above all, preparing to negotiate with the US – the single biggest bilateral deal that could benefit Britain.

161. Why is this so important?

162. Because the opportunities for Britain abroad have never been so big. And we need to work harder than ever before to seize them. Yes, competition for every job and every contract has increased. The last ten years has seen the extraordinary rise of powerful new economies in Latin America and Asia. And the globalisation of supply has meant new competitors making products, and more jobs going abroad. But now these countries aren't just producers; they are consumers too.

168. As nations get richer they spend more money on products where Britain excels. On everything from financial services and pharmaceuticals to jet engines, music and computer games.

171. The globalisation of demand means new countries demanding our products, fuelling new jobs at home. If we make the most of this, there is a huge opportunity to secure a great future for our country. And that is why as we **get through the crisis,** I believe we can look ahead with confidence.

Conclusion

175. I cannot predict how this crisis will end for others. And I cannot pretend that Britain will be immune from the consequences, either. But this I can promise: that we know what needs to be done and we are doing it.

178. Get the deficit under control, get the foundations for recovery in place, defend the long-term interests of our country and **hold our course**.

180. As Prime Minister, I will do whatever it takes **to keep Britain safe from the storm**.

In Cameron's Eurozone speech, JOURNEY/WEATHER metaphors cluster most intensely towards the beginning of the speech in lines 1–15. In this macro-slot, these occurrences thus function to define a conceptualization from the start which will be reoriented to periodically, and more or less explicitly, throughout the speech. Clustering, though to a lesser extent, at the end of the speech, the complex blend 'helps to persuade readers to accept a preferred metaphoric model' (Koller 2004: 91).

In the first paragraph, metaphorical expressions 'perilous economic times' and 'keep Britain safe' do not immediately invoke images of bad weather but allude instead to some non-specified danger. Conceptually, they seem to place 'on hold' a mental space for this unspecified danger which is populated by the WEATHER frame only further into the text when it becomes clear that the 'danger' is strong winds or a storm. The complex blend that is built up 'logo-genetically' (Halliday and Matthiessen 1999) as the text unfolds to conceptualize the financial crisis and Britain's economic recovery is modelled in Figure 5.5.[20]

The blend seems to be a contemporary version of another metaphor with a long history in Western political thought: the SHIP OF STATE metaphor.[21] In this version, however, the image invoked, prompted by 'turbulence' and 'headwinds', is aeronautical.[22] In the blend constructed, input space₁ is populated by information from both a JOURNEY frame and a WEATHER frame. The JOURNEY frame is accessed initially by the phrase 'not to take the easy course – but the right course'. The WEATHER frame is first accessed by 'turbulence', whose meaning, like *headwind*, involves the activation of both WEATHER and JOURNEY frames. It is then strengthened by repeated references to 'storms'. Input space₂ is populated by information from POLITICS and ECONOMICS frames. In the scenario that

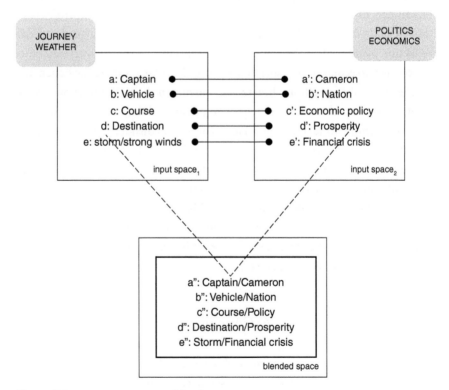

Figure 5.5. CAPTAIN CAMERON blend

emerges in the blended space, David Cameron, standing metonymically for the Government, is the captain of the vehicle whose social and economic policies will 'steer' Britain through the storms/financial crisis to return once more to prosperity.

There are a number of ideological implications of this blend. Construing the financial crisis as bad weather legitimates free-market economics by presenting economic fluctuation as naturally occurring and therefore unavoidable rather than being man-made. There is no reference to any culpable causers of the crisis. The blend thereby conceals the role that particular institutions and political systems played in bringing it about. Moreover, the blend legitimates the Government's particular deficit reduction plan in at least two ways. In the first place, knowledge recruited through completion from the JOURNEY/WEATHER frames informs us that the only rational thing to do in the face of a storm, in order to keep safe, is to 'batten down the hatches' and 'maintain course'. In the blend, this equates to implementing the Government's deficit reduction plan. This plan is, of course, controversial and by no means the only course of action available. However, the metaphor presents the policy as, if not necessarily desirable, logical and essential. Similarly, in the second place, drawing exclusively from the JOURNEY frame, the blend legitimates the Government's particular deficit reduction plan based on the 'logic' that there is only one route which can return the country to economic prosperity and the quicker we get there the better. This is reflected in the speech in phrases like 'moving in the right direction', 'on the right economic path' and 'the only path to prosperity'. Any 'deviation' from this path or attempts to take an 'alternative course' is considered foolhardy ('The idea that high deficit countries can borrow and spend their way to recovery is a dangerous delusion'). Finally, it is also worth noting that the blend contains an inherent assumption that the destination – the economic situation as it was before the financial crisis – is socially desirable. This assumption not only legitimates the socio-economic conditions we are returning to but also the Coalition's cuts where the blend 'implies that hardships are to be tolerated because the goals are worthwhile' (Charteris-Black 2004: 93).

6. Conclusion

In this chapter we have introduced conceptual blending as a construal operation invoked by metaphor in discourse. Metaphor, we have seen, is a means of simultaneously representing and evaluating actions and events. The conceptualizations that metaphors invoke result in rich, imagined scenarios which, through compression, reduce complex social phenomena to simple, tangible event models. These models provide a particular ideologized world view and act as heuristics legitimating social action. We have explored the ideological and legitimating functions of metaphor in three discursive contexts: media reactions to the London riots, David Cameron's response to the London riots and David Cameron's speech addressing the financial crisis in Britain and the Eurozone. What the metaphors in all three cases have in common, drawing on frames such as FIRE, PATHOGENICS and WEATHER, is that they naturalize social phenomena. Such desocialization makes it possible to think about social actions without necessarily thinking about their human impact.

Deixis, Distance and Proximization

1. Introduction

In Chapter 3, we saw how images can present to the viewer alternative vantage points from which the scene depicted is experienced. In Chapter 4, we saw how certain grammatical constructions may similarly invoke, as an inherent component of their semantic values, a particular spatial point of view. This semantically encoded point of view forms part of a viewing arrangement with a mental space in which the specific event described is conceptualized. In this chapter, we take up a deictically motivated model of conceptualization to account for meaning construction in discourse as 'language above the sentence' and to account for more pragmatic forms of positioning which are anchored in the broader context of the text and more dependent on an intersubjective consensus of values. This framework, known as Discourse Space Theory (Chilton 2004), accounts for discourse-level meaning construction in terms of an abstract, three-dimensional configuration in a mental 'discourse' space which provides a conceptual coherence to whole texts as entities and events are mapped out across axes representing socio-spatial, temporal and evaluative (epistemic and axiological) 'distance'.[1] A major advantage of this model, then, is that it can account for different types of pragmatic positioning within a single framework. In its evaluative dimension, it provides a cognitive account of modal and axiological positioning and therefore has the potential to unite more functionally oriented research on evaluation (e.g. Bednarek 2006) with Cognitive Linguistic research on the representation of space and time. In this chapter, we introduce this framework and show how different types of pragmatic positioning strategy are effected within the three-dimensional model proposed. In Section 2, we introduce the architecture of the basic model. Then, in Section 3, we see how alternative DISTANCE/PROXIMITY values invoked in discourse reflect (and reinforce) shared ideological world views and how the dynamic process of 'proximisation' (Cap 2006, 2013) may function rhetorically in legitimating social action. In Section 3, we see how all this plays out in Tony Blair's outline of the threat from Iraq in his foreword to the Government's now discredited dossier *Iraq's Weapons of Mass Destruction: The Assessment of the British Government*. In Section 4, we see how distance, proximity and proximization feature in the Mission Statement of the English Defence League.

2. Discourse Space Theory

The central claim of Discourse Space Theory (DST) is that during discourse we open up a particular kind of mental space in which the 'world' described in the discourse is conceptually represented. This **discourse space** consists of three intersecting axes around which the **discourse world** is constructed by positioning ideational elements in the text in ontological relations with one another as well as with the speaker inside this space. Each of these axes represents a scale of relative 'distance' from a **deictic centre**. The three axes are a spatial or socio-spatial axis (S), a temporal axis (T) and an evaluative axis which is simultaneously engaged in both an epistemic (E_e) and an axiological (E_a) aspect.[2] The deictic centre represents the speaker/hearer's current **point of view** in social, temporal, epistemic and axiological 'space'. The zone immediately surrounding the deictic centre represents what the speaker/hearer takes as their socio-spatial, temporal, epistemic and axiological **ground**.

Deixis is at root spatial and, as traditionally conceived, relates to the coding of distance relative to the speaker's situational coordinates at the moment of utterance. This is reflected most obviously in adverbs *here* versus *there* and demonstratives *this* versus *that*. Deixis is also known to show up in relation to time (*now* versus *then*) and person (*us* versus *them*).[3] The deictic nature of evaluation is less recognized.[4] In the DST model, the notion of deixis is de-coupled from immediate situational dependencies and is extended to cover the speaker/hearer's broader conceptualization of what counts as 'we', 'here', 'now', and 'acceptable' within the arena of geo-politics taking in such ideas as national identities, collective memories, historical moments or time periods, political systems, religious beliefs and epistemological truths. The socio-spatial axis can be seen as a conflation of traditional deictic categories place and person extending a deictic conceptualization to geo-political relations. The temporal axis represents a time line from 'now' to 'distant past' and 'distant future'. In its evaluative dimension, DST presents a deictic account of epistemic modality and moral evaluation. The evaluative axis represents a deictic conceptualization of 'right' versus 'wrong' both in their epistemic and in their moral sense. We can therefore think of each axis as having antonymic reference points with various intermediate stations. In so far as the evaluative axis engaged in its axiological guise concerns moral evaluation, we can think of its two ends as representing positive versus negative JUDGEMENT values. In its epistemic aspect, the evaluative axis has connections with the system of ENGAGEMENT in Appraisal Theory. The magnitude at which a proposition is placed on the E_e axis corresponds with the opening or closing of dialogic space. The conceptualizer exists by default at the deictic centre co-located with concepts US, HERE, NOW and RIGHT. This idealized cognitive model is shown in Figure 6.1.

Although this cognitive model does not represent the axes of the human body, it is certainly tempting to see the basic configuration and the process of meaning construction involved as embodied, ultimately rooted in cognitive systems responsible for locating objects in the physical space surrounding the body.[5] Research in cognitive science has shown that people keep track of the objects around their selves by constructing a mental reference frame made up of extensions of the three body axes (Tversky 1998; Tversky et al. 1999). This necessarily involves visual processes and in particular stereoscopic vision as

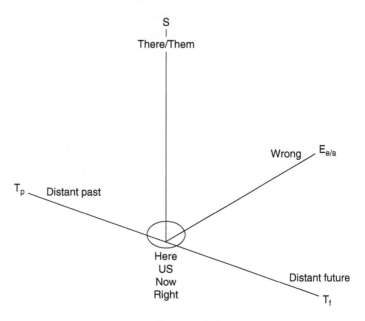

Figure 6.1. Discourse space: basic model

well as motor simulations. The mental configuration in discourse space can be seen as a further abstraction from the three body axes, experienced from within the constraints of our field of vision, to yield a three-dimensional conceptual structure which language is able to appropriate in meaning-making processes. The socio-spatial, temporal and evaluative axes in the discourse space may therefore reflect the coronal, sagittal and transversal axes of the body, respectively, as experienced in the field of view.[6] This is not to say, however, that there is any principled relation between the semantic values of the axes in the discourse space and the particular body axes. Only that the body provides an abstract conceptual structure to which the semantic values important for meaning-making at the discourse level may be arbitrarily assigned and conceptualized metaphorically in terms of distance.[7] The notion of ground in this extra-deictic account of conceptualization may then correspond at a higher level of abstraction with peripersonal space in situated cognition. And the conceptual process of constructing a discourse world within this mental discourse space may be a specific incarnation of a more general cognitive capacity for egocentric spatial location which language has co-opted. Construing elements at different 'distances' in discourse space may be a linguistic analogue of depth perception. Such an embodied model of conceptual representation is well founded in light of Cognitive Linguistic research highlighting the primacy of spatial cognition in human language (e.g. Lakoff 1987; Lakoff and Johnson 1999; Levinson 2003). There is also systematic lexical evidence pointing to spatialized conceptualizations, in the form of conceptual metaphors, of social, temporal, and epistemic relations: '*close* friends/*distant* enemies', '*near* future/*remote* past', '*close* to the truth/*far* from the truth' (Chilton 2004: 56–61). The case for a spatialized, deictic conceptualization of axiological evaluation is more complex but lexical evidence can be found in expressions like '*beyond* reproach' and '*bring* to justice'.[8]

In the course of discourse, the basic model is populated by entities, events, times and places represented (explicitly or implicitly) in the text. These conceptual elements get mapped out within the three-dimensional space relative to one another and in relation to the topography of the basic model to create a 'discourse world'. The relative positions of certain elements within the conceptual space may be inscribed in discourse by grammatical features like tense and modal markers, pronouns, and prepositional phrases, which Fauconnier (1994) would refer to as 'space builders'. The relative position of other elements may only be invoked, organized by presupposed knowledge and value-orientations in shared cognitive frames. Elements in the discourse space are linked either by **connectors** or by **vectors**. Connectors represent various kinds of relation including attribution and possession. Vectors represent material processes between elements including the conceptualizer at deictic centre as well as abstract movements through the space. Crucially, the mapping out of elements inside the discourse space is subject to **construal**. It therefore does not directly reflect reality but rather constructs it. The populated discourse space constitutes a world view which hearers are presumed to share or are invited to accept and, through back-projection to the frames that structure the discourse space, update their encyclopaedic knowledge bases accordingly.

Emerging from the general framework of DST, Cap (2006, 2008, 2010, 2011, 2013) presents an elaborated theory of **proximization**. For Cap, proximization is a rhetorical-pragmatic strategy in which the speaker, in order to legitimate immediate counter action, presents an actor, situation or event, construed as a 'threat' to the Self, as entering, along spatial, temporal or axiological dimensions, the conceptualizer's ground and therefore being of personal consequence (2006: 6). It is primarily conceived as a feature of interventionist discourse (Cap 2010: 119). In what follows, I approach proximization from an explicitly Cognitive Linguistic perspective grounded in the geometric model of DST and offer some further elaborations and refinements of the framework. I do so in the context of two case studies: Tony Blair's justification for intervention in Iraq and the English Defence League's discourse against 'Islamisation'.

3. Proximization in Tony Blair's justification for action in Iraq

In this section, we explore the cognitive dimensions of proximization in the context of Tony Blair's discourse surrounding Britain's military involvement, alongside the United States, in Iraq. Military action in Iraq began on 18 March 2003. Prior to this, there had been a long discursive attempt to make the case for, and gain public support for, military intervention. A major premise of this discursive campaign was the threat posed to national and international security by Iraq's possession of weapons of mass destruction. As part of this campaign, on 24 September 2002, the UK Government published a document outlining the details of Iraq's weapons capability. The text in Box 6.1 is an extract from the foreword to this document written by Tony Blair.[9] In this section, we illustrate proximization as a deictic construal operation realizing positioning strategies with this text as well as with supporting examples taken from a speech to parliament on 18 March 2003[10] and an address to the nation on 20 March 2003 announcing that military action in Iraq had commenced. The text in Box 6.1 is marked up for spatial, temporal and epistemic proximization.

Bold = spatial
<u>Single underline</u> = temporal
<u>Double underline</u> = epistemic

Box 6.1. Extract from Blair's foreword to the September dossier

<u><u>I am in no doubt</u></u> that the threat is serious and <u>current</u>, that he has made progress on WMD, and that he has to be stopped.

Saddam has used chemical weapons, not only against an enemy state, but against his own people [SPATIAL¹]. <u><u>Intelligence reports make clear that</u></u> **he sees the building up of his WMD capability, and the belief overseas that he would use these weapons, as vital to his strategic interests, and in particular his goal of regional domination** [SPATIAL²]. And <u><u>the document discloses that</u></u> his military planning allows for some of the WMD to be ready <u>within 45 minutes</u> of an order to use them.

<u><u>I am quite clear that</u></u> Saddam will go to extreme lengths, indeed has already done so, to hide these weapons and avoid giving them up.

In today's inter-dependent world, a major regional conflict does not stay confined to the region in question [SPATIAL³]. Faced with someone who has shown himself capable of using WMD, I believe the international community has to stand up for itself and ensure its authority is upheld.

The threat posed to international peace and security, when WMD are in the hands of a brutal and aggressive regime like Saddam's, <u><u>is real</u></u>. **Unless we face up to the threat, not only do we risk undermining the authority of the UN, whose resolutions he defies, but more importantly and in the longer term, we place at risk the lives and prosperity of our own people** [SPATIAL⁴].

3.1 Spatial proximization

Spatial proximization relies on a script involving an interaction between an ANTAGONIST and a PROTAGONIST.[11] Specifically, it consists in a representation of the ANTAGONIST entering the PROTAGONIST's spatial ground, or 'territory', resulting in corporeal harm to the PROTAGONIST. In the discourse presented by Tony Blair in the build-up to the Iraq War, the role of ANTAGONIST is filled by Saddam Hussein, the Iraqi regime or terrorists while the role of PROTAGONIST is

filled by Britain or the British people (who the audience is presumed to belong
to) and other Western democratic countries. By way of example, consider the
following extract from Tony Blair's speech to the nation announcing Britain's
intervention in Iraq:[12]

(1) [T]his new world faces a new threat of disorder and chaos born either
of brutal states like Iraq armed with weapons of mass destruction or of
extreme terrorist groups. Both hate our way of life, our freedom, our
democracy. My fear, deeply held, based in part on the intelligence that
I see, is that [these threats $_{antagonist}$] come together and [deliver $_{motion}$]
[catastrophe $_{result}$] [to $_{direction}$] [our country and our world $_{protagonist}$]. (Tony
Blair, 20 March 2003)

Proximization effects are not aroused by any single lexical item but, rather, are
invoked by a combination of functional units, such as found in the final line of (1),
which together serve to fulfil the proximization script. In (1), the ANTAGONIST
is 'these threats' referring anaphorically to 'brutal states like Iraq armed with
weapons of mass destruction' and 'extreme terrorist groups'. The PROTAGONIST is
the British people, including the addressee, whose spatial ground is represented
by 'our country and our world'. Proximization is effected as 'these threats' are
construed as entering, realized in 'deliver' and 'to', the PROTAGONIST's territory
resulting in 'catastrophe', which, in the context, can be taken as denoting physical
impact. It thus becomes possible to provide a 'grammar' of spatial proximization
made up of the following functional units (cf. Cap 2006: 60):

> Noun phrases (NPs) conceptualized as ANTAGONISTS.
> NPS conceptualized as PROTAGONISTS
> Verb phrases (VPs) conceptualizing action/motion of ANTAGONISTS
> Prepositional phrases (PPs) conceptualizing direction of action/motion
>   towards PROTAGONISTS
> NPs conceptualizing impact of action/motion on PROTAGONISTS

Conceptually, the discourse world as defined by (1) is modelled in Figure 6.2.[13]
Elements 'Iraq' and 'terrorist groups' are located at the remote end of S
constituting an Us versus Them polarization. Iraq is linked by means of a
connector representing both attribution and possession with elements 'brutal'
and 'weapons of mass destruction'. These elements, which inscribe/invoke,
respectively, negative JUDGEMENT: PROPRIETY evaluations, are located at the
remote end of E engaged in its axiological gear. There seems to be a general
correspondence in distance values on the socio-spatial and the axiological axis

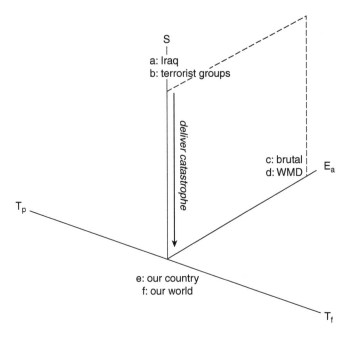

Figure 6.2. Spatial proximization

where what is geo-politically distant is also construed as morally distant (Chilton 2004: 172). Proximization as a dynamic simulation is based on an ACTION or MOTION PLUS IMPACT image schema. In the discourse space, this is represented by a force vector along the spatial axis whose tail is located at the remote end of S with ANTAGONISTS 'Iraq' and 'terrorist groups' as the source of the threat but whose head, where the impact will be felt, points to the conceptualizer's ground at deictic centre.

The proximization construal in (1) is invoked by a single sentence. We can refer to this means of realization as **phraseological**. In phraseological proximization, the vector that connects the ANTAGONIST as the source of the threat and the PROTAGONIST as the ultimate target is evoked all at once where the full 'extent' of the vector is made explicit within the utterance. Spatial proximization, however, is not restricted in its realization to single sentences. It may instead be built up logo-genetically as discourse unfolds. We can refer to this form of spatial proximization as **narrative**. In narrative proximization, the vector connecting the ANTAGONIST with the PROTAGONIST is not evoked all at once but *evolves* progressively through spatial or geo-political frames of reference towards the conceptualizer's ground. The proximising effect in narrative realization is not so easily attributable to the interaction of specific functional units and is not necessarily made explicit in the discourse. Rather, it relies on intra-textual relations between utterances, the generation of implicatures and common deictic positioning of elements on the S axis. Consider the following lines highlighted in the text in Box 6.1.

(2) Saddam has used chemical weapons, not only against an enemy state, but against his own people.
(3) [H]e sees the building up of his WMD capability, and the belief overseas that he would use these weapons, as vital to his strategic interests, and in particular his goal of regional domination
(4) In today's inter-dependent world, a major regional conflict does not stay confined to the region in question.
(5) Unless we face up to the threat, not only do we risk undermining the authority of the UN, whose resolutions he defies, but more importantly and in the longer term, we place at risk the lives and prosperity of our own people.

We can identify the people and places located on the S axis as: 'Saddam', 'an enemy state', 'his own people', the broader 'region', 'the UN', 'we' and 'our own people'. Based on background beliefs and attitudes presumed to be shared, these elements are likely to be organized on the S axis as modelled in Figure 6.3. At the deictic centre is 'our own people' to whom the conceptualizer is presumed to belong but to whom they are also positioned as belonging by the inclusive pronouns 'we' and 'our'. At the remote end of S is Saddam Hussein, the source of the threat and therefore the 'departure point' for the vector representing proximization. Saddam is explicitly linked to elements 'chemical weapons', 'WMD capability' and 'strategic interests' remote on the axiological axis. Other elements are positioned at various points in between reflecting construed geo-political distance and, by implication, axiological distance. Hence, 'the UN' is closer than 'the region' (which presumably refers to the Middle East). These elements and the geo-political frames they access are introduced as the discourse unfolds. Interestingly, then, this socio-spatial deictic organization is signalled iconically in the order in which elements occur in the text. The threat originating at the remote end of S is thus presented as evolving through consecutive geo-political 'locations' extending first to 'enemy states' and 'his own people' and then to 'the region'. The evolution of the threat is indexed in the text by the predicate 'used . . . against' in (2) connecting the source of the threat to 'enemy states' and 'his own people'. Taking into account the temporal dimension, the events in (2) are designated as having taken place in the past and so the vector representing the process has an (unspecified) value somewhere on T_p. In (3), the threat is extended to 'the region' by the nominalized predicate 'regional domination'. The threat presented in (3), however, has not yet been realized and pertains instead to a future scenario. The vector representing the process in this scenario therefore has some value on T_f. Through temporal proximization strategies deployed elsewhere in the text and operating over the spatial dimension (see subsequent section), this vector is positioned close to now within the conceptualizer's temporal ground. Further evolution of this vector in (4) is the result of an implicature arising from 'does not stay confined'. The implicature is that, unless something is done to impede it, the threat will continue to extend towards the conceptualizer's spatial ground at deictic centre. The implicature is reinforced in (5) by 'we place at risk the lives and prosperity of our own people'. This proximization is modelled in Figure 6.3.

The overall effect of this proximization strategy is to arouse an AFFECT: INSECURITY appraisal which in turn helps to legitimate some pre-emptive action. Rather than waiting for the threat to arrive we must 'meet it head on'. Conceptually, this defusion involves a COUNTER-FORCE schema in which the continued progression of the threat is prevented by a neutralizing force. This schema is instantiated in expressions like 'face up to' in (5) and 'must be stopped' in the opening line of the text. The COUNTER-FORCE schema is modelled in Figure 6.4.

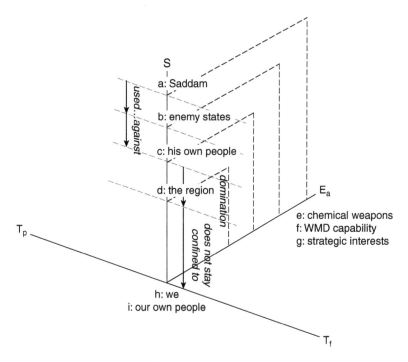

Figure 6.3. Narrative spatial proximization

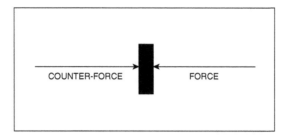

Figure 6.4. COUNTER-FORCE schema

3.2 Temporal proximization

The legitimating effects of spatial (as well as axiological) proximization are further enhanced by temporal proximization. Temporal proximization thus operates over spatial (and axiological) proximization as a form of intensification. In temporal proximization, the scenario presented on the spatial or axiological plane is construed as close to and continuing towards or already part of the conceptualizer's temporal ground. We can distinguish two types of temporal proximization: **past-oriented** and **future-oriented**. Past-oriented temporal proximization involves a conceptual shift or evolution along the T axis from some point on T_p towards 0 at deictic centre while future-oriented temporal proximization involves a conceptual shift from some point on T_f towards deictic centre. In both cases, temporal proximization can be characterized as a narrowing of conceptual space between events on the T axis and the conceptualizer's *now*.

Cutting across this distinction, we can identify two alternative forms of realization: **phraseological** and **analogical**. In the case of the latter, which tends to occur in past-oriented temporal proximization, culturally salient events in collective memory are brought closer to 'now' for purposes of (dis)analogy. This form of temporal proximization relies on our phenomenological experience of time as something that can be protracted or contracted (Flaherty 1999). We can experience events in the past 'as if they happened only yesterday' (contracted time). Conversely, recent events can 'feel like a lifetime ago' (protracted time). In temporal proximization, of course, time is experienced as contracted. Events in the past are made salient on the T axis to inform, by comparison, the conceptualizer's present context (Cap 2013: 85). As an example, consider the following from Blair's 2003 announcement of military engagement:

(6) War between the big powers is unlikely, Europe is at peace, the Cold War already a memory. But this new world faces a new threat of disorder and

chaos born either of brutal states like Iraq armed with weapons of mass destruction or of extreme terrorist groups. (Tony Blair, 20 March 2003)

Although Blair confines the Cold War to a distant memory, its very mention causes it to be phenomenologically experienced as closer to 'now' in construed time (Cap 2013). The COLD WAR frame is thus, in the discourse moment, brought closer in memory. This is represented by the vector in Figure 6.5. The vector here is not a force vector as in spatial proximization but a translation vector. It does not represent contact between elements but an abstract movement through the discourse space. The COLD WAR frame, which includes a deictic polarization between the East and the West and, axiologically, between Capitalism and Communism, is linked by means of an analogical connecter to a frame for the current WAR ON TERROR. This comparison serves to construct a similar polarization in the discourse space between the new (Western) world on the one hand and Iraq and terrorists on the other hand, as well as, axiologically, between values of peace possessed by the West and values of disorder and chaos possessed by Iraq and terrorist groups. This configuration, through back-projection to the WAR ON TERROR frame, helps construct an ideology of Us

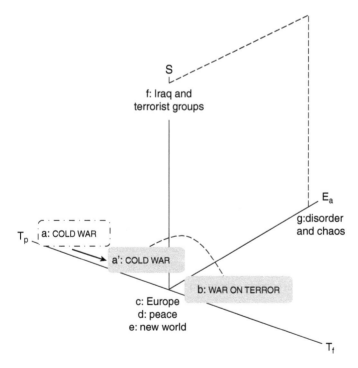

Figure 6.5. Analogical temporal proximization

versus Them which in turn helps legitimate action in the name of the war on terror.

In phraseological forms of realization, proximization is indexed by tense and aspect, temporal deictics, adjectives and prepositional phrases construing the occurrence of an event as close to now, adverbs indicating speed of motion and motion verbs which include within their meaning a high speed of motion (leading to a contracted time frame in which an event will 'complete'). In future-oriented temporal proximization (which may also be realized or analogically), the event is construed as not only momentous but imminent thus requiring immediate counter-action (Cap 2006, 2013). In past-oriented temporal proximization, a situation or event starting in the past is construed as still occurring. This involves a progression along the T axis towards the deictic centre. In the September dossier, with reference to Saddam Hussein's weapons capability, temporal proximization is indexed by the use of verb phrases expressing unbroken duration from some unspecified point in the past to the 'present' moment in political time. Consider (7)–(9) for example:

(7) Saddam <u>has continued</u> to produce chemical and biological weapons.
(8) [D]espite sanctions, despite the damage done to his capability in the past, despite the UN Security Council Resolutions expressly outlawing it, and despite his denials, Saddam Hussein <u>is continuing</u> to develop WMD.
(9) [H]e <u>continues</u> in his efforts to develop nuclear weapons.

(7)–(9) are all expressed in the present tense which locates a situation in the speaker's temporal ground, from where the events described are viewed (see Radden and Dirven 2007). The difference between (7)–(9) is in **aspect**. (7) is in the perfective or non-progressive aspect while (8) is in the imperfective or progressive aspect. (9) is in the simple present tense and so does not formally mark aspect. However, aspect is encoded in the semantics of simple present tense forms. Semantically, aspect has to do with the **boundedness** of events (ibid.). In the perfective aspect, an event is construed as bounded seen from the 'outside'. It is bounded in the sense that it has an endpoint. In the present perfective, that endpoint is the conceptualizer's *now*. The duration of the event is broken only by its 'arrival' at *now*. The present perfect therefore leaves at least the possibility that the situation will continue after now. This is in contrast with the past perfect in the invented example (10):

(10) Saddam <u>had continued</u> to produce chemical and biological weapons
(*invented example*)

In (10), the endpoint of the event is at some time earlier than *now*. In other words, the duration of the event is broken before *now*. The conceptual distinction between the present perfect and the past perfect is modelled in Figure 6.6. The vector represents an event unfolding in time with its magnitude denoting the duration of the event. The box represents the boundedness of the event. In the discourse space, this is represented as in Figure 6.7.

In the present imperfective in (8) and the simple present in (9), which here encodes an imperfective aspect, the event is conceptualized as unbounded seen from 'inside' the situation as it is happening. The event is unbounded in the

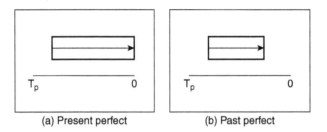

(a) Present perfect   (b) Past perfect

Figure 6.6. Present versus past perfective

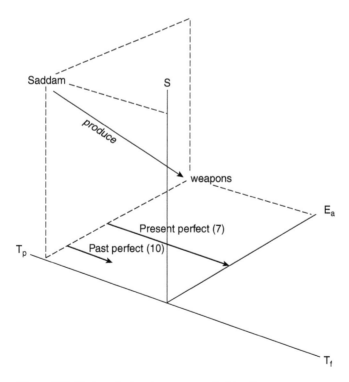

Figure 6.7. Past perfect and present perfect in discourse space

sense that it is presented without any endpoint. The focus is not on the event as a whole but on the process that makes up the event, which is seen as currently unfolding. In construing the situation as presently ongoing, the imperfective aspect not only 'conveys greater immediacy' (Radden and Dirven 2007: 190) but also strongly encourages the possibility that the situation will continue to endure unless impeded.[14] The conceptualization invoked by the imperfective aspect is modelled in Figure 6.8. The dashed line after the temporal region construed broadly as 'now' represents the situation's potential continuation. This is represented in the discourse space as in Figure 6.9.[15]

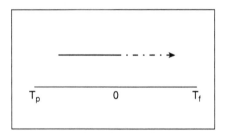

Figure 6.8. Imperfective aspect

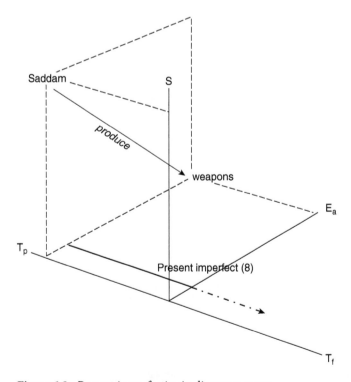

Figure 6.9. Present imperfective in discourse space

Let us now turn to future-oriented instances of temporal proximization. In future-oriented temporal proximization, the speaker presents an undesirable situation or event as either current or imminent. That is, in the discourse space, as either already inside the conceptualizer's temporal ground or located close to and continuing towards it. Since activities unfold in time (conceptualized as movement through space (Lakoff and Johnson 1999)), some previously held discourse world is necessarily presupposed in which the scenario described was further off in the future. Consider the following example:

(11) Some of these countries are now a short time away from having a
      serviceable nuclear weapon. (Tony Blair, 18 March 2003)

Proximization is realized in (11) by the phrase 'a short time away from' which locates the threat at the perimeter of the conceptualizer's temporal ground. The presence of 'now' serves explicitly to index a discourse world in which 'these countries' were further away from 'having a serviceable nuclear weapon'. Proximization lies in the translation from this previous world to the one presented by the speaker resulting in a relative compressed time frame on T_f. This is modelled in Figure 6.10.

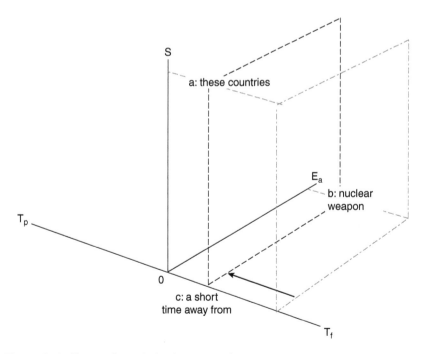

Figure 6.10. Temporal proximization as translation

In (11), the threat refers to the ambitions of 'these countries' (anaphorically 'dictatorships with highly repressive regimes' including Iraq) to acquire nuclear weapons technology. In (12) and (13), 'the threat' refers to non-nuclear weapons of mass destruction which Saddam Hussein is presented as already in possession of.

(12) [T]he threat is serious and <u>current</u>. (Tony Blair, 24 September 2002)
(13) The threat to Britain <u>today</u> is not that of my father's generation. (Tony Blair, 20 March 2003)

The temporal adjective 'current' and the deictic 'today' both serve to explicitly locate 'the threat' at point 0 on the T axis. In these examples, therefore, the process is taken a stage further so that we are not so much dealing with *proximization* as a dynamic conceptualization but temporal *proximity*. Temporal proximity is closely connected with epistemic modality where what is now is also real. We turn to epistemic proximization below.

3.3 Epistemic proximization

Several researchers in Cognitive Linguistics have suggested a conceptual relation between temporal and epistemic distance (e.g. Dancygier 2004; Langacker 1991, 2009). There is, as Langaacker (2009: 206) points out, a strong philosophical or embodied basis to this connection – 'since the future has not yet been determined, it cannot yet be real or known'. At the same time, temporal proximity, that which is now, is part of current reality and so can be known with surety. This correlation is reflected in linguistic behaviour through the grammaticized tense-modal system in which formally defined tense markers (e.g. the English present) express epistemicity and formally defined modal markers (e.g. *will*) are used to express tense. This correlation, however, is also reflected in discourse in the collocational behaviour of temporal and epistemic expressions. Consider the following example:

(14) The possibility of ... terrorist groups in possession of weapons of mass destruction or even of a so-called dirty radiological bomb – is now, in my judgment, a <u>real and present</u> danger to Britain and its national security. (Tony Blair, 20 March 2003)

In epistemic proximization, the evaluative axis is seen in its epistemic aspect representing a scale of reality-irreality. (14) encodes both temporal and epistemic proximization with corresponding values on the T_f and E_e axes. In other words, epistemic proximization, in this and other similar examples, seems to be directly proportionate to temporal proximization.[16] Epistemic proximization can be characterized as a conceptual shift along the epistemic axis so that a situation comes to form part of the conceptualizer's epistemic ground. In a mental discourse space, this involves a previous discourse world (again, explicitly indexed by 'now' in (14)) with a distal value along E_e being translated into a current discourse world with a more proximal E_e value. The epistemically remote world then represents a world construed as counterfactual relative to the world entertained as 'real'. The conceptualization invoked by (14) is modelled in Figure 6.11. The vector represents proximization in both the epistemic and the temporal dimension.

Epistemic proximization operates ideologically to attain legitimacy where public support would not normally be granted on the basis of remote possibilities. Political speakers must therefore do discursive work to establish a conceptualization in which their premises for action are treated as true (Chilton 2004). One way to do this is through existential presuppositions which assume an intersubjective reality space in which certain propositions are established fact. In the text in Box 6.1, this is exemplified by the definite noun phrase 'the threat'. Another is to ask the audience to place their trust in the speaker's evaluation. This can be explicitly as in 'in my judgement' in (14) as well as 'I am in no doubt that ...' and 'I am quite clear that ...' in Box 6.1. Alternatively, it may only be implicitly

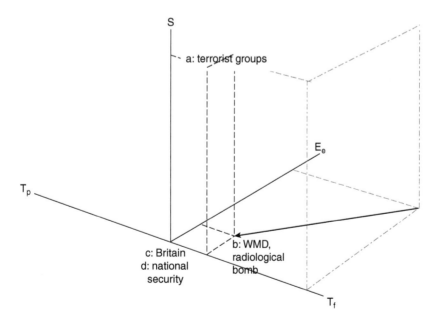

Figure 6.11. Epistemic and temporal proximization

as in 'is real' in Box 6.1 (see Marín Arrese 2011). In the case of the latter, the evaluation is still grounded in the speaker's subjective assessment but there is no explicit appeal to the speaker's own credibility – in Langacker's (1991) terms, the speaker, as the source of predication, remains 'offstage'. Finally, where, as van Dijk (2011: 53) states, 'speakers are more credible when they are able to attribute their knowledge or opinions to reliable sources, especially if some of the recipients may doubt whether they are well grounded', some third party may be stated as the original source of predication. Particularly prevalent in political discourse are independent reports which the audience are expected to regard as reliable. Examples of such attribution are found in the extract in Box 6.1 in 'intelligence reports' make clear that . . . and 'the document discloses that . . . ' These forms of **evidentiality** may act as metaphorical forces propelling a proposition towards the conceptualizer's epistemic ground along E_e (cf. Sweetser 1990; Talmy 2000).

3.4 Axiological proximization

The final form of proximization is axiological proximization. Axiological proximization relies on an ability to imagine opposing axiological world views. In DST, this is based on a mirror image of one's own deictic coordinates in socio-spatial, temporal and, crucially, axiological space (Chilton 2014). In discourse surrounding the war on terror, the axiological opposition is typically between democratic values of the West, including the United Kingdom, and non-democratic values of countries in the Middle East, including Iraq. This ideological cognitive model is represented in Figure 6.12. The solid architecture is a base space representing the world view of the PROTAGONIST. The dashed architecture is a second space, derived by a mirror transformation (ibid.), representing the world view of the ANTAGONIST (recall from Chapter 4 that mental spaces can be nested). In both spaces, the evaluative axis is seen engaged in its axiological gear. Values which are 'remote' for Britain constitute the axiological ground for Iraq. Conversely, values which make up the axiological ground for Britain are located at the remote end of E_a for Iraq.

Axiological proximization, as defined by Cap (2010: 130), consists in a 'narrowing of the gap between two different and opposing ideologies'. I take the closing of this gap to represent the axiological ground of the PROTAGONIST and the ANTAGONIST becoming more alike. Axiological proximization thus amounts to social transformation.[17] This can involve a shift in the axiological ground of the PROTAGONIST or the ANTAGONIST. From the perspective of the protagonist, we can therefore refer to **stable ground** or **shifting ground**

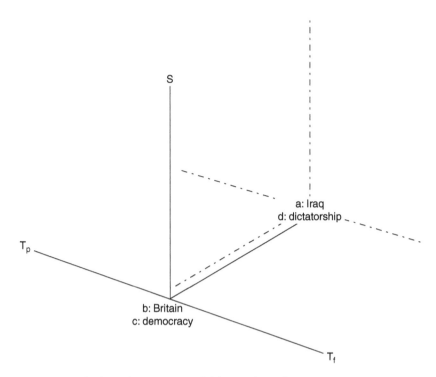

Figure 6.12. Ideological cognitive model for axiological opposition

axiological proximization.[18] Moreover, seen again from the perspective of the PROTAGONIST, axiological proximization can be categorized as **positive** or **negative**. At the level of speech acts, positive proximization occurs in acts of promising or offering while negative proximization occurs in acts of warning (Wiezcorek 2008). Typically, positive axiological proximization is based on a shift in the ANTAGONIST's axiological ground towards that of the PROTAGONIST while negative axiological proximization is predicated on a shift in the PROTAGONIST's axiological ground towards that of the ANTAGONIST. The distinction is reflected in nominalized forms like 'democratisation' (of Them) and 'radicalisation' (of Us) which represent positive, stable ground versus negative, shifting ground axiological proximization, respectively. In the discourse space, this again involves a translation from a starting set of coordinates to a target set.

    In official discourse on the war in Iraq, we tend to find positive instances of stable ground axiological proximization. By way of example, consider (15):

(15) [W]e shall help Iraq move towards democracy. (Tony Blair, 20 March 2003)

This positive form of proximization is used as a moral justification for intervention based on political norms and principles accepted as universal standards in the

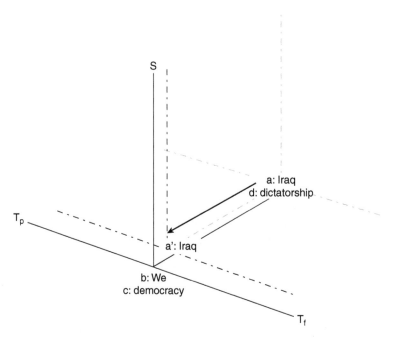

Figure 6.13. Positive axiological proximization

West. It appeals to a 'rescue' scenario rather than a 'defence' scenario.[19] The conceptualization invoked by (15) is modelled in Figure 6.13. In the starting space, Iraq is co-located with values of dictatorship. In the translated or target space, Iraq's axiological ground has shifted 'closer' to values of democracy.[20]

Different Discourses rely on different types of proximization strategy. Discourses which are interdiscursively connected with Discourses of the war on terror but which rely more heavily on negative axiological proximization are extreme-nationalist Discourses of far-right organizations. Here, negative axiological proximization is used to represent a perceived threat to national, legal and political identities. In the following section, we briefly consider proximization in the Mission Statement of the English Defence League. We focus on axiological and temporal proximization.

4. Proximization in the Mission Statement of the English Defence League

The English Defence League (EDL) is a far-right protest movement which campaigns against a perceived 'intrusion' of Islamic beliefs and practices into British politics, law and culture. This world view is based on an axiological opposition between British and Islamic traditions. The organization argues for a 'halt' to the further 'Islamisation' of the United Kingdom. This argument relies on a conceptualization of negative, shifting ground axiological proximization. Consider the following excerpts from the organization's Mission Statement:[21]

(16) These radicals dominate Muslim organisations, remain key figures in British mosques, and are steadily <u>increasing their influence</u>.

(17) The operation of Islamic courts, the often unreasonable demand that Islam is given more respect than it is due, and the stealthy <u>incursion</u> of halal meat into the food industry, all demonstrate that sharia is already <u>creeping into our lives</u>.

(18) In order to ensure the continuity of our culture and its institutions, the EDL stands opposed to the <u>creeping Islamisation</u> of our country, because intimately related to the <u>spread of Islamic religion</u> is the political desire to <u>implement an undemocratic alternative to our cherished way of life: the sharia</u>.

The discourse world constructed by (16)–(18) is modelled in Figure 6.14. In this case, it is the axiological ground of the PROTAGONIST which is construed as shifting. Element a: Britain in the base space, which is also the source space

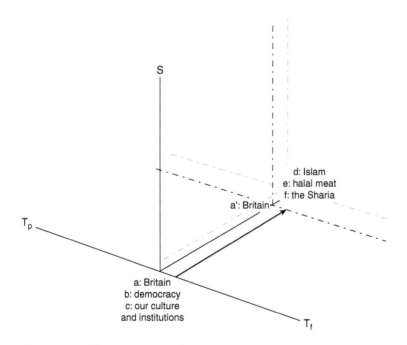

Figure 6.14. Negative axiological proximization

in shifting ground axiological proximization, is translated as element a': Britain in the target space having moved 'further away' from 'democracy' and 'British culture' and 'closer' to 'Islamic culture' and 'the Sharia'. Interestingly, in these examples, this process of social transformation is presented as happening now through the present imperfective construction 'is already creeping into our lives' and the nominalizations 'creeping Islamisation' and 'spread of Islamic religion'. The axiological proximization strategy is therefore supported by a temporal proximization strategy. Worth noting, however, is that although anchored to the conceptualizer's temporal ground, the time frame in which the process is unfolding is construed as protracted. This is indexed by the pace of motion encoded in the semantics of *creep*. The image presented is of a social transformation taking place without notice but which will eventually arrive at a tipping point by which time it will be too late. The argument advanced therefore seems to be that we must intervene now before 'things have gone too far'.

5. Conclusion

In this chapter, we have focused on the deictic positioning of actors and events seen from a contextually specified point of view. In line with Chilton (2004), we have suggested that, in the course of discourse, elements referred or alluded to in the text get positioned at relative distances from the conceptualizer's socio-spatial, temporal, epistemic and axiological ground in a mental discourse space. We have subsequently illustrated a range of proximization strategies in which speakers present elements in the discourse world as encroaching on the conceptualizer's ground in four dimensions. Crucial to the theory of proximization, therefore, is that the conceptualizer, their territory or their social identity, is placed onstage as part of the conceptualization. Proximization is conceptually represented in different types of vectors denoting abstract movement in the discourse space. In the case of spatial proximization, this vector is a force vector which stands, symbolically, for movement through physical space making contact with the conceptualizer's physical ground. In the case of temporal, epistemic and axiological proximization, the vector is a translation vector which represents movement through metaphorical space. In each case, the vector represents a compression in magnitude along the S,T or $E_{e/a}$ axes. In spatial proximization, this compression construes a physical threat as close to or capable of reaching *here*. In axiological proximization, it construes changing social values. Both strategies are aimed at legitimating interventionist action. Temporal proximization operates over spatial and (negative) axiological proximization so that the threat of corporeal harm or loss of identity is construed as close to *now* or current and thus requiring immediate counter-action. Temporal proximization may therefore be thought of as a kind of intensification strategy. Finally, epistemic proximization operates over the whole of the discourse world to construe the scenario expressed in the other three dimensions as a faithful model of reality.

Afterword

The fact that texts are imbued with ideology has been more than adequately demonstrated in CDA since its inception in Critical Linguistics. This book has therefore not sought to show *that* language encodes ideology but, rather, *how* ideology may be enacted through discourse. Specifically, it has been an attempt to show how grammar constitutes a locus of ideology and how grammars, as models of language or image, provide theoretical and analytical handles on some of the discursive features which, in certain contexts of use, are responsible for the expression and reproduction of ideology. In the first half of this book, we have explored the utility of systemic functional models of grammar, including as their categories can be extended to describe meaning in images and thus contribute to a grammar of visual design. A grammar of visual design, we also saw, necessarily includes additional categories relating to space. In the second half of this book, we have explored more cognitively oriented theories of grammar and meaning construction inspired by developments in Cognitive Linguistics. Here, similarly, we suggested that conceptual structures evidenced by language, in particular conceptual metaphors, may also function in the meaning of images. At the same time, however, we have argued that the meaningful basis of much of language, including grammatical constructions, is provided by the kind of visuo-spatial experience that is captured in a multimodal grammar. From a cognitive perspective, therefore, the relation between linguistic and multimodal grammars is more bidirectional with parameters previously considered unique to visual grammar forming part of a cognitive linguistic grammar too. This points not to two distinct grammars in the linguistic and visual realms but to a single conceptual system which operates in both linguistic and visual discourse. From such a cognitive perspective, a recurring theme in both the linguistics and visual discourse analyses presented has been the role played by the body, as well as the conceptualizer's 'situatedness' in mental representations of space, in processes of meaning construction. The notion of situatedness is also extended to include the conceptualizer's point of view in metaphorical representations of temporal and evaluative 'space'.

The extent to which SFG and Cognitive Linguistic approaches are competing or complementary remains unanswered. Both emphasize in their characterization of grammar choice, function, meaning and the construal of experience. In this sense, they are at least compatible. SFG is more text- and speaker-focused while Cognitive Linguistics is more discourse-focused taking into account the hearer as well as the speaker. They may therefore be deployed in complement with one another in description- versus interpretation-stage analysis, respectively. However, it seems unlikely on economic grounds that we have in our minds two distinct grammars responsible for the alternative tasks of discourse production and consumption. Moreover, there are some crucial epistemological differences between SFG and Cognitive Linguistics. For example, SFG models grammar as a procedural navigation through a functional network. By contrast, Cognitive Linguistics sees grammar as a system of symbolic assemblies in which grammatical constructions, as units of the language, invoke holistic patterns of conceptual representation. Similarly, although both SFG and Cognitive Linguistic analyses point to many of the same grammatical features as ideologically load-bearing, in some cases they suggest alternative ideological functions. As accurate characterizations of grammar, then, there do seem to be some fundamental incommensurabilities and critical discourse analysts, for the sake of scientific integrity, may have to choose between them.

Chronologically, of course, SFG precedes Cognitive Linguistics as a method in CDA. This is reflected in the organization of this book. It has not been my intention, however, to suggest that SFG should necessarily be superseded by Cognitive Linguistics in CDA. Through the different data analyses presented, I hope to have demonstrated that both frameworks are effective tools in the CDA box, each with their own merits.

SFG has a number of distinct advantages. In its stark delineation of functional categories and their text-level realizations, for example, SFG allows for clear classifications to be made in textual deconstruction. It is, in turn, especially congenial to comparative forms of analysis. Its extension in Appraisal Theory provides an inventory of lexical resources for the expression of different types of evaluation thus enabling clear and systematic analyses of stance in discourse – an area which CDA would benefit from attending to in more detail. More generally, the model of grammar advanced in SFG is more intimately connected to the social functions of language and its particular situations of use than in Cognitive Linguistics where grammar is grounded in more general cognitive principles. SFG is therefore a particularly neat fit with the philosophical orientation of CDA. At the same time, however, SFG has its limitations as a method of CDA. Some researchers, for example, might find that the strict classificatory nature of SFG is not always amenable to analysing authentic textual data. SFG also presents no account of semantic metaphor which, it seems, is closely connected with grammar and which constitutes a particularly fertile site for the reproduction of ideology.

Cognitive Linguistics, by contrast, is more flexible. The categories it proposes are 'fuzzy' and allow for more or less prototypical forms of realization as well as border-line cases. Moreover, Cognitive Linguistics incorporates grammar and semantic metaphor under the same general principles. In fact, Cognitive Linguistics is generally more encompassing. It addresses many of the same phenomena as SFG, often at finer levels of specification, but from a psychological perspective. For example, Cognitive Linguistics can account for information structure and grammatical metaphor in terms of point of view shifts and consequent differences in distribution of attention. Similarly, Cognitive Linguistics offers an account of 'transitivity' in terms of the different image schemas imposed on the scene conceptualized. However, it also naturally incorporates other pragmatically significant phenomena such as metaphor, deixis and implied or connotative meaning within a single, coherent theoretical framework. Moreover, while SFG is primarily speaker-oriented and does not explicitly address the role of the audience in meaning-making processes, Cognitive Linguistics is concerned with modelling the construction of an intersubjective conceptual space jointly attended to by both the speaker and hearer in the course of discourse. A major advantage of Cognitive Linguistics for CDA, then, is that it can address the problem of cognitive equivalence and at least begin to theorize the conceptual import of grammatical structures already identified as potentially ideological as well as reveal the ideological qualities of others. Cognitive Linguistics presents a psychologically plausible model of grammar. It is founded upon what is already known about the way the mind works in other domains of cognition. However, the claims advanced in the Cognitive Linguistic Approach would be further strengthened by experimental evidence. CDA has already witnessed a cognitive turn in the study of discourse and ideology. What may be needed now is an experimental turn.

SFG is an established methodology with a long tradition of application in CDA. Its utility as a descriptive tool for textual analysis is not in doubt. The Cognitive Linguistic Approach is more novel and many of its theoretical and analytical claims are still to be borne out. It does, however, raise questions concerning the view of grammar in SFG. Whether Cognitive Linguistics will in the end come to succeed SFG as a method of CDA or whether the two can be coherently worked together in a new combined framework only time and further research will tell.

Notes

Introduction

1   Some work in CDA concentrates more on developing this macro-level social critique, theorizing the social and political conditions which allow language to function as an instrument of power. Other work, such as this one, concentrates more on detailed critical linguistic analysis. van Dijk (2009: 62) therefore prefers to use the label Critical Discourse Studies (CDS) to equally capture the fact that a critical approach involves critical theory and critical analysis. This book, however, is very much situated at the applied linguistics end of the spectrum, concentrated on grammar in use. I therefore retain the label CDA throughout in order to reflect the micro-level, text-analytical perspective pursued. This is not to say, of course, that this book does not contribute to *linguistic* theory.

2   Critique in this sense can be most immediately traced to the Critical Theory of the Frankfurt School which suggests that social theory should not only be aimed at understanding and explaining society but also at transforming and improving it (Wodak and Meyer 2009: 6).

3   A similar relation can be seen between scientists and the journals they publish in.

4   Difficult philosophical questions arise here as to whether the values of CDA, as a largely European school, are inherently 'Western' and whether there can be a universal ethics to which CDA can be oriented (Chilton 2011; Chilton et al. 2010).

5   Grammars, of course, are not the only useful tools in the CDA box. Other invaluable methods have been developed, focused on more pragmatic, thematic or interactional features of discourse which are equally important in the expression of ideology and the legitimation of social action (e.g. Reisigl and Wodak 2001). These approaches have drawn up typologies and inventories of linguistic categories which also allow systematic analysis.

6   By strategy, I mean, following Reisigl and Wodak (2001), a more or less intentional/institutionalized plan of discourse practices, including in grammatical selection, whose deployment achieves some linguistic, cognitive and ultimately social action effect.

7   Other, more content-related approaches include the discourse-historical approach (e.g. Reisigl and Wodak 2001) and the socio-cognitive approach (e.g. van Dijk 1998).

8   The methods of multimodal CDA are not restricted to the grammar of visual design but extend further to account for argument, intertextuality and interdiscursivity in visual discourse (e.g. Richardson and Wodak 2009).

9 The Cognitive Linguistic Approach is not to be confused with the Socio-Cognitive Approach, although some researchers have sought to unify them. While the Socio-Cognitive Approach develops a general cognitive framework combining traditional semantic and pragmatic notions with psychological theory on memory, the Cognitive Linguistic Approach applies a range of more narrowly defined linguistic theories sourced specifically from Cognitive Linguistics. Moreover, while the cognitive structures that are constitutive of ideology in the Socio-Cognitive Approach are taken as propositional in nature, in the Cognitive Linguistic Approach they are taken as conceptual (Chilton 2004; Hart 2010).

Chapter 1

1 Although it is recognized that any aspect of linguistic structure can be a marker of values (Fowler 1991: 66), the significance of articulation, prosody and so on tends to be the province of variationist sociolinguistics rather than CDA (cf. O'Grady 2012).

2 The term lexicogrammar reflects the treatment in SFG of lexis and grammar as two poles of a single cline rather than as discrete systems (Halliday and Matthiessen 2004: 43). Grammar and vocabulary, on this account, are intimately bound in the expression of meaning. We discuss this idea further in relation to Cognitive Grammar in Chapter 4.

3 Note that the term 'process' in SFG is not restricted to actual processes (material, mental, verbal, behavioural) but also covers states (existential, relational).

4 Note that the categories ACTOR/GOAL from SFG and AGENT/PATIENT, which are taken from semantics, represent slightly different ways of looking at the clause and do not necessarily always coincide with one another. We flit between both perspectives in the course of our analyses.

5 The so-called Battle of Orgreave, one of the bloodiest and saddest events in the year-long strike, occurred a month later on 18 June.

6 See Montgomery et al. (2000: 90–2) for a classic transitivity analysis of how events on the picket line during the 1983 Miners' Strike were constructed in *The Daily Mail* versus *The Morning Star*.

7 We may distinguish between 'creative', 'transactive' and 'intransactive' material processes: creative processes bring a GOAL into existence; transactive processes act on an already existing GOAL; and intransactive processes do not involve a second participant but only an ACTOR.

8 Available at http://www.telegraph.co.uk/finance/g20-summit/5089870/G20-protests-Rioters-loot-RBS-as-demonstrations-turn-violent.html and http://www.guardian.co.uk/world/2009/apr/01/g20-summit-protests, accessed 26 April 2013.

9 The two texts are broadly similar in length with *The Telegraph* article containing 1009 words and *The Guardian* article 1059 words. Processes in reported clauses have not been included so as to maintain a picture of the 'institutional voice'. However, the content and selection of quotatives in news articles are ideologically significant.

10   For many readers, 'storm' in this context may conjure intertextual associations with the 'storming of the Bastille' in the French Revolution and thus invoke positive evaluations. This intertextual link is likely to have been recently reinforced as the French Revolution has been brought to the fore of public consciousness through the popularity of the film production of Victor Hugo's *Les Misérables*.

11   Such expressions may instantiate a conceptual metaphor PROTEST IS WAR (see Chapter 5 for a further discussion of metaphor).

12   We discuss this 'spatialisation' strategy in more detail, defining a finer semantic analysis of process types from a cognitive perspective, in Chapter 4.

13   Although originally outlined in Critical Linguistics (Fowler et al. 1979; Kress and Hodge 1979), van Leeuwen points out that mystification analysis has continued to be 'an important part of CDA' (1996: 38).

14   Note that the Theme does not necessarily coincide with Subject and PARTICIPANT but may be realized by Adjunct and thus CIRCUMSTANCE for example.

15   It should be noted that removing responsible agents is by no means the only potential ideological function of the agentless passive. In the context of the 'global economy', for example, Fairclough (2000) shows how a sentence such as 'goods can be made in low cost countries', which occurred in a 1998 New Labour White Paper on 'Building the Knowledge-driven Economy', can serve to conceal who is making those goods and in what circumstances (see also Merkl-Davies and Koller 2012). Neither are material processes the only processes that can undergo agentless passivization.

16   In grammatical metaphor, the relationship between the semantic structure and its marked realization in lexicogrammar is sometimes described as 'incongruent'. Grammatical metaphor and lexical metaphor are related in so far as both involve a choice between 'transparent' and more 'opaque' forms of representation.

17   The corpus collates articles from across the British press published between 2000 and 2006, a period in which the European Union twice expanded and two general elections were fought with a focus on issues relating to immigration.

18   The 'critical instinct' issue concerns 'how easily or not the human mind can be tricked, deceived or manipulated through the use of language' (Chilton 2005: 41) and is raised in light of recent research in the evolution of communication (e.g. Sperber 2001).

Chapter 2

1   See Hunston and Thompson (2000) for an overview. Following Hunston and Thompson (2000), we will maintain the term 'evaluation' as an umbrella for the various kinds of stance-taking acts that speakers perform.

2   Two recent studies applying features of Appraisal Theory in CDA are Bednarek and Caple (2010) and Fuoli (2012).

3 Martin and White (2007) distinguish here between 'particulate' and 'prosodic' realizations.

4 It is important to note that the scope of individual lexical items is not necessarily limited to particular appraisal functions. Certain forms may perform alternative functions in different contexts.

5 Indeed, in critical accounting research, this form of impression management is often explained in terms of Legitimacy Theory (Campbell et al. 2003; Deegan 2002).

6 This is not to say, of course, that the assertion is necessarily truth-conditionally felicitous, only that the speaker, in the current communicative context, is refusing to recognize and engage with any alternative assessments.

7 Contraction can thus be seen as functionally closer to monogloss than expansion.

8 This move is referred to as an 'authorization' strategy by van Leeuwen and Wodak (1999).

9 Note that for Martin and White (2007), the dominion of GRADUATION is not restricted to systems of APPRAISAL. For example, it can also be seen to operate on the output of TRANSITIVITY to code the speaker's assessment of the intensity of material, mental and verbal processes.

10 At this point in the sequence of events, the coalition was operating on the premise that chemical, biological and nuclear weapons existed in Iraq and that Saddam Hussein had access to these weapons. This was in spite of conflicting evidence from a United Nations investigation led by Hans Blix. Shortly after the invasion, the Iraq Survey Group confirmed that no such weapons existed in Iraq.

11 Only isolated instances of GRADUATION: FORCE are marked since infused FORCE, as an inherent meaning component of many words, is so densely distributed in any text. However, we will discuss some significant instances of infused FORCE.

12 See Chapter 6 for further discussion of this 'warrant' in terms of 'proximization'.

13 They are probably contained within cognitive frames (see Chapter 4).

14 Technically, co-occurance counts as collocation when measured at a rate which exceeds chance and which is therefore statistically significant.

15 The claim in this last point, from a usage-based perspective, would be that speakers learn the connotative value of words by monitoring discourse and somehow 'logging' their typical contexts of use.

16 It is in this sense that 'the systematic study of corpora yields information about language use that is not available to unaided intuition' (Deignan 1999: 178).

17 http://bncweb.lancs.ac.uk, accessed 4 March 2012.

Chapter 3

1 See Richardson and Wodak (2009) for a discourse-historical approach to multimodal CDA.

2　The means of realization across the two modalities are clearly very different but equivalences can be drawn based on the communicative functions they perform (Kress and van Leeuwen 2006).

3　Evaluations cannot be *inscribed* in an image in the way that they can in language. The connection between particular meanings and forms in multimodal discourse is less bound. Evaluations are, thus, more context-specific and dependent on predefined values. We can therefore only speak of *invoked* evaluations when analysing images.

4　Search conducted on 3 June 2013.

5　More technically, this is a visual realization of a lower-bounding implicature (Horn 2004).

6　See Kress and van Leeuwen (2006: 72) for details on how this contrast is achieved through different options in COLOUR and DEEP SPACE.

7　Machin (2007) sees such low resolution as a visual realization of low MODALITY.

8　The source of the vector is referred to as 'the tail'. The endpoint of the vector is referred to as 'the head'.

9　A quintessential example would be the famous Alfred Leete recruitment poster from the First World War analysed by Kress and van Leeuwen (1996: 117–18).

10　See Chapter 5 on conceptual metaphor.

11　This is not the only system available to languages, as Levinson (2003) shows. It is, however, the predominant system in English.

12　Hence, whether 'the bike' is described as *next to*, *in front of* or *behind*, 'the tree' depends on where the speaker is in relation to the bike and the tree.

13　See subsequent chapters for further discussion of embodiment in language.

14　The ability to 'see' from another's perspective is based on an underlying capacity known as Theory of Mind (Baron-Cohen 1995; Tomasello 1999).

15　The London G20 protests occurred around the G20 Summit on 2 April 2009. The protests addressed a range of issues, including current economic policy, the banking system, the continued war on terror and climate change. The Trades Union Congress protest took place on 26 March 2011 and was primarily concerned with planned public spending cuts. The Student Fee protests consisted of a number of protests organized by the National Union of Students in response to rises in higher education tuition fees. The two most significant of these took place on 10 and 24 November 2010. All of these protests saw violence with injuries sustained by both the police and protestors.

16　Getty is in fact the world's largest image bank with 25 per cent of the overall market in an industry worth $2 billion (Machin 2004: 318).

17　It should be noted that this interpretation is in conflict with the polysemy we find in the word *right*.

18　Alternatively, it may be related to that fact that logical operations are typically dealt with by the left hemisphere of the brain and more emotive processes typically occur in the right hemisphere.

19 Of course, in another conceptual metaphor, UP is associated with admiration as when we say 'look *up* to someone'. Views from cardinal point -1 may therefore connote admiration. This may be why, for example, war memorials are typically built with soldiers aloft (Abousnouga and Machin 2011). Whether the point of view suggests admiration or subjugation depends on other features in the representation of the participant, including not only transitivity features but also bodily features like posture and facial expression.

20 It is worth noting that the image is among the first returned in a simple Google search for 'Muslims' (search conducted on 19 September 2013).

21 Goatly (2011a) refers to this as the 'multivalency' of source concepts in conceptual metaphors.

22 Extreme close-ups are often used in support of racist ideologies (Richardson 2008; Richardson and Wodak 2009). Given the context of the image, it may be argued that the image is inter-discursive, instantiating both a Discourse of political protests and an anti-Muslim, and perhaps more generally an anti-immigration Discourse. It would be interesting to compare typical values for PERSPECTIVE in images of Muslim protesters and non-Muslim protesters published in the British press.

23 This contextualization is an example of a 'myth' (in Barthes' sense) being reused to frame a contemporary situation (cf. Kelsey 2012).

Chapter 4

1 This chapter borrows from Hart (2013a/b).

2 It should be noted at this point that a cognitive approach is not a totalizing one intended to supersede other approaches to CDA. Rather, it complements and can be integrated with other approaches (Hart 2010).

3 This is not, of course, to say that conceptualization *is* perception but, rather, that the two are parallel manifestations of more general cognitive systems (Langacker 1999, 2008). In other words, the kinds of things that we do in perception we also do in conceptualization.

4 This typology is a modified version of earlier ones presented in Hart (2011a/b and 2013a/b).

5 It is semantic positioning that we discuss in this chapter. We discuss pragmatic positioning in Chapter 6.

6 Depending on the verb choice, direction and rate of motion may also be elaborated. Alternative grammatical structures may also invoke the same basic structure but prompt for elaboration of only specific elements of it (see next section for discussion).

7 These data are made up of two articles from each of the following newspapers: *The Times, The Telegraph, The Guardian, The Independent, The Express* and *The Daily Mail.*

8 It was also found that newspapers supposedly more central politically, such as *The Independent* and *The Times*, steered closer to the narrative presented by right-wing newspapers like *The Telegraph* than they did to left-wing publications like *The Guardian.*

9 At this point, a note is needed on the status of diagrams in Cognitive Linguistics (cf. Langacker 2008: 9–12). It is not suggested that language users have in their minds images of precisely the forms presented. The diagrams are a notational device intended to *model* on paper conceptual structures held in the mind. Alternative notational devices could be conceived and alternative diagrammatic notations can be used to capture the same phenomena. However, the particular use of diagrams in Cognitive Linguistics is well motivated if, as is claimed, meaning is imagistic in nature. While it may be challenged, then, that the diagrams fall short of the rigour of a mathematical formalism, they are intended to model fundamental elements of meaning such as topology, sequence and causation in a way that is intuitive and psychologically plausible and in a way that is systematic rather than ad hoc. They are not heuristics to help analysts interpret meaning but attempts at modelling meaning as it is represented in cognition.

10 See Hart (2011a) for an analysis of force-interactions in immigration discourse.

11 The qualitative analyses presented in this section supersede those given in Hart (2013b: 171–4).

12 Given the visuo-spatial qualities of conceptualization, it is more than mere analogy to use the term *viewer* to refer to the conceptualizer and to borrow, in describing some of the meaningful properties of language, vocabulary from grammars of visual design such as found in film and other media studies (cf. Langacker 1999: 203–6).

13 This positioning is also partly achieved by the distal modal in 'could be seen'.

14 There is also now a growing body of neuroscientific and experimental psycholinguistic evidence in support of this hypothesis (see Bergen 2012 for an overview).

15 This can be heard in the intonation if one reads the example aloud.

16 This goes for passive constructions in which the entity encoded as Subject is a THEME as well as those in which the PATIENT is the Subject.

17 See also Chapter 6 for further discussion of proximization.

18 This analysis is similar to but not quite the same as Langacker's (2002: 78–9) analysis of nominalization as invoking a *summary* rather than *sequential* scanning of an event.

19 Imagine the view of a field you get in an aerial shot.

20 See also Talmy (2000) on 'windowing of attention'.

21 Ergative constructions can similarly be analysed as a shift in point of view on the DISTANCE plane.

22 This exact same construction is repeated in articles published in three different newspapers. This is doubtless down to those newspapers buying in their copy from third-party press agencies such as Reuters and failing to make any alterations to the text.

23 Most causal interactions do not in reality, of course, start from nowhere. Rather, for any event there is a potentially infinite chain of causal interactions which precede it. We cannot therefore speak felicitously about the viewing frame covering the complete scene but only about it covering the complete schema which is invoked by the linguistic instantiation.

24 The form of mystification analysis presented here is deployed at a level above the clause encompassing larger text units and inferences made across adjacent clauses (cf. criticisms of mystification analysis from Widdowson 2004).

Chapter 5

1 This chapter cannot do justice to the wealth of work that now exists on the ideological functions of metaphor in discourse across a range of social and political contexts (e.g. Charteris-Black 2004, 2006a; Chilton 1996; Goatly 2011b; Koller 2004; Musolff 2004; Santa Ana 2002). Our purpose is to just highlight the role that metaphor plays in ideological reproduction and show how metaphor fits within the broader cognitive linguistic approach to CDA presented in Part 2 of this book.

2 Blending is not restricted to metaphor but is also invoked by other forms of figurative language (Fauconnier and Turner 2002).

3 Fauconnier and Turner (2002) also suggest a fourth **generic space** which captures more general structure shared by elements in the two input spaces. Following Radden and Dirven (2007), however, we leave aside the generic space in the proceeding examples since its inclusion would not add much to the analyses.

4 In this way, metaphor often constitutes a *topos* (Reisigl and Wodak 2001). In this instance, the metaphor represents a topos of burden (see Hart 2010).

5 This is not, of course, to say that grammar is the sole source of metaphor in discourse.

6 A quick search using Webcorp (www.webcorp.org.uk) confirms this.

7 The lexemes highlighted are not restricted in their usage profiles to the FIRE domain. In isolation, the extent to which these examples invoke the FIRE frame may therefore be challenged (O'Halloran 2007). However, the various lexemes

are more or less prototypically associated with fire and intertextually they point to a systematic understanding of the situation in terms of fire. Once established through intertextual experience as a conventional mode of understanding, the conceptual metaphor RIOTS AS FIRE licenses an interpretation in the sense of fire as the one most immediately accessible (and therefore 'relevant' – see Sperber and Wilson 1995).

8 See also Semino's (2008: 118–23) discussion of a BNP leaflet associating Muslim asylum seekers with explosions.

9 Full speech is available at: https://www.gov.uk/government/speeches/pm-statement-on-violence-in-england.

10 Full speech is available at: https://www.gov.uk/government/speeches/pms-speech-on-the-fightback-after-the-riots.

11 A similar blend used by Cameron is the BROKEN BRITAIN blend instantiated in examples like: 'Do we have the determination to confront the slow-motion moral collapse that has taken place in parts of our country these past few generations?' and 'In my very first act as leader of this party I signalled my personal priority: to mend our broken society'. Although the blend does not make use of BIOLOGY and MEDICINE frames, it possesses much of the same 'logic' sourced from BUILDING and ENGINEERING frames. For example, in both blends society is seen as damaged and in need of restoring.

12 It is easy to imagine a counter-discourse in which social conditions such as poverty are seen as the 'disease' responsible for the riots as a symptom of this disease. The 'cure' in such a counter-discourse would then consist in addressing issues like poverty.

13 In Lakoff's (1996) terms, we might say that Cameron is promoting a CONFIDENT SURGEON rather than a CARING NURSE medical frame.

14 As represented, for example, in recent popular TV shows like *Skint* and *Benefits Street*.

15 Full speech is available at: https://www.gov.uk/government/speeches/prime-minister-a-speech-on-the-economy.

16 Interestingly, in his study of metaphor in financial reporting, Charteris-Black (2004) did not find evidence of a conceptual metaphor ECONOMIC CONDITIONS ARE WEATHER.

17 The primary metaphor PURPOSEFUL ACTIVITY IS MOVEMENT TOWARDS A DESTINATION, for example, is also at the root of the by now much studied conceptual metaphor LIFE IS A JOURNEY (Grady 1997).

18 Mixing metaphors, of course, is usually held up as an example of 'poor' grammar. Mixing conventional metaphors, however, is pervasive and highly productive in political argumentation creating rich and integrated conceptualizations rather than awkward clashes of imagery (Kimmel 2010).

19 On the EU IS A CONTAINER metaphor, see Chilton and Ilyin (1993), Drulák (2006), Musolff (2004) and Šarić et al. (2010).

20 In the text, Cameron refers to both the 'journey' that Britain must take and to the ones that other member States must take.

21 It has its origins in Plato's *Republic*.

22 To the extent that it has an intertextual or recontextualizing link with the SHIP OF STATE metaphor, the blend may achieve cognitive and cultural resonance based on geo-psychological traits of British English speakers (as islanders) and nostalgic associations with British maritime history (Charteris-Black and Ennis 2001).

Chapter 6

1 Although originally outlined by Chilton (2004), this framework has since been taken up and developed in a number of new directions (Cap 2006, 2013; Cienki et al. 2010; Dunmire 2011; Filardo Llamas 2013; Kaal 2012).

2 In Chilton (2004), the third axis is simultaneously epistemic and deontic. Cap (2006) does away with the epistemic aspect and replaces the deontic axis with an axiological axis. I follow Cap in favouring axiological over deontic where the former is a broader category able to account for a wider range of specific value-types. However, I retain the dual-functionality of the third axis in light of the central significance of epistemic evaluation in political communication.

3 For detailed treatments of deixis see Fillmore (1975) and Levinson (1983).

4 However, see Frawley (1992) and Langacker (1991) for deictic accounts of epistemic modality.

5 Although Chilton (2004) does not make this connection, something very similar is suggested in Chilton (2009) and in personal communication.

6 The fact that the evaluative axis in the discourse space is only a half-line (the sagittal axis extends behind the body too) can be accounted for by the constraints imposed by our field of view, which allows only a 160–180° panorama, on our visual experience of the space around the body.

7 Indeed, the basic model could be arranged any which way, for example, with the socio-spatial axis as the X axis, the evaluative axis as the Y axis and temporal axis as the Z axis; the topological relation between elements in the discourse space would be maintained. The only constraint seems to be that the socio-spatial and the evaluative axes are half-lines.

8 It may also be argued for on the basis of the polysemous relation between deontic modals, which are bound with concepts of legality, morality and so on, and epistemic modals which are more intuitively theorized in terms of deictic distance (Chilton 2004: 60).

9   Full text is available at http://www.archive2.official-documents.co.uk/document/reps/iraq/foreword.htm.

10 Full text is available at http://www.publications.parliament.uk/pa/cm200203/cmhansrd/vo030318/debtext/30318-06.htm.

11 The term ANTAGONIST is being used in the more classical sense here compared to in Chapter 4.

12 Full speech is available at http://news.bbc.co.uk/1/hi/uk_politics/2870581.stm.

13 For the sake of illustration, temporal and epistemic dimensions are not taken into account in this analysis. The presumption, however, from Blair's point of view, is that the actual occurrence of this scenario is not too far removed in terms of time or possibility.

14 Fausey and Matlock (2011) demonstrate in an empirical context the ideological import of the perfective versus imperfective aspect. They gave participants sentences about a fictional politician's infidelity and corruption. One group was given sentences in the imperfective aspect such as 'Last year, Mark was having an affair with his assistant and was taking hush money from a prominent constituent'. The other group was given sentences in the perfective aspect such as 'Last year, Mark had an affair with his assistant and took hush money from a prominent constituent'. The two groups were then asked to rate the politician's chances of re-election. Over 75 per cent of readers who were given the imperfective construction said they were confident the politician would not be re-elected while only around 50 per cent of readers given the perfect construction reported the same. This was attributed to the fact that the imperfective allows the possibility that the action is still happening while the perfective aspect confines the event to the past.

15 Where the tail of the vector is construed as located in these models is a matter of contextual knowledge. Grammatically, however, the use of *continue to* in (7) and (8) suggests an origin at a greater distance along T_p than present perfective and imperfective forms 'has produced' and 'is developing'.

16 This is not a condition of the relation between temporal and epistemic distance.

17 This is a slightly different interpretation to the one found in Cap (2010, 2011).

18 Of course, there is a third possibility in which the axiological ground of both the PROTAGONIST and ANTAGONIST is shifting in axiological convergence. However, this is not normally a feature of justificatory, interventionist discourse.

19 It is worth noting at this point that following the invasion of Iraq it was discovered that the intelligence findings reported in the September document were massively flawed and Iraq was not in possession of any weapons of mass destruction. The September dossier came to be known as the 'dodgy dossier'. With the initial premise for going to war in Iraq debunked, there was a discursive shift away from a Discourse of defence to one of 'responsibility' to the Iraqi people. In the context of US discourse, Cap (2006) shows that a defining feature of this discursive shift

was a marked move away from a reliance on spatial proximization strategies to a compensatory reliance on axiological proximization strategies instead.

20 There is some lexical evidence to suggest that the conceptualization involved here might not be based on a mirror transformation of the base space followed by a translation but on a 180^0 rotation of the base space followed by a rotation back in the target space: for example, 'come round to our way of thinking'. However, this form of expression appears to be relatively idiomatic.

21 Full text is available at http://www.englishdefenceleague.org/mission-statement/.

Bibliography

Abousnnouga, G. and D. Machin (2011). Visual discourses of the role of women in war commemoration: A multimodal analysis of British war monuments. *Journal of Language and Politics* 10 (3): 322–46.

Austin, J. L. (1962). *How to Do Things with Words*. Oxford: Clarendon Press.

Baker, P., C. Gabrielatos, M. KhosraviNik, M. Krzyzanowski, T. McEnery and R. Wodak (2008). A useful methodological synergy? Combining critical discourse analysis and corpus linguistics to examine discourses of refugees and asylum seekers in the UK press. *Discourse & Society* 19 (3): 273–306.

Baron-Cohen, S. (1995). *Mindblindness: An Essay on Autism and Theory of Mind*. Cambridge, MA: MIT Press.

Bednarek, M. (2006). *Evaluation in Media Discourse: Analysis of a Newspaper Corpus*. London: Continuum.

Bednarek, M. and H. Caple (2010). Playing with environmental stories in the news: Good or bad practice? *Discourse & Communication* 4 (1): 5–31.

Beer, F. A. and C. De Landtsheer (eds) (2004). *Metaphorical World Politics*. East Lansing: Michigan State University Press.

Bergen, B. K. (2012). *Louder than Words: The New of Science of How the Mind Makes Meaning*. New York: Basic Books.

Biber, D. and E. Finegan (1989). Styles of stance in English: Lexical and grammatical marking of evidentiality and affect. *Text* 9 (1): 93–124.

Billig, M. (2003). Critical discourse analysis and the rhetoric of critique. In G. Weiss and R. Wodak (eds), *Critical Discourse Analysis: Theory and Interdisciplinarity*. Basingstoke: Palgrave Macmillan. pp. 35–46.

— (2008). The language of critical discourse analysis: The case of nominalization. *Discourse & Society* 19: 783–800.

Bounegru, L. and C. Forceville (2011). Metaphors in editorial cartoons representing the global financial crisis. *Visual Communication* 10 (2): 209–29.

Caldas-Coulthard, C. R. (1994). On reporting reporting: The representation of speech in factual and factional narratives. In M. Coulthard (ed.), *Advances in Written Text Analysis*. London: Routledge. pp. 295–308.

Campbell, D., B. Craven and P. Shrives (2003). Voluntary social reporting in three FTSE sectors: A comment on perception and legitimacy. *Accounting, Auditing & Accountability Journal* 16 (4): 558–81.

Cap, P. (2006). *Legitimization in Political Discourse*. Newcastle: Cambridge Scholars Publishing.

— (2008). Towards a proximisation model of the analysis of legitimization in political discourse. *Journal of Pragmatics* 40 (1): 17–41.

— (2010). Proximizing objects, proximizing values: Towards an axiological contribution to the discourse of legitimization. In U. Okulska and P. Cap (eds), *Perspectives in Politics and Discourse*. Amsterdam: John Benjamins. pp. 119–42.

— (2011). Axiological proximisation. In C. Hart (ed.), *Critical Discourse Studies in Context and Cognition*. Amsterdam: John Benjamins. pp. 81–96.

— (2013). *Proximization: The Pragmatics of Symbolic Distance Crossing*. Amsterdam: John Benjamins.

Charteris-Black, J. (2004). *Corpus Approaches to Critical Metaphor Analysis*. Basingstoke: Palgrave Macmillan.

— (2006a). Britain as a container: Immigration metaphors in the 2005 election campaign. *Discourse & Society* 17 (6): 563–82.

— (2006b). *Politicians and Rhetoric: The Persuasive Power of Metaphor*. Basingstoke: Palgrave Macmillan.

Charteris-Black, J. and T. Ennis (2001). A comparative study of metaphor in English and Spanish financial reporting. *English for Specific Purposes Journal* 20: 249–66.

Chilton, P. (1996). *Security Metaphors: Cold War Discourse from Containment to Common House*. New York: Peter Lang.

— (2004). *Analysing Political Discourse: Theory and Practice*. London: Routledge.

— (2005a). Missing links in mainstream CDA: Modules, blends and the critical instinct. In R. Wodak and P. Chilton (eds), *A New Research Agenda in (Critical) Discourse Analysis: Theory, Methodology and Interdisciplinarity*. Amsterdam: John Benjamins. pp. 19–52.

— (2005b). Manipulation, memes and metaphors: The case of *Mein Kampf*. In L. de Saussure and P. Schulz (eds), *Manipulation and Ideologies in the Twentieth Century*. Amsterdam: John Benjamins. pp. 15–44.

— (2007). Geometrical concepts at the interface of formal and cognitive verbs: Aktionsart, aspect, and the English progressive. *Pragmatics & Cognition* 15 (1): 91–114.

— (2010). From mind to grammar: Coordinate systems, prepositions, constructions. In V. Evans and P. Chilton (eds), *Language, Cognition and Space: The State of the Art and New Directions*. London: Equinox Publishing. pp. 331–70.

— (2011). Still something missing in CDA. *Discourse Studies* 13 (6): 769–81.

— (2014). *Language, Space and Mind: The Conceptual Geometry of Linguistic Meaning*. Cambridge: Cambridge University Press.

Chilton, P. and M. Ilyin (1993). Metaphor in political discourse: The case of the 'Common European House'. *Discourse & Society* 4 (1): 7–31.

Chilton, P., H. Tian and R. Wodak (2010). Reflections on discourse and critique in China and the West. *Journal of Language and Politics* 9 (4): 489–507.

Coffin, C. and K. O'Halloran (2006). The role of APPRAISAL and corpora in detecting covert evaluation. *Functions of Language* 13 (1): 77–110.

Croft, W. and D. A. Cruse (2004). *Cognitive Linguistics.* Cambridge: Cambridge University Press.

Dancygier, B. (2004). *Conditionals and Prediction: Time, Knowledge and Causation in Conditional Constructions.* Cambridge: Cambridge University Press.

Deegan, C. (2002). Introduction: The legitimising effect of social and environment disclosures – A theoretical foundation. *Accounting, Auditing & Accountability Journal* 15 (3): 282–311.

Deignan, A. (1999). Corpus-based research into metaphor. In L. Cameron and G. Low (eds), *Research and Applying Metaphor.* Cambridge: Cambridge University Press. pp. 177–202.

Dessalles, J.-L. (1999). *Why We Talk: The Evolutionary Origins of Language.* Oxford: Oxford University Press.

Dirven, R., R. Frank and M. Putz (2003). Introduction: Categories, cognitive models and ideologies. In R. Dirven, R. Frank and M. Putz (eds), *Cognitive Models in Language and Thought: Ideology, Metaphors and Meanings.* Berlin: Mouton de Gruyter. pp. 1–24.

Drulák, P. (2006). Motion, container and equilibrium: Metaphors in the discourse about European integration. *European Journal of International Relations* 12 (4): 499–531.

Dunmire, P. (2011). *Projecting the Future through Political Discourse.* Amsterdam: John Benjamins.

Eagleton, T. (1991). *Ideology: An Introduction.* London: Verso.

El Refaie, E. (2001). Metaphors we discriminate by: Naturalized themes in Austrian newspaper articles about asylum seekers. *Journal of Sociolinguistics* 5 (3): 352–71.

— (2003). Understanding visual metaphor: The example of newspaper cartoons. *Visual Communication* 2 (1): 75–96.

Evans, V. (2004). *The Structure of Time: Language, Meaning and Temporal Cognition.* Amsterdam: John Benjamins.

Evans, V. and M. Green (2006). *Cognitive Linguistics: An Introduction.* Edinburgh: Edinburgh University Press.

Fairclough, N. (1989). *Language and Power.* London: Longman.

— (1992). *Discourse and Social Change.* Cambridge: Polity.

— (1995a). *Critical Discourse Analysis: The Critical Study of Language.* London: Longman.

— (1995b). *Media Discourse.* London: Edward Arnold.

— (1996). A reply to Henry Widdowson's 'Discourse Analysis: A Critical Review'. *Language and Literature* 5: 1–8.

— (2000). *New Labour, New Language?* London: Routledge.

— (2003). *Analyzing Discourse: Textual Analysis for Social Research.* London: Routledge.

— (2005). Critical discourse analysis in transdisciplinary research. In R. Wodak and P. Chilton (eds), *A New Agenda in (Critical) Discourse Analysis: Theory, Methodology and Interdisciplinarity.* Amsterdam: John Benjamins. pp. 53–70.

Fauconnier, G. (1994). *Mental Spaces: Aspects of Meaning Construction in Natural Language*. Cambridge: Cambridge University Press.

— (1997). *Mappings in Thought and Language*. Cambridge: Cambridge University Press.

Fauconnier, G. and M. Turner (1996). Blending as a central process of grammar. In A. E. Goldberg (ed.), *Conceptual Structure, Discourse and Language*. Stanford, CA: CSLI Publications. pp. 113–30.

— (2002). *The Way We Think: Conceptual Blending and the Mind's Hidden Complexities*. New York: Basic Books.

Fausey, C. M. and T. Matlock (2011). Can grammar win elections? *Political Psychology* 32 (4): 563–74.

Filardo Llamas, L. (2013). 'Committed to the ideals of 1916'. The language of paramilitary groups: The case of the Irish Republican Army. *Critical Discourse Studies* 10 (1): 1–17.

Fillmore, C. (1975). *Lectures on Deixis*. Stanford, CA: CSLI Publications.

— (1982). Frame semantics. In Linguistics Society of Korea (eds), *Linguistics in the Morning Calm*. Seoul: Hanshin Publishing Co. pp. 111–37.

Forceville, C. (1996). *Pictorial Metaphor in Advertising*. London: Routledge.

Fowler, R. (1991). *Language in the News: Discourse and Ideology in the Press*. London: Routledge.

Fowler, R. (1996). On critical linguistics. In C. R. Caldas-Coulthard and M. Coulthard (eds), *Texts and Practices: Readings in Critical Discourse Analysis*. London: Routledge. pp. 3–14.

Fowler, R., R. Hodge, G. Kress and T. Trew (1979). *Language and Control*. London: Routledge and Kegan Paul.

Franklin, N. and B. Tversky (1990). Searching imagined environments. *Journal of Experimental Psychology: General* 119: 63–76.

Frawley, W. (1992). *Linguistic Semantics*. Hillsdale, NJ: Lawrence Erlbaum.

Fuoli, M. (2012). Assessing social responsibility: A quantitative analysis of Appraisal in BP's and IKEA's social reports. *Discourse & Communication* 6 (1): 55–81.

Gabrielatos, C. and P. Baker (2008). Fleeing, sneaking, flooding: A corpus analysis of discursive constructions of refugees and asylum seekers in the UK press 1996–2005. *Journal of English Linguistics* 36 (1): 5–38.

Gee, J. P. (1990). *Social Linguistics and Literacies: Ideology in Discourses*. London: Falmer Press.

Glasgow Media Group (1976). *Bad News*. London: Routledge and Kegan Paul.

Goatly, A. (2011a). *The Language of Metaphors*. 2nd edn. London: Routledge.

— (2011b). *Washing the Brain: Metaphor and Hidden Ideology*. Amsterdam: John Benjamins.

Grady, J. (1997). Foundations of meaning: Primary metaphors and primary scenes. Unpublished Ph.D dissertation. University of California, Berkeley.

— (1999). A typology of motivation for conceptual metaphor: Correlation vs. resemblance. In G. Steen and R. Gibbs (eds), *Metaphor in Cognitive Linguistics*. Amsterdam: John Benjamins. pp. 79–100.

— (2005). Primary metaphors as inputs to conceptual integration. *Journal of Pragmatics* 37: 1595–614.

Grady, J., S. Coulson and T. Oakley (1999). Blending and metaphor. In G. Steen and R. Gibbs (eds), *Metaphor in Cognitive Linguistics*. Amsterdam: John Benjamins. pp. 101–24.

Habermas, J. (1977). A review of Gadamer's Truth and Method. In F. R. Dallmayr and T. A. McCarthy (eds), *Understanding and Social Inquiry*. Notre Dame: University of Notre Dame Press. pp. 335–61.

Halliday, M. A. K. (1967). Notes on transitivity and theme in English: Part 2. *Journal of Linguistics* 3: 199–244.

— (1973). *Explorations in the Functions of Language*. London: Edward Arnold.

— (1978). *Language as Social Semiotic: The Social Interpretation of Language and Meaning*. London: Edward Arnold.

— (1985). *An Introduction to Functional Grammar*. London: Edward Arnold.

— (1994). *An Introduction to Functional Grammar*. 2nd edn. London: Edward Arnold.

— (2007). Language as social semiotic: Towards a general sociolinguistic theory. In M. A. K. Halliday, *Language and Society*. Edited by J. Webster. London: Continuum. pp. 169–202.

Halliday, M. A. K. and C. M. I. M. Matthiessen (2004). *Construing Experience through Meaning: A Language-based Approach to Cognition*. 2nd edn. London: Continuum.

Hampe, B. and J. Grady (eds) (2005). *From Perception to Meaning: Image Schemas in Cognitive Linguistics*. Berlin: Walter de Gruyter.

Hart, C. (2008). Critical discourse analysis and metaphor: Toward a theoretical framework. *Critical Discourse Studies* 5 (2): 91–106.

— (2010). *Critical Discourse and Cognitive Science: New Perspectives on Immigration Discourse*. Basingstoke: Palgrave Macmillan.

— (2011a). Force-interactive patterns in immigration discourse: A Cognitive Linguistic approach to CDA. *Discourse & Society* 22 (3): 269–86.

— (2011b). Moving beyond metaphor in the Cognitive Linguistic Approach to CDA: Construal operations in immigration discourse. In C. Hart (ed.), *Critical Discourse Studies in Context and Cognition*. Amsterdam: John Benjamins. pp. 171–92.

— (2011c). Legitimising assertions and the logico-rhetorical module: Evidence and epistemic vigilance in media discourse on immigration. *Discourse Studies* 13 (6): 751–69.

— (ed.) (2011d). *Critical Discourse Studies in Context and Cognition*. Amsterdam: John Benjamins.

— (2013a). Event-construal in press reports of violence in political protests: A Cognitive Linguistic Approach to CDA. *Journal of Language and Politics* 12 (3): 400–23.

— (2013b). Constructing contexts through grammar: Cognitive models and conceptualisation in British Newspaper reports of political protests. In J. Flowerdew (ed.), *Discourse in Context*. London: Bloomsbury. pp. 159–84.

Hart, C. and P. Cap (2014). Introduction. In C. Hart and P. Cap (eds), *Contemporary Critical Discourse Studies*. London: Bloomsbury.

Hart, C. and D. Lukeš (eds) (2007). *Cognitive Linguistics in Critical Discourse Analysis: Application and Theory*. Newcastle: Cambridge Scholars Publishing.

Haynes, J. (1989). *Introducing Stylistics*. London: Hyman.

Herman, E. S. and N. Chomsky (1988). *Manufacturing Consent: The Political Economy of the Mass Media*. New York: Pantheon Books.

Hodge, R. and G. Kress (1993). *Language as Ideology*. 2nd edn. London: Routledge.

Horn, L. R. (2004). Implicature. In L. R. Horn and G. Ward (eds), *The Handbook of Pragmatics*. Oxford: Blackwell. pp. 3–28.

Hunston, S. and G. Thompson (eds) (2000). *Evaluation in Text: Authorial Stance and the Construction of Discourse*. Oxford: Oxford University Press.

Johnson, M. (1987). *The Body in the Mind: The Bodily Basis of Meaning, Imagination, and Reason*. Chicago, IL: University of Chicago Press.

Kaal, B. (2012). Worldviews: Spatial ground for political reasoning in Dutch election manifestos. *CADAAD* 6 (1): 1–22.

Kelsey, D. (2012). Remembering to forget: Supporting and opposing the war on terror through the myth of the Blitz spirit after the July 7th bombings. *CADAAD* 6 (1): 23–37.

KhosraviNik, M. (2010). Actor descriptions, action attributions, and argumentation: Towards a systematization of CDA analytical categories in the representation of social groups. *Critical Discourse Studies* 7 (1): 55–72.

Kimmel, M. (2010). Why we mix metaphors (and mix them well): Discourse coherence, conceptual metaphor and beyond. *Journal of Pragmatics* 42: 97–115.

Koller, V. (2004). *Metaphor and Gender in Business Media Discourse: A Critical Cognitive Study*. Basingstoke: Palgrave Macmillan.

— (2010). The integration of other social domains into corporate discourse: The case of political metaphors. In H. Kelly-Holmes and G. Mautner (eds), *Language and the Market*. Basingstoke: Palgrave Macmillan, pp. 238–50.

— (2011a). 'Hard-working, team-oriented individuals': Constructing professional identities in corporate mission statements. In J. Angouri and M. Marra (eds), *Constructing Identities at Work*. Basingstoke: Palgrave Macmillan. pp. 103–26.

— (2011b). Analysing lesbian identity in discourse. In C. Hart (ed.), *Critical Discourse Studies in Discourse and Cognition*. Amsterdam: John Benjamins. pp. 97–141.

Koller, V. and P. Davidson (2008). Social exclusion as conceptual and grammatical metaphor: A cross-genre study of British policy-making. *Discourse & Society* 19 (3): 307–31.

Koller, V. and G. Mautner (2004). Computer applications in critical discourse analysis. In C. Coffin, A. Hewings and K. O'Halloran (eds), *Applying English*

Grammar: Functional and Corpus Approaches. London: Hodder and Stoughton.
pp. 216–28.

Kress, G. (1989). *Linguistic Processes in Sociocultural Practice.* 2nd edn. Oxford: Oxford
University Press.

Kress, G. and R. Hodge (1979). *Language as Ideology.* London: Routledge and Kegan
Paul.

Kress, G. and T. Van Leeuwen (2006). *Reading Images: The Grammar of Visual Design.*
2nd edn. London: Routledge.

Lakoff, G. (1987). *Women, Fire and Dangerous Things: What Categories Reveal about the
Mind.* Chicago, IL: University of Chicago Press.

— (1996). *Moral Politics: How Liberals and Conservatives Think.* Chicago, IL: University
of Chicago Press.

— (2008). The neural theory of metaphor. In R. W. Gibbs (ed.), *The Cambridge
Handbook of Metaphor and Thought.* Cambridge: Cambridge University Press.
pp. 17–38.

Lakoff, G. and M. Johnson (1989). *Metaphors We Live by.* Chicago, IL: University of
Chicago Press.

— (1999). *Philosophy in the Flesh: The Embodied Mind and its Challenge to Western
Thought.* New York: Basic Books.

Lakoff, G. and M. Turner (1989). *More than Cool Reason: A Field Guide to Poetic
Metaphor.* Chicago, IL: University of Chicago Press.

Langacker, R. W. (1987). *Foundations of Cognitive Grammar, Volume I: Theoretical
Prerequisites.* Stanford, CA: Stanford University Press.

— (1991). *Foundations of Cognitive Grammar, Volume II: Descriptive Application.*
Stanford, CA: Stanford University Press.

— (2002). *Concept, Image, and Symbol: The Cognitive Basis of Grammar.* 2nd edn.
Berlin: Mouton de Gruyter.

— (2008). *Cognitive Grammar: A Basic Introduction.* Oxford: Oxford University Press.

— (2009). *Investigations in Cognitive Grammar.* Berlin: Mouton de Gruyter.

Lee, D. (1992). *Competing Discourses: Perspectives and Ideology in Language.* London:
Longman.

Levinson, S. (1983). *Pragmatics.* Cambridge: Cambridge University Press.

— (2003). *Space in Language and Cognition: Explorations in Cognitive Diversity.*
Cambridge: Cambridge University Press.

Lim, F. V. (2004a). Problematising 'semiotic resource'. In E. Ventola, C. Charles and
M. Kaltenbacher (eds), *Perspectives on Multimodality.* Amsterdam: John Benjamins.
pp. 51–64.

— (2004b). Developing an integrative multisemiotic model. In K. L. O'Halloran (ed.),
Multimodal Discourse Analysis. London: Continuum. pp. 220–46.

Louw, B. (1993). Irony in the text or insincerity in the writer? The diagnostic potential
of semantic prosodies. In M. Baker, G. Francis and E. Tognini-Bonelli (eds), *Text
and Technology.* Amsterdam: John Benjamins. pp. 157–76.

Machin, D. (2004). Building the world's visual language: The increasing global importance of image banks in corporate media. *Visual Communication* 3 (3): 316–36.

— (2007). *An Introduction to Multimodal Analysis*. London: Bloomsbury.

— (2009). Multimodality and theories of the visual. In C. Jewitt (ed.), *Handbook of Multimodality*. London: Sage. pp. 181–90.

Machin, D. and A. Mayr (2012). *Critical Discourse Analysis: A Multimodal Approach*. London: Sage.

Mandler, J. M. (2004). *The Foundations of Mind: Origins of Conceptual Thought*. Oxford: Oxford University Press.

Marín Arrese, J. (2011). Effective vs. epistemic stance and subjectivity in political discourse: Legitimising strategies and mystification of responsibility. In C. Hart (ed.), *Critical Discourse Studies in Context and Cognition*. Amsterdam: John Benjamins. pp. 193–224.

Martin Rojo, L. and T. A. van Dijk (1997). 'There was a problem, and it was solved!' Legitimating the expulsion of 'illegal' immigrants in Spanish parliamentary discourse. *Discourse & Society* 8 (4): 523–67.

Martin, J. R. (1995). Reading positions/positioning readers: Judgement in English. *Prospect: A Journal of Australian TESOL* 10: 27–37.

— (2000). Close reading: Functional linguistics as a tool in critical discourse analysis. In L. Unsworth (ed.), *Researching Language in Schools and Communities: Functional Linguistics Approaches*. London: Cassell. pp. 275–303.

Martin, J. R. and P. R. R. White (2007). *The Language of Evaluation: Appraisal in English*. Basingstoke: Palgrave Macmillan.

Merkl-Davies, D. and V. Koller (2012). 'Metaphoring' people out of this world: A critical discourse analysis of a chairman's statement of a UK defence firm. *Accounting Forum* 36 (3): 178–93.

Mithen, S. J. (1998). *Creativity in Human Evolution and Prehistory*. London: Routledge.

Montgomery, M. (1986). *An Introduction to Language and Society*. London: Routledge.

Montgomery, M., A. Durant, N. Fabb, T. Furniss and S. Mills (2000). *Ways of Reading: Advanced Reading Skills for Students of English Literature*. 2nd edn. London: Routledge.

Murdock, G. (1973). Political deviance: The press presentation of militant mass demonstration. In S. Cohen and J. Young (eds), *The Manufacture of News: Deviance, Social Problems and the Mass Media*. London: Constable. pp. 206–25.

Musolff, A. (2003). Ideological functions of metaphor: The conceptual metaphors of health and illness in public discourse. In R. Dirven, R. M. Frank and M. Pütz (eds), *Cognitive Models in Language and Thought: Ideology, Metaphors and Meanings*. Berlin: Mouton de Gruyter. pp. 327–52.

— (2004). *Metaphor and Political Discourse: Analogical Reasoning in Debates about Europe*. Basingstoke: Palgrave Macmillan.

Nuyts, J. (2007). Cognitive linguistics and functional linguistics. In D. Geeraerts and
H. Cuyckens (eds), *The Oxford Handbook of Cognitive Linguistics*. Oxford: Oxford
University Press. pp. 543–65.

O'Grady, G. (2012). The use of prosody in generating negative inferences in televised
electoral debate. Paper presented at CADAAD 2012, University of Minho, 4–6 July.

O'Halloran, K. (2003). *Critical Discourse Analysis and Language Cognition*. Edinburgh:
Edinburgh University Press.

— (2007). Critical discourse analysis and the corpus-informed interpretation of
metaphor at the register level. *Applied Linguistics* 28 (1): 1–24.

— (2011). Multimodal discourse analysis. In K. Hyland and B. Paltridge (eds),
Companion to Discourse. London: Continuum. pp. 120–37.

Origgi, G. and D. Sperber (2000). Evolution, communication and the proper function
of language. In P. Carruthers and A. Chamberlain (eds), *Evolution and the Human
Mind: Modularity, Language and Meta-Cognition*. Cambridge: Cambridge University
Press. pp. 140–69.

Radden, G. and R. Dirven (2007). *Cognitive English Grammar*. Amsterdam: John
Benjamins.

Reisigl, M. and R. Wodak (2001). *Discourse and Discrimination: Rhetorics of Racism and
Anti-Semitism*. London: Routledge.

Reyes, A. (2011). Strategies of legitimization in political discourse: From words to
actions. *Discourse & Society* 22 (6): 781–807.

Richardson, J. E. (2008). 'Our England': Discourses of 'race' and class in party election
leaflets. *Social Semiotics* 18 (3): 321–35.

Richardson, J. E. and R. Wodak (2009). The impact of visual racism: Visual arguments
in political leaflets of Austrian and British far-right parties. *Contraversia* 6 (2):
45–77.

Rizzolatti G., L. Fadiga, L. Fogassi and V. Gallese (1997). The space around us. *Science*
277 (5323): 190–1.

Santa Ana, O. (2002). *Brown Tide Rising: Metaphors of Latinos in Contemporary
American Public Discourse*. Austin: University of Texas Press.

Šarić, L., A. Musolff, S. Manz and I. Hudabiunigg (eds) (2010). *Contesting Europe's
Eastern Rim: Cultural Identities in Public Discourse*. Bristol: Multilingual Matters.

Searle, J. R. (1975). A taxonomy of speech acts. In K. Gunderson (ed.), *Minnesota
Studies in the Philosophy of Science 9: Language, Mind and Knowledge*. pp. 344–69.

Semino, E. (2008). *Metaphor in Discourse*. Cambridge: Cambridge University Press.

Sharrock, W. W. and D. C. Anderson (1981). Language, thought and reality, again.
Sociology 15: 287–93.

Shimko, K. L. (2004). The power of metaphors and the metaphors of power: The
United States in the Cold War and after. In F. A. Beer and C. De Landtsheer
(eds), *Metaphorical World Politics*. East Lansing: Michigan State University Press.
pp. 199–216.

Simpson, P. (1993). *Language, Ideology and Point of View*. London: Routledge.

— (2004). *Stylistics: A Resource Book for Students*. London: Routledge.

Sinclair, J. (1991). *Corpus, Collocation, Concordance*. Oxford: Oxford University Press.

— (1996). The search for units of meaning. *TEXTUS* IX (1): 75–106.

Sperber, D. (2001). An evolutionary perspective on testimony and argumentation. *Philosophical Topics* 29: 401–13.

Sperber, D. and D. Wilson (1995). *Relevance: Communication and Cognition*. 2nd edn. Oxford: Blackwell.

Stubbs, M. (1995). Collocations and semantic profiles: On the cause of the trouble with quantitative studies. *Functions of Language* 2 (1): 23–55.

— (1997). Whorf's children: Critical comments on critical discourse analysis (CDA). In A. Ryan and A. Wray (eds), *Evolving Models of Language*. Clevedon: British Association for Applied Linguistics. pp. 100–16.

Suchman, M. (1995). Managing legitimacy: Strategic and institutional approaches. *The Academy of Management Review* 20 (3): 571–610.

Sweetser, E. (1990). *From Etymology to Pragmatics: Metaphorical and Cultural Aspects of Semantic Structure*. Cambridge: Cambridge University Press.

Talmy, L. (2000). *Toward a Cognitive Semantics*. Cambridge, MA: MIT Press.

Tendhal, M. and R. Gibbs (2008). Complementary perspectives on metaphor: Cognitive linguistics and Relevance Theory. *Journal of Pragmatics* 40: 1823–64.

Titscher, S., M. Meyer, R. Wodak and E. Vetter (2000). *Methods of Text and Discourse Analysis: In Search of Meaning*. London: Sage.

Tomasello, M. (1999). *The Cultural Origins of Human Cognition*, Cambridge, MA: Harvard University Press.

Toolan, M. (1991). *Narrative: A Critical Linguistic Introduction*. London: Routledge.

Trew, T. (1979). Theory and ideology at work. In R. Fowler, R. Hodge, G. Kress and T. Trew (eds), *Language and Control*. London: Routledge and Keegan Paul. pp. 94–116.

Tversky, B. (1998). Three dimensions of spatial cognition. In M. A. Conway, S. E. Gathercole and C. Cornoldi (eds), *Theories of Memory II*. Hove, East Sussex: Psychological Press. pp. 259–75.

Tversky, B., J. B. Morrison, N. Franklin and D. J. Bryant (1999). Three spaces of spatial cognition. *Professional Geographer* 51: 516–24.

van Dijk, T. A. (1991). *Racism and the Press*. London: Routledge.

— (1993). Principles of critical discourse analysis. *Discourse & Society* 4 (2): 243–89.

— (1997). Cognitive context models and discourse. In M. Stamenow (ed.), *Language Structure, Discourse and the Access to Consciousness*. Amsterdam: John Benjamins. pp. 189–226.

— (1998). *Ideology: A Multidisciplinary Approach*. London: Sage.

— (1999). Context models in discourse processing. In H. Oostendorp and S. Goldman (eds), *The Construction of Mental Models during Reading*. Mahwah, NJ: Erlbaum. pp. 123–48.

— (2008). *Discourse and Context: A Sociocognitive Approach.* Cambridge: Cambridge University Press.

— (2009). Critical discourse studies: A sociocognitive approach. In R. Wodak and M. Meyer (eds), *Methods of Critical Discourse Analysis.* 2nd edn. London: Sage. pp. 62–86.

— (2010). *Society and Discourse: How Social Contexts Influence Text and Talk.* Cambridge: Cambridge University Press.

— (2011). Discourse, knowledge, power and politics: Towards critical epistemic discourse analysis. In C. Hart (ed.), *Critical Discourse Studies in Context and Cognition.* Amsterdam: John Benjamins. pp. 27–64.

Van Leeuwen, T. (1996). The representation of social actors. In C. R. Caldas-Coulthard and M. Coulthard (eds), *Texts and Practices: Readings in Critical Discourse Analysis.* London: Routledge. pp. 32–70.

— (2005). *Introducing Social Semiotics.* London: Routledge.

— (2007). Legitimation in discourse and communication. *Discourse & Communication* 1 (1): 91–112.

— (2008). *Discourse and Practice: New Tools for Critical Discourse Analysis.* Oxford: Oxford University Press.

Van Leeuwen, T. and R. Wodak (1999). Legitimizing immigration control: A discourse-historical analysis. *Discourse Studies* 10 (1): 83–118.

Voloshinov, V. N. (1995). *Marxism and the Philosophy of Language* (trans. L. Matejka and I. R. Titunik). London: Routledge.

Weiss, G. and R. Wodak (2003). Introduction: Theory, interdisciplinarity and critical discourse analysis. In G. Weiss and R. Wodak (eds), *Critical Discourse Analysis: Theory and Interdisciplinarity.* Basingstoke: Palgrave Macmillan. pp. 1–35.

Widdowson, H. G. (1995). Discourse analysis: A critical view. *Language and Literature* 4 (3): 157–72.

— (2000). On the limitations of linguistics applied. *Applied Linguistics* 21 (1): 3–25.

— (2004). *Text, Context, Pretext: Critical Issues in Discourse Analysis.* Oxford: Blackwell.

Wiezcorek, A. (2008). Proximisation, common ground and assertion-based patterns for legitimisation in political discourse. *CADAAD* 2 (1): 31–48.

Williams, G. (ed.) (2009). *Shafted: The Media, the Miners' Strike and the Aftermath.* London: Campaign for Press & Broadcasting Freedom.

Wittgenstein, L. (1953). *Philosophical Investigations.* Oxford: Blackwell.

Wodak, R. (2001). What is CDA about: A summary of its history, important concepts and its developments. In R. Wodak and M. Meyer (eds), *Methods of Critical Discourse Analysis.* London: Sage. pp. 1–13.

— (2006). Mediation between discourse and society: Assessing cognitive approaches in CDA. *Discourse Studies* 8 (1): 179–90.

Wodak, R. and M. Meyer (eds) (2009). *Methods of Critical Discourse Analysis.* 2nd edn. London: Sage.

Young, L. and C. Harrison (2004). Introduction. In L. Young and C. Harrison (eds),
    Systemic Functional Linguistics and Critical Discourse Analysis. London: Continuum.
    pp. 1–14.
Zacks, J., B. Rypma, J. D. E. Gabrieli, B. Tversky and G. H. Glover (1999). Imagined
    transformations of the body: An fMRI study. *Neuropsychologia* 37 (9): 1029–40.
Zwaan, R. A. (2004). The immersed experiencer: Toward an embodied theory of
    language comprehension. In B. H. Ross (ed.), *The Psychology of Learning and
    Motivation, Volume 44*. New York: Academic Press. pp. 35–62.

Index

Lightning Source UK Ltd.
Milton Keynes UK
UKHW020223101019
351310UK00009B/186/P